Google and the Digital Divide

D1523145

CHANDOS INTERNET SERIES

Chandos' new series of books are aimed at all those individuals interested in the internet. They have been specially commissioned to provide the reader with an authoritative view of current thinking. If you would like a full listing of current and forthcoming titles, please visit our website www.chandospublishing.com or email info@chandospublishing.com or telephone +44 (0) 1223 891358.

New authors: we are always pleased to receive ideas for new titles; if you would like to write a book for Chandos, please contact Dr Glyn Jones on email gjones@chandospublishing.com or telephone number +44 (0) 1993 848726.

Bulk orders: some organisations buy a number of copies of our books. If you are interested in doing this, we would be pleased to discuss a discount. Please email info@chandospublishing.com or telephone +44 (0) 1223 891358.

Google and the Digital Divide

The bias of online knowledge

ELAD SEGEV

Chandos Publishing

Oxford • Cambridge • New Delhi

Chandos Publishing
TBAC Business Centre
Avenue 4
Station Lane
Witney
Oxford OX28 4BN
UK
Tel: +44 (0) 1993 848726
Email: info@chandospublishing.com
www.chandospublishing.com

Chandos Publishing is an imprint of Woodhead Publishing Limited

Woodhead Publishing Limited
Abington Hall
Granta Park
Great Abington
Cambridge CB21 6AH
UK
www.woodheadpublishing.com

First published in 2010

ISBN:
978 1 84334 565 7

© Elad Segev, 2010

British Library Cataloguing-in-Publication Data.
A catalogue record for this book is available from the British Library.

The Publishers make no representation, express or implied, with regard to the accuracy of the information contained in this publication and cannot accept any legal responsibility or liability for any errors or omissions.

The material contained in this publication constitutes general guidelines only and does not represent to be advice on any particular matter. No reader or purchaser should act on the basis of material contained in this publication without first taking professional advice appropriate to their particular circumstances. All screenshots in this publication are the copyright of the website owner(s), unless indicated otherwise.

Cover design by Hutchins Creative and Itamar Daube.
Typeset by Domex e-Data Pvt. Ltd.
Printed in the UK and USA.

025.04
Seg

Contents

List of figures and tables

Figures

Tables

About the author

Elad Segev is a postdoctoral fellow and lecturer of media and communications at the Hebrew University of Jerusalem and visiting lecturer at Tel Aviv University and Ben Gurion University in Israel. He dedicated his doctorate work at the Research Institute for Law, Politics and Justice at Keele University in England to the study of search engine biases and their social and political implications. He also publishes studies on online news biases, Americanisation, cultural diversity, the digital divide, and new applications and methodologies to utilise data-mining for new media research.

The author may be contacted at:

Elad Segev
PO Box 4092
Zichron Yaaqov 30900
Israel
E-mail: *info@eladsegev.com*

Acknowledgments

I would like to convey my sincere gratitude and appreciation to Professor Costas Constantinou for his insightful intellectual comments and suggestions. A very special thank to Professor Menahem Blondheim who read the entire manuscript and provided a lot of support. Many thanks to Professor Niv Ahituv, Dr Elizabeth Carter and Professor Gadi Wolfsfeld, who provided tremendous assistance with improving the empirical chapters and offered some very useful suggestions. Many thanks to Professor John Vogler and the reflection group at Keele University for the intriguing ideas and scholarly atmosphere. Thanks to Dr Glyn Jones from Chandos Publishing for his useful suggestions and comments, and to Marion Lupu and John Tresman for their beautiful and careful proofreading of the entire manuscript.

A very special dedication and thanks to Yuko Hori for her admirable patience, encouragement and support during the process of writing. This book would never have commenced without her. Thanks to Professor Robert Smith for his friendly company and academic inspiration. A warm thank you to my parents, who encouraged and supported my curiosity and eagerness to pursue knowledge from a very early age. Endless thanks to Regula Miesch who apart from linguistic comments and brilliant ideas, always gave me a lot of courage, love and a listening ear in the most critical moments. Finally, thanks to my charming little brothers and friends who kept on reminding me of the 'other life' beyond the book. I would like to dedicate this book to all these very dear people who made it possible.

Preface

> Technologies are often developed in response to the agendas of powerful social actors. Initially, they shape themselves to the contours of custom; ultimately, they follow paths selected through struggles among groups seeking to turn technologies to their own interests. (DiMaggio et al., 2001: 327 on McGuire and Granovetter, 1998)

One of the current concerns of socially informed studies of the internet is to understand the reasons for the so-called digital divide and to assess its implications for everyday life. In this sense, the internet, which is an almost unlimited and expanding information source, increasingly becomes a useful and powerful instrument for the acquisition of knowledge, and such knowledge brings social, political and economic advantages. When searching for information, people turn first, and increasingly only, to the internet (Hinman, 2005). This suggests that using the internet in general and search engines in particular can increase information opportunities but also information inequalities – something that should be carefully studied.

As a field of research, the internet provides a rich site to study socio-technological practices, as well as to look at their power implications during the early stages of the diffusion and institutionalisation of a new medium. The internet is a unique medium as it combines a variety of methods and forms of communication, such as mutual interaction, broadcasting, self-searching for information, forum groups, human–computer interaction, and various types of content, e.g. text, image, voice and video (DiMaggio et al., 2001). This variety of methods provides skilled users with a wide range of opportunities to translate information into knowledge and develop new social networks and ethnoscapes. A historical perspective is also crucial in this respect, given that dominant actors have historically exploited media and communication technologies to disseminate forms of knowledge, promote their interests and maintain or challenge specific social orders.

Popular search engines and internet companies such as Google and Yahoo! play a particularly important role as the new and increasingly dominant agents and hubs of information. They have gained worldwide popularity by producing, organising, distributing, customising and manipulating online information. These companies have acquired a strategic position by addressing the insatiable need of the information society – the need for immediate and relevant information. Governments, organisations, companies and individuals depend on obtaining and producing immediate and relevant online information to meet daily tasks and demands. Thus, both information providers and information retrievers often turn to search engines in order to support their functions and gain or retain a competitive advantage over their competitors.

The most common way for individuals to retrieve online information and for governments and corporations to maximise publicity and reach more audiences is through search engines. It has been indicated that search engines are one of the major ways to reach websites worldwide (Hopkins, 2007; see also Appendix A). From this perspective, popular search engines that are visited by millions every day are the 'gatekeepers' to online information. The term 'gatekeeper' refers to the 'process of controlling information as it moves through a gate' (Barzilai-Nahon, 2006a: 3). Directory services for online information and search engines such as Google, MSN and Yahoo! are classic examples of online gatekeepers, as they control the flow of information and provide a gate to the online world. Search engines are not only agents that index, organise and customise information in the chaotic online network, but also instruments for navigating and exploring new territories on the web (Introna and Nissenbaum, 2000). On the one hand, they provide more opportunities for information production and consumption but, on the other, as will be further indicated, they also produce information inequalities by promoting certain actors (i.e. states, companies and skilled users), while marginalising others.

This book focuses mainly on Google, the leading search engine and one of the most visited internet properties nowadays, which has more than 770 million unique users[1] every month, i.e. half of the world internet users (comScore, 2009a; Kopytoff, 2007a). This tremendous rating of Google and other popular search engines, directories, portals and gatekeepers (hereafter, information agents) elevates them to be 'authority sites' (Hurlbert, 2004), with the power to channel, control and manipulate the information flow. Over the last ten years, therefore, Google has grown from being a popular brand[2] to a dominant information agent, whose practices need to be critically engaged and assessed.

This raises the question of technological and information inequalities, which are often related to other social, economic and political inequalities, also known as the 'digital divide'.[3] It may be that the internet provides more opportunities for individuals and groups to express themselves and retrieve relevant information. However, various examples in this book will suggest that the greatest ability to produce and disseminate information lies in the hands of popular information agents (such as Google), and their advanced customisation mechanisms may also create dependence and progressively 'lock' users into their services. Moreover, their growing ability to collect and store personal data potentially also threatens the privacy of their users. In other words, together with greater empowerment and control, information agents also increase their ability to construct 'realities' and maintain dependency among their users.

The phrase 'politics of online information' appears throughout the book, where the word 'politics' is used in its broader sense as 'an aspect of all social relations, rather than activity centred on the institutions of government' (Gamble, 1990: 412). C. Anderson (1977) defined the political act as the decision we make on behalf of others, the setting of rules and standards and the distribution of resources among rival human needs and purposes. In this sense, 'politics of online information' refers to the information and communication rules and standards, which are often developed and shaped by communication corporations, and the allocation and distribution of informational resources among online users, companies and states with diverse needs and interests.

From the bottom-up view, the politics of online information is the ability of *individuals* to exercise information skills and utilise search engine interfaces to find relevant information or use their skills so that they themselves can be found online (Introna and Nissenbaum, 2000). From the top-down view, it is the operation of *corporations* and *organisations* that own 'authority sites' that provide, organise and customise online information. It is argued that those who can employ an advanced politics of online information also shape the information society, and thus their strategies and tactics require investigation.

The politics of online information employed by search engines is often driven by commercial motives, and although not always intentional, carries several political and social implications. Hinman (2005) identifies three main ethical problems that search engines pose: (a) the lack of transparency in their search algorithm and their organisation of information, (b) their ability to monitor the search history of their users, and (c) their engagement in local censorship. As an example he gives the photographs of Iraqi prisoner abuse in Abu Ghraib that were omitted from Google Image Search in December 2004. Deriving from a similar concern, the later chapters of this book examine the extent of these problems in specific search channels, such as Google News and Google Earth, which have not been subject to sustained research in this context. While Hinman focuses on the implications of search mechanisms on privacy issues, the main purpose of this book is to examine the implications of the organisation of information in Google (and its uses) also on the digital divide and the biased understandings of the world.

The main argument of the book is that search engines very often intensify the digital divide by organising the world's information with a clear, if not always intentional, bias towards commercial and popular trends, which in many cases take the form of US-centric or mainstream views.[4] The concepts of bias and the dominance of certain views in the context of search engines and their various social, political and economic implications will be further discussed. In this respect, an important goal of this book is to provide a critical view on the implications of search engines and their users on the development and dissemination of the digital divide.

The digital divide and online information

Although many scholars have claimed that the digital divide is not only about inequality in accessing the network (Hargittai, 2000; 2003; Norris, 2001; DiMaggio et al., 2001; Ciolek, 2003; Castells, 2004; R. Rogers, 2004; Barzilai-Nahon, 2006b), the various information uses and skills are a relatively new aspect in the study of the digital divide.[5] This book attempts to address a particular aspect of the digital divide of uses, looking at Google and some of its less-examined search channels. It suggests that the diverse uses of online information have different implications, which can eventually benefit certain actors and shape information order in specific contexts and ways.

From a macro perspective, through the ongoing process of commercialisation and privatisation, it has been argued that some governments are losing a degree of control over the production and consumption of information, while private corporations are becoming increasingly more dominant and powerful actors (Mosco, 1996; Hirst and Thompson, 1999). From a micro perspective, some suggest that information-skilled individuals, such as the so-called 'hackers', play a crucial role in the emergence but also the challenge of the digital divide (Graham, 1998; Himanen, 2001; Kellerman, 2002; Ciolek, 2003). Hence, various actors may benefit or lose from the new technological opportunities, and one of the current challenges of internet researchers is to explore and identify those opportunities and thus gradually unveil the new complex characteristics of the digital divide.

In line with literature on international political economy (e.g. Cox, 1987; Gilpin, 1987; Mosco, 1996), it is believed that social and economic powers, particularly the capitalist system, influence national and international politics. Commercial practices (communication oligopolies and mega-corporations) as well as social and cultural practices (the dominance of the English language and education for information skills) are seen as important reasons for the digital divide, not only between individuals, but also between states. These inequalities, which can be displayed through the different uses of information in different countries, can therefore have significant implications. Countries with greater economic power are expected to have more developed and integrated information and communication technologies (ICTs), and thus more developed and diverse uses of online information.

Together with economic interests, there are various political interests in operation (such as freedom of expression and national security) that sometimes conflict with each other and continuously shape the global and local information flow. While some online networks allow free information flow, other networks censor and restrict the free access to online information. At the national level, this is especially strong in some Middle Eastern countries, as well as China and North Korea (Sussman, 2000), where governments constantly restrict and filter any expression that may threaten their national security. At the organisational level, firewalls prevent employees from accessing 'irrelevant' information that may distract concentration and harm productivity. Finally, at the family level, parents may install software to limit the access of their children to pornography or other undesirable online content. These examples, some of which will be developed in the following chapters, demonstrate that the technology is available and can be used by states and corporations to control and manipulate the intractable flow of information, and even more so than is currently the case.

Yet, even in countries where the access to online information is relatively advanced and free, it is wrong to expect the development of online communities with equal opportunities to produce and consume information. First, the digital divide emerges as a result of the commercialisation of the internet as well as the operation of dominant information agents such as search engines and popular 'authority' sites.

Studies have indicated that the access range is gradually shrinking, i.e. more online users visit fewer websites (Waxman, 2000; Webster and Lin, 2002). This tendency is strongly supported by the ability of the more dominant and popular websites to customise information for the specific interests of their online users, and thus to consensually narrow their view and purview.

Second, the digital divide emerges as a result of the operation of information-skilled users. Considerable responsibility lies with online users and their habits. Chapter 4 will indicate, for example, that most popular search queries are about entertainment rather than social, political and economic information. Although an online political panel may be theoretically free and open for everyone to participate, in practice it is visited by very few online users, who understand its potential and want to take part in local and global discussions (Norris, 2001). To this end, advanced customisation mechanisms enable online users to focus on their specific interests, but at the same time perpetuate the digital divide within the online community (Sunstein, 2001). The use of search engines in this context intensifies online inequalities between those with and those without information skills, and those who are aware and not aware of the benefits of political and economic information.

The digital divide of access to information, i.e. between the online and the offline societies, and the digital divide of information uses, i.e. within the online community itself, constitute the current information order. This order is shaped by dominant communication corporations and information agents that organise, customise and divide the information society, and by the growing gap between different information-skilled users in different states.

US dominance and global communications

It is impossible to examine the digital divide without taking into account global economic, political and cultural processes. Thompson (1995) suggests looking at the complex global interaction between human, material and symbolic flows. In this context, Thompson defines the concept of 'power' as:

> [the] ability to act in pursuit of one's aims and interests, the ability to intervene in the course of events and to affect their outcome. In exercising power, individuals employ the resources available to them; resources are the means, which enable them to pursue their aims and interests effectively. (Thompson, 1995: 13)

Subsequently, Thompson identifies four types of power: economic power, political power, military power and symbolic power. While the first three types may be self-explanatory, symbolic power refers to the production, transmission and retrieval of information, symbols and cultures through media channels, and thus is directly related to the problem of the digital divide and the increasing importance of search engines in this context. However, maybe the most important idea that Thompson puts forward, and which is crucial to this book, is that symbolic power constantly corresponds with the other types of power.

While there is obvious significance to each of these forces, Mattelart and Mattelart (1998) suggest that the process of 'globalisation' initially grew out of the notion of 'financial globalisation' and the restructuring of the international financial sphere. Regulating and maintaining the economic order on a global scale have clear political and social implications (Hirst and Thompson, 1999). Similarly, Van der Pijl (1984) and Cox (1987) indicate the growing development of transnational corporations and international markets, and their economic and political significance. It has been estimated that multinational corporations account for 20 per cent of world production and 70 per cent of world trade (Perraton et al., 1997). The new global economy is characterised by its capacity to work as a unit in real time on a global scale (Castells, 2000). This is possible mainly due to the existence of a global network of communication that makes possible an immediate flow of information.

The growing connectivity and flow of information, people and commodities on a global scale have led to the development of the concept of 'cultural imperialism' (Schiller, 1992), which describes a network of force, pressure and influence of the dominant values, practices and structures of the centre. This process is characterised by the transition of most of the developing world from political subordination to political independence yet combined with economic dependence. Global media and communications play a particularly important role in the process. Unlike other industries, the communication industry has direct implications on human consciousness and therefore also on politics, society and culture. Thus, in Schiller's view, the worldwide penetration of the Western (predominantly US) media industry leaves little room for the development of opposing or even alternative views and agendas.[6]

From the cultural point of view, globalisation can be seen through the increased use of a few dominant languages across the globe. In the 1990s, De Swaan found that 10–12 languages account for the first language of over 60 per cent of the world's population (De Swaan, 1991). The dominance of English nowadays is a significant manifestation of political and economic globalisation (Crystal, 2003), reflecting the symbolic power of the USA and perhaps other English-speaking countries. This trend could be further intensified on the internet, where English is evidently the dominant language (Lazarus and Mora, 2000; Pastore, 2000; O'Neill et al., 2003; UNESCO, 2006). Indeed, the interactive nature of the internet, and the increasing popularity of Web 2.0 applications in particular may provide a fruitful ground for smaller languages as well (Danet and Herring, 2007). However, the current situation is still in favour of large languages and particularly English, which is at the core of all internet technologies (Paolillo, 2007). Language is therefore one of the major reasons for the digital divide within the online community, providing an advantage to those who master English.

Looking at the internet in a broader sense, Kroes (2003) agrees that it is predominantly American in nature, suggesting that 'anyone who is surfing the net is drawn into a world of information, blending commercial and other messages, that in most cases is clearly of American origin, or is at least cast in an American mould' (Kroes, 2003: 245). Yet, he also suggests that the interactivity of the internet sometimes enables the 'periphery' to 'strike back at the empire' and promote local views. In any case, he believes that commercial and capitalist forces dominate the online network, making its content fit the sensibility of users from the USA and other Western countries.[7] Thus, US dominance is seen primarily through the dominance of its symbolic power in global media channels, which is also supported by global economic structures and institutions.

During the 1970s, UNESCO was the first international organisation to study and address the asymmetry of communication flow between states and to outline its implications. As a result of the policies of the Reagan administration to adopt the theory of 'free flow' as well as the overshadowing problems of the Cold War, the various initiations of international organisations to balance and equalise the information flow eventually turned into a 'dialogue of the deaf' (Mattelart and Mattelart, 1998). In the 1980s, the USA and the UK withdrew from UNESCO in protest, believing that it had become politically and socially hostile to their interests. The UK rejoined in 1997 following a change of government, and the USA rejoined in 2003, but only after UNESCO had implemented considerable organisational reforms (Ofori-Attah, 2007).

A recent example in this context was the proposal introduced during the World Summit of the Information Society (WSIS) to establish the Internet Governance Forum. Not surprisingly, the USA has strongly rejected the idea of global control over the internet, and particularly the role of assigning domain names (which is in the hands of the US-based ICANN).

Eventually, it was agreed that the Internet Governance Forum would be an international organisation with a purely consultative role (Mattelart, 2008). During the summit, the US delegation advocated a strong private sector and the rule of law as the critical foundations for the development of national ICTs (Porter, 2003).

As such, despite the growing international concern over the USA's online dominance, it seems that the ability to counterbalance this trend is still limited. The following chapters will provide empirical support to this view, suggesting that the USA often displays higher capacity to interact with and influence internet corporations and particularly search engines in order to disseminate certain views and agendas among many online users.

Internet commercialisation

Together with the US dominance of global communications, this work is also concerned with the growing commercialisation of the internet. Various theorists have outlined the implications of media commercialisation (Beniger, 1986; Mosco, 1989; Babe, 1995), and particularly the commercialisation of the internet (Hinton, 1999; Webster and Lin, 2002), which significantly shape the online information flow and its content.

Looking at earlier mass media channels (i.e. the press, radio and television), Adorno (1991) indicated the development of a global uniform taste, on the basis that companies searching for profits tend to produce homogeneous programmes or texts in order to attract maximum audiences. Similarly, previous studies have shown that commercial concerns and dependence on a small number of similar sources of news and opinions lead to the production of homogeneous content and views (Gaunt, 1990; McManus, 1993; Underwood, 1993; Jamison and Campbell, 1998; Picard, 1998).

Bagdikian (2004) has also indicated that the growing competition over media control and dependence on advertisements affect the production of content that often serves the interests of economically and politically dominant actors. This is to suggest that commercialisation of media is directly related to the problem of information inequality. Herman and Chomsky (2002) believe that even in states where the media are privately-owned and there is very little formal censorship, it is possible to trace the economic and, also, often the political motives behind filtering out certain items of news, marginalising dissenting content and allowing dominant actors a greater exposure and audience reach.

At the beginning, the emergence of the internet was thought to counterbalance this trend, as it made possible all types of social communication, combining all types of media (Negroponte, 1995; Barlow, 1996). Chapter 1 delineates the various opportunities that the internet offers in terms of information production and consumption, and the current debate regarding its role in producing a more equal information society or, on the other hand, preserving and even intensifying information inequalities based on commercial, political and technological considerations. The results of the experimental chapters that follow, however, will support the latter view. Although entrance barriers to the network may be low, competitors can channel and monopolise the attention of users (Barzilai-Nahon, 2006a). In fact, an early study has already found that 80 per cent of visits are to only 0.5 per cent of websites (Waxman, 2000). Popular portal sites act as 'gatekeepers', as they index online information, and create links and searching possibilities to other websites (Hargittai, 2000). This is precisely why it is important to recognise the commercial motives of search engines and examine the various ways in which they shape their organisation and manipulation of online information.

As will be detailed, apart from channelling the attention of online users to specific websites, customisation plays an important role in the inequality of information production through media channels in general and search engines in particular. Turow (2005) argues that the ability of advertisers to reach narrow and specific audiences depends on the ability of media companies to narrowcast and customise their distribution of information. The main factors used by advertisers to build up audiences are demographic, which in return influence the production of content and increase the socio-economic inequality (Bagdikian, 2004). The demassification process is especially interesting in the context of search engines and their advertising mechanisms, which provide relevant advertisements for each search query,[8] and therefore introduce a narrow customisation of content, enhancing the fragmentation of audiences. The practice of product customisation has recently been embraced by global companies in general and communication companies in particular following the development of the long-tail theory (C. Anderson, 2006), which suggests that products that are less in demand collectively compose a market share that exceeds the relatively few popular products.

The following chapters will suggest that US dominance and internet commercialisation are reflected through and intensified by the organisation of online information by search engines. These trends are also related to the structural bias of search engines, which is often a result of their being commercial companies.

On bias and monopoly of knowledge

The digital divide is related to the concept of *information bias*, which is examined and assessed in this book through the information produced by and retrieved in Google. Harold Innis (1951) developed this concept in his work, *The Bias of Communication*, referring to the unequal production, distribution and retrieval of information.[9] When it comes to search engines, information bias is related to its advanced customisation mechanisms as well as its organisation of information based on economic and political considerations, where certain actors are promoted and others are marginalised. Various studies have indicated, for example, that search results are dominated by US and commercial websites (Cho and Roy, 2004; Introna and Nissenbaum, 2000; Mowshowitz and Kawaguchi, 2002; Walker, 2002; Gerhart, 2004; Hurlbert, 2004; Kavassalis et al., 2004; R. Rogers, 2004; Van Couvering, 2004; Vaughan and Thelwall, 2004; Battelle, 2005). This trend is a result of their automatic page-ranking mechanism, which prioritises bigger and more popular websites.[10]

Information bias corresponds with another concept of Innis (1951): 'the monopoly of knowledge'. By monopoly of knowledge, Innis refers to the dominance and control of certain forms of communications, but also to the dominance of certain views and discourses (e.g. US or commercial) within that information. Driven by a similar concern, Mattelart (1980) develops the concept of a 'dominant ideology', Schiller (1992) writes about 'cultural imperialism', and Bagdikian (2004) writes about 'media monopolies'. In all cases, the authors describe a process of economic consolidation of media companies, resulting in biases and unequal production and distribution of information. This is to suggest that the bias of information and the monopoly of knowledge are directly linked. These terms are used throughout the book in order to describe the growing dominance of certain views and agendas in the information produced by search engines, and the inevitable political and cultural implications of this bias.

One of the main problems with information bias in search engines is the lack of transparency. Hinman (2005) suggests that recent page-ranking algorithms incorporate hundreds of hidden factors, and thus online users can never know what information is included and promoted, and what is excluded and marginalised. Search algorithms are considered as a top trade secret and, in most cases, online users are not even aware of the biases in their search results (Introna and Nissenbaum, 2000). This is particularly worrying as recent studies indicate that online users tend to trust search engines and are influenced by the order of search results rather than by their relevancy (Pan et al., 2007). Thus, most online users do not question or critically evaluate the search results: they rarely look at the second page of results and are often satisfied with visiting one document within the result set (Jansen et al., 2000).

Theoretically, a less biased search engine will be one that equally provides alternative (i.e. non-mainstream) and less popular websites on the first page of results, in which information will not be dominated by commercial and US sources, and will allow easy access to more local and vernacular political, economic and social information rather than to entertainment. Most important, it will be transparent, i.e. display the various considerations that lead to a certain organisation and prioritisation of search results, will be subject to public review and users will have the power to control them.[11] However, as the following chapters indicate, it is unreasonable to expect commercial search engines to reveal their trade secrets or to risk the relevancy of their ranking by prioritising less popular websites.

The point is that popularity, and particularly popularity of links, which is the core principle of the page-ranking mechanism, does not necessarily mean relevancy, and definitely not importance. Search engines are far from providing the exact answer for each individual, and much farther from understanding what each individual intended to find. Although search engines work constantly on personalisation and customisation of their results, there is still a gap between the information needed and the information provided, particularly when users search for specific or esoteric information. The dominance of certain information at the top of the search results has further implications on the way in which online users understand and construct their knowledge. This is particularly crucial for those who do not know exactly what they are seeking or do not possess advanced information skills and therefore use relatively general search queries.

As will be shown though the study of Google News and Google Maps, the principle of popularity, which is based on commercial considerations, systematically brings to the user's attention certain political, economic and social issues (e.g. US and commercial content), while marginalising other issues (e.g. alternative and local views). Moreover, Chapter 4 will indicate that online users in some countries are less interested in retrieving diversity of content, and increasingly seek popular entertainment. Thus, it is a bidirectional rather than unidirectional process, in which people design technologies to promote and distribute popular and commercial content, and in return reinforce and shape their own information needs. In short, popularisation and customisation of information by search engines contribute and shape the emerging monopoly of knowledge.

Search engines and the digital divide

As indicated earlier, the main claim being addressed throughout the book is that search engines in general and Google in particular play an increasingly significant role in the production, dissemination and often intensification of the digital divide. This is mainly due to their ability to *customise* information and organise it according to its *popularity*. Customisation is one of the important mechanisms employed by search engines, enabling online users to type any search query and obtain unique and personalised search results. Search engines constantly increase their ability to provide more specific and personalised search results based on the search history of their users and other individual and personal preferences. Subsequently, customisation has significant implications for the digital divide, and Chapter 4 will shed light on some of them, while comparing the popular search queries put to Google in different countries.

The organisation of online information according to its popularity is another feature of search engines with implications for the digital divide. In its most basic form, it refers to the specific organisation of search results, where out of millions and sometimes billions of webpages that contain the user's search queries, search engines prioritise and display an eclectic list of webpages. Obviously, online users cannot read all the results; in most cases they never go beyond the first page of results (Jansen et al., 2000; Jansen and Spink, 2003).

The principle of popularity dominates every customised individual search and is embedded in the organisation of information in every specific search channel (images, books, articles, news and even maps). Chapters 5 and 6 examine the organisation of information and its implications in the specific search channels for news and maps. Findings show a clear bias in Google News and Google Earth, which provides an obvious informational and political advantage for the USA and some other capitalist countries, and thus perpetuates and intensifies the digital divide.

In short, both customisation and popularisation, the core principles of the search engine mechanism, have clear implications on the production and intensification of the digital divide. As will be shown, this divide is not concerned with the unequal access to online information as much as with the unequal use of this information, and particularly the dominance of certain technological, economic and political patterns within that use.

The structure of the book

As the most popular search engine, Google was chosen to be the main object of study in the investigation of search engine biases and their implications on the digital divide. Subsequently, various methods and analytical approaches have been employed. The first chapters provide an up-to-date account of media theory and critique with respect to the digital divide and the historical use of communications in support of social, economic and political domination. An internet survey, particularly in online news archives, provided a useful resource to study the expanding search engine market, the remarkable rise of Google and its recent developments, operations and relationships with governments, organisations and individuals. Finally, the last three chapters process and analyse some of the data published in Google and its specific services (e.g. popular search queries, news articles and maps) to test their biases and implications regarding the digital divide of information uses.

Although many studies that look at the biases of media content use qualitative methods (Torfing, 1991; Laclau, 1994; Smith, 1994; Renkema, 2004; Izadi and Saghaye-Biria, 2007), this book takes a mainly quantitative approach (see also Beardsworth, 1980). The decision to apply quantitative methods derives from the nature of the data in Google as well as the author's background in the field of information studies. To this end, the book also offers some new methods to analyse search queries and specific search channels in order to conceptualise and shed light on the digital divide of information uses.

Chapter 1 looks at the political role of communications through history (mainly utilising the analyses of Innis, McLuhan and Mattelart), as well as of the internet and the digital divide today. The growing integration of ICTs into the daily life of billions of people around the world brings about new qualities and possibilities in the information society (e.g. immediacy, customisation and a decentralised network structure). This increases the importance not only of financial resources but also of information resources and skills, i.e. the ability of individuals, organisations and states to employ online information and utilise interfaces to enhance their positions within the global network. This chapter provides a theoretical basis for the following chapters, which continue to explore the digital divide and the politics of online information in the search engine context.

Chapter 2 explores the operation and technical potential of search engines and their social implications and challenges. It explains why search engines can only cover a small part of the web, and examines the concept of the 'deep web'. The deep web has significant implications for the digital divide, as websites that are not indexed by search engines can be reached only if users know about their existence, have potential access or pay fees to access them, or demonstrate especially high information skills (e.g. hackers). Nevertheless, making the deep web accessible and searchable does not necessarily mean bridging the information gap. Being indexed by search engines, the popularity of websites depends on their ability to pay for promotion, as well as on the inclusion/exclusion mechanisms of search engines. These mechanisms are highly biased in favour of commercial and US-based websites, where popular information is further popularised and less-popular information is further marginalised. The implications of such biases (particularly on students and scholars) are further discussed. Similarly, the social and ethical aspects concerning search engines are examined, i.e. resolving the growing number of conflicts on the regulation of public and private information, and mediating between the various politics of online information exercised by individuals, organisations and governments.

Chapter 3 focuses more specifically on the operation of Google, the leading search engine and internet property at present. It is proposed that by organising and manipulating online information better than other companies, Google has not only acquired tremendous worldwide popularity, but has also become a powerful information agent. The ability to prioritise and customise information also empowers Google's users, who can edit their own stories, focus on their interests and exclude any undesirable content. This in return strengthens the position of Google, creating a cycle of dependence. The growing number of additional services offered by Google, including Google Books, Google Scholar and iGoogle (personalised search), are examined in the light of the 'locking mechanism' concept. In addition, this chapter examines the interaction between Google and local governments, where mutual political and/or economic interests often outbalance the privacy interests of individuals on the one hand, and their freedom of information production and retrieval on the other.

Together, the first three chapters provide an analytical framework for the empirical chapters that follow. They address mainly the question of how online communication is used to gain economic and political advantages, thus widening the gap between the information-rich and the information-poor.

Chapter 4 develops a methodology to study what information is being sought in different countries and to what extent this information is politically and economically related, thus providing comprehensive advantages to certain countries over others, reinforcing or challenging the digital divide. It analyses the most popular search queries in Google and Yahoo! over a period of two years.

It is suggested that certain information uses (e.g. search queries about news, government, science, education or business) can provide economic and socio-political advantages (e.g. help online users find jobs, compare prices of products and services, establish online business, acquire an education, increase their social and political involvement, and so on). The analysis includes 27 countries, and examines three different aspects of their information uses: content, heterogeneity of information uses and accuracy of search. Together, these various aspects compose the information skills and the popular information trends in each country. It is argued that countries in which users demonstrate greater information skills also have greater potential to maximise the benefits of the internet and gain political and economic advantages over other countries.

Chapter 5 examines the biases in Google News, a multilingual interface that pulls articles from thousands of popular online news sources. The growing popularity of Google News and its global spread make it an influential channel, which can have important implications on the way people perceive the world. Mass media theories, such as those of Anderson, Mattelart and Bagdikian, provide a theoretical support for this assumption. Subsequently, an experimental methodology is developed to analyse the top news articles in Google News, and the 'imagined international communities' that are being shaped by this putatively global and unbiased information. It tries to find out which countries have been mentioned more frequently in Google News, and which issues have dominated world news.

Findings indicate that the USA is a dominant actor in most popular news sources, and that both English and non-English online news display US-centric priorities and agendas. It is therefore suggested that those who possess better language skills and more economic resources dominate the production and dissemination of information in global media channels and can therefore maintain control over the global information order. By prioritising commercial, English or US-based websites as more popular and authoritative, search engines such as Google further polarise the information society and increase the digital divide.

Chapter 6 explores Google Earth and Google Maps. Similar to Google News, these services are increasingly used by scholars, students and the lay public, who are not always aware of their structural biases. The study of Google Earth, which provides high-resolution aerial images from all over the world, leads to an interesting discussion about private and public information. In this context, Google Earth apparently poses a threat for some governments as it displays images of military installations. In practice, it seems that some governments manage to censor Google Earth, while others have less control. Subsequently, those maps and images significantly shape our perceptions and understandings of the world as we know it.

Boundaries and limitations of scope

The main scope of this book is search engines in general and Google in particular, and their impact on the digital divide. Although search engines generate the highest online traffic and are currently used as the dominant online navigation tool, a number of other important online actors have recently grown in terms of popularity and influence. These include weblogs, social network services, and information and media-sharing websites, such as Wikipedia, YouTube and Flickr to name but a few. As they gradually develop and become online hubs, they introduce their own accreditation mechanisms to frame knowledge (often based on similar commercial principles of customisation and popularisation of information), which also have specific social and political implications and similarly require careful investigation.

It is important to bear in mind that the book covers a limited period in the early phase of the internet's diffusion and institutionalisation. Available in its commercial format only from the beginning of the 1990s, the internet is still considered a relatively young medium, which may develop in predictable but also in unpredictable directions. There is, for example, a growing online population in Asia, which accounts for almost 40 per cent of internet usage. Currently, there are more than 700 million online users in Asia compared with 400 million online users in Europe and 250 million online users in North America (Internet World Stats, 2009). As will be suggested, this trend may challenge the dominance of English online, and introduce growing online communities of Chinese, Spanish and Arabic speakers. This, in return, may counterbalance some of the current online biases and inequalities.

Media and information critiques provide the framework for this study of the online digital divide produced by search engines and their users. These critiques also aim to reveal patterns and meanings in the information flow. Less attention, however, is paid to the various processes involved in the production of information, the business models and the strategies of search engine companies. Although search engines are perceived first of all as profit-making entities, they are also organisations composed of thousands of individuals. They have specific structures, hierarchies and diverse interests. To this end, there is a need to investigate these organisation and management structures, and to understand the various relations involved in the process of production and design of search mechanisms. This perspective can be especially challenging for scholars, as search engine companies tend to be very secretive when it comes to guarding their corporate information.

Finally, there is further need to engage in an anthropological study of the online users themselves and the process of information retrieval. The studies presented in this book are based on the longitudinal collection of data available through search engines, and thus the analysis does not fully account for the complexity of factors involved in the search process itself as well as the historical, social, economic, political and cultural background of the online users in each country. Taking into account these various conditions will require further monitoring, interviews and surveys in order to get a better grasp of the user's need for information and the adoption of various strategies and techniques to acquire online information. When combined, these studies will complement one another and deepen our understanding of the digital divide of information uses.

Notes

1. The term 'unique users' refers to the number of different individuals that have used Google in a specific period. Marketers and website owners track the number of unique users in any given period by registering their IP addresses, browser IDs and other details (SearchCIO, 2006).
2. In April 2007, Google was claimed to be the most valuable brand, with a value of $66,434 million (Millward Brown, 2007).
3. The concept of the digital divide and particularly the digital divide of information uses will be broadly discussed in Chapter 1.
4. By 'US-centric views' I mainly refer to the asymmetrical flow of online information from the USA and therefore also to the dominance of US priorities and agendas in popular online channels (as will be displayed in Google News and Google Maps). Similarly, some other leading countries other than the USA play a significant role in the production and dissemination of information reflected by search engines. See also the section on US dominance, and the experiments in Chapters 5 and 6.
5. See Chapter 1 for more recent studies on the digital divide of information uses.
6. The term 'alternative views' is used hereafter to refer to non-mainstream views. In the context of the US dominance discourse, alternative views often take the form of views that oppose US priorities and agendas.
7. The term 'Western countries' is used hereafter to refer to Western European countries, as well as the USA, Canada, Australia and New Zealand.
8. See Chapter 3 for a detailed discussion on Google's AdWords advertising programme.
9. See Chapter 1 for further elaboration on Innis's concepts (e.g. bias of communication and the monopoly of knowledge).
10. See Chapter 3 for a detailed explanation of the page-ranking mechanisms in search engines.
11. See also the section on the future of search engines in the conclusion.

Power, communication and the internet

The study of the digital divide has its roots in the historical investigation of the social and political ramifications of media and communications. This chapter looks at the evolution of ICTs and the contribution of new ICTs to the emergence of the so-called 'information society' with its inevitable inequalities and biases. It highlights the central role of information in the production of power as it has been argued that when information becomes 'useful' and productive, it turns into knowledge (Borgmann, 1999; Roberts, 2000) and so into a potentially powerful social and political tool. The internet is currently one of the main media through which one can transfer and diffuse information worldwide. It is also an important channel used by dominant actors within the information society to exercise and expand their control, and thus produce information and knowledge inequalities.

In exploring the asymmetry of information production and diffusion, one finds that contemporary disciplinary and cross-disciplinary studies offer a range of understandings, assessments and critiques. The internet is a relatively new technology, and it is therefore not always simple to evaluate its social impact, especially while it is still in the process of diffusion and institutionalisation. Nonetheless, given that the internet was developed from previous technologies and within an existing social context, it is wise to observe the history of media and the use of information first, rather than to rush into forming new theories and frameworks of analysis. Exploring how media and communications were historically used to gain social, economic and political power, this chapter delineates the background to understand the significant role of the internet and search engines today, suggesting that in line with previous patterns they offer limitations as well as possibilities for social change. The following chapters will examine more specifically the role of search engines and Google in this context, particularly their contribution to the digital divide of information uses.

Communication and power

Over the years, dominant actors have used communication in order to exert power and control, and communication practices have in return shaped the way in which power is exerted. Two leading media and communication theorists, Harold Innis and Armand Mattelart, provide an historical account of the relation between communications and political power and, in many ways, construct the foundations of the concept of the digital divide. The writings of Innis are particularly relevant for his development of the key concepts of communication bias and monopoly of knowledge. Mattelart provides a comprehensive and wide analysis of the political aspects of communications, the information society and the digital divide, which will be used throughout the book.

Innis was one of the first to examine the operation of empires from a media and communication perspective. His basic proposition is that the 'effective government of large areas depends to a very important extent on the efficiency of communication' (Innis, 1972: 7). He defines 'empire' as an institution within a civilisation that promotes a monopoly of communication and therefore also a *monopoly of knowledge*. Monopoly of knowledge has three applications in his work: (a) monopoly of knowledge by one dominant form of communication (such as oral or written communication); (b) monopoly of knowledge by one dominant resource and technology (such as printing and paper, papyrus or parchment); and (c) monopoly of knowledge by one dominant class or group (such as the clergy or the middle class). Innis finds similar communication patterns among empires throughout history. He believes that the monopoly of knowledge eventually threatens the stability of the empire, suggesting that successful and efficient empires could usually maintain a certain balance between a variety of media forms, resources and users.

From a different perspective, Mattelart (1980) explains the role of communication in reinforcing dominant social and political norms and structures. Using a Marxist framework, Mattelart describes how the mass media of radio and television were used to reinforce the dominant bourgeois ideology in Chile in the mid-1970s. The Marxist notion of 'dominant ideology' shows similarities to the 'monopoly of knowledge' described in many of Innis's texts. While Innis provides various applications of the 'monopoly of knowledge', Mattelart focuses mainly on class hegemony. Both Innis and Mattelart argue that this dominant ideology, disseminated through media channels and 'unifying' people under similar knowledge patterns, eventually forms imperial power. Interestingly, Mattelart claims that a long-lasting empire is one that can maintain a *plurality* of expressions, while Innis talks about heterogeneous media that have both time and space orientations, and a balance between writing and oral traditions.[1] The plurality of Mattelart is somewhat different from that of Innis: it is a plurality that offers the opportunity to express different opinions. Only media that allow the receiver to transmit can obtain and maintain this plurality.

Innis's 'monopoly of knowledge' is related to a useful (though not problem-free) distinction between two types of media. The first type is concerned with duration over *time*, while the second deals with extension in *space*. Time-biased media and communication tools refer to heavy materials such as stone that lasts for a long time but has a limited diffusion. For example, the ancient theocratic empires used stone architecture to communicate 'authority' and to exert control locally. Innis also considers the spoken language as a time-biased communication tool as it is inherited locally and not so easily diffused. Space-biased media and communication tools refer to lighter materials such as paper, which has a relatively short life but great diffusion. Later empires used the press and other light technologies to communicate and exert control globally.

The development of monopolies of knowledge (based on dominant media forms, resources or class) and their inevitable biases can be seen throughout history. The invention of paper and later the press, a spaced-biased medium à la Innis, contributed to urbanisation, as paper could be produced cheaply, primarily in cities. Ultimately, this is why when the innovation of paper reached Europe, it transferred control over media production from rural monasteries to urban cathedral schools and universities. It also encouraged the revival of a vernacular literature, rather than one dominated by Latin, and consequently helped in the development of a collective feeling of a national 'imagined community' (Anderson, 1983) as well as a new political bureaucracy. Together with the popularity of paper as a medium, the printing press emerged, leading to the mass production of texts in many languages. At first, these texts were predominantly religious, but gradually prose, science and politics also benefited from the Gutenberg revolution (McLuhan, 1962). Newspapers, published daily, became a force in disseminating current events as well as strengthening public awareness and engagement in social and political life.

For the British Empire, the press helped to reinforce literary activities, and the English language was employed to establish cultural domination within its colonies (Ngugi, 1986). The invention of the telegraph and the telephone linked distant places and worked toward the expansion and control of greater areas. By 1880, the British Empire had an extensive international telecommunications system that provided economic and geopolitical control (Headrick, 1991; Hills, 2002). The emergence of radio and wireless technology increased the economic and military coordination and efficiency across the oceans and later also in the air. This technology was employed by the USA and Germany to a greater extent than by the UK, which was still counting mainly on its global telegraph and cable systems. Thus, McMahon (2002) believes that the failure of Britain to lead the development of radio was a factor in the reduction of its global power and influence. In contrast, Hills (2002) suggests that it was not the lack of technological capabilities as much as Britain's insistence of retaining radio broadcasting under state ownership, unlike in the USA where companies began broadcasting worldwide on a commercial basis.

The mass production of newspapers and radio provided fertile ground for advertisements and propaganda, as well as for nationalism and communism. Their unidirectional nature served the conflicting interests of dominant actors leading to the Second World War. By the beginning of the Cold War, the USA had invested heavily in developing ICTs, which translated into global economic and political advantages. In 1975, satellites and microwave technologies provided the USA with the possibility of full global coverage and control over information worldwide, carrying voice, telex, television, fax and other data simultaneously. Furthermore, satellite technology was so expensive and complex that the supply of equipment was dominated by the USA, the Soviet Union and a few wealthy Western countries. Encouraged by governmental support, US corporations, particularly communication companies, gradually formed worldwide dominant monopolies and oligopolies (e.g. IBM, Motorola and AT&T), which, in turn, provided not only business and private services, but also military and political advantages, furnishing the USA with the power to shape the international order (McMahon, 2002).

However, although technological advantages increased US dominance in world politics and economy, they were supported by the fact that the USA already had specific economic, political and military advantages. Various scholars suggest that the international political, economic and technological advantages of the USA are interrelated and very much prevail globally (Kennedy, 1989; Schiller, 1992, 1996; Mosco, 1996; Hardt and Negri, 2000; Hills, 2002; Ignatieff, 2003). Thus, the monopoly of knowledge is now characterised by the popularity of light media channels (e.g. space-biased electronic communication, mobile phones and the internet), which are often dominated by commercial and US actors. Time-biased media have not yet arisen in response to challenge this trend seriously.

The emergence of the internet

The duality of time and space gets an interesting twist in the information age, where technological developments enable people to communicate and 'work as a unit in real time on a planetary scale' (Castells, 1996: 92). The internet in this view is a major and paradigmatic medium of the information age. Its lightness, diffusion, penetration and immediacy have a considerable influence on social relations and communication practices (Baron, 2008), and therefore also on the continuous developments and changes of the monopoly of knowledge and its biases.

The immediacy and global dissemination of online information make the internet a very useful space-biased medium, yet its potential to serve as a time-biased medium, i.e. its potential for storing this information, is not always fully exploited. One of the initial rationales for designing computer network infrastructure in the 1960s was to create an indestructible information system that could survive a heavy offensive (Norris, 2001). The decentralised and resistant network structure was considered as a possible solution. Unlike heavy stone and ephemeral paper, digital data are light, mobile and can theoretically exist forever. There is no difference between the original and the copy of a digital product and, like the virus that can be duplicated, the digital product can be produced and maintained in a growing network of online carriers. It is very likely that the ideal infrastructure to preserve data is the internet. Sending e-mails, searching for information and even creating websites are all seemingly ephemeral or temporal activities. However, it is also possible to store and archive this information and, as will be suggested, this has already been partly done by Google and other search engines. This opportunity in return has significant implications for the emerging monopolies of knowledge à la Innis.

Another way to store information is through peer-to-peer (P2P) technology. Supported by the internet infrastructure, P2P technology enables users to share information and download files directly from one another in a way that provides a 'natural' duplication and dissemination of information. This technology was designed to provide a direct communication line between individuals, but as a by-product it also deposits information in the network and maintains it as long as the network exists.[2] Thus, P2P and similar technologies that enhance the connectivity of the online network can be technically adapted to provide an answer to the limited expectancy of online information.

Hence, the internet (especially with the help of online applications such as search engines) embodies both time and space-biased media. It is the

5

lightest media tool as it spreads and diffuses with the speed of light. It also has the ability to store information for unlimited time. From this perspective, the internet along with other new ICTs can potentially develop and prove to be an even more powerful instrument of control than is currently the case, or generally imagined. The time-space theory of Innis, when applied to the internet and its information agents such as Google, reveals their potentially tremendous power in shaping the global informational order.

Yet it leaves open some questions regarding the nature of this power, i.e. the nature of the emerging monopoly of knowledge. Innis (1951) argues that the contemporary empire is much more abstract and mostly based on our mind. The 'imperial' act of invasion and penetration is of ideas into human minds, through the bombardment of information, advertisements and spin. Thus, dominant communication corporations (particularly search engines) that organise and customise the intractable flow of information contribute to the emergence of a monopoly of knowledge. Additionally, information-skilled users, who produce and utilise interfaces to promote personal, group or corporate interests, play an important role in this process.

Another way to look at the new monopoly of knowledge is through the growing dominance of the internet as a form of communication. A recent report revealed, for example, that people in Britain spend more time on the internet than watching television (B. Johnson, 2006). The internet not only serves as an information channel, but also shapes, tightens and maintains social relations, facilitating a global network structure. This is particularly important in the light of the argument by Innis (1951) that the more a medium of communication is used, the stronger its influence on the creation of a monopoly of knowledge. Hence, online communication, as it spreads and penetrates every aspect of life, has great potential to shape the next monopoly of knowledge in the contemporary world.

It is impossible to point to a single factor that exclusively shapes the new monopoly of knowledge, but rather one should look at the emerging system of interactions between the various actors (i.e. internet companies, information-skilled users and the internet infrastructure). In this way, the society of today can be perceived as a network with key junctures where crucial and powerful information is stored. Those who can access the junctures and the hubs can influence others politically, financially and culturally. As will be shown later, search engines are understood in this context as the main interfaces that mediate between online users and the internet (although they are also an integral part of the network). Being in such a strategic position, search engines have become information 'authorities' that often define the important and the less important, and even the private and the public in terms of online information. A new monopoly of knowledge is therefore emerging as a result of this constant interaction between dominant actors.

It is believed that the commercialisation of the internet, particularly the dominance of commercial search engines, has a significant influence on this monopoly of knowledge. As was previously suggested, as much of the online production comes from the USA, the new monopoly of knowledge is also strongly influenced by US views and agendas. Hence, although the internet offers various methods and opportunities to express and communicate, this does not always translate into equality. Various examples in this book will indicate that both commercial and US considerations often shape the organisation of information, the inclusion and exclusion mechanisms and the various asymmetries of information production and distribution.

The various faces of the digital divide

The term 'digital divide' originally referred to the gap and inequality in accessing online information, the capacity and skills of ICT use, the technical quality of the network, the governmental and social investment for online infrastructure and education, the overall ability to translate and evaluate information, and the social diversity of users (Anderson et al., 1995). The internet is one of the most significant media in which the digital divide emerges, allowing different opportunities for individuals to find jobs, acquire education, access governmental information, and participate in political panels and support groups. People who are unable or less able to access the internet therefore have fewer political, economic and social opportunities and find themselves in a disadvantageous position.

Pippa Norris (2001) specifies three types of digital divide: *the global divide*, which is the difference in access to the internet and its infrastructure among different countries; *the social divide*, which is the difference in access among diverse social groups; and *the democratic divide*, which refers to the different applications and uses of online information to engage, mobilise and participate in public life. Her comprehensive study uses data from 179 countries and a variety of social groups, and indicates that the inequality of access, which although may gradually decrease over time, is subject to and powerless to overturn other fundamental inequalities, such as endemic social stratifications and world poverty. Her study indicates that in the period between 1996 and 1999, the digital divide in Europe expanded. The inequalities of access on the basis of income, education, occupation and age increased, whereas only the gender gap decreased over time. The results of her study describe the first years of internet institutionalisation, and some aspects may indeed change in the longer term when the use of the internet becomes even more entrenched. However, internet diffusion may also slow down and stop at a certain point of saturation, as has happened with all previous information technologies. Indeed, information inequality is not limited to the internet; similar inequalities exist with other information technologies such as television, fax machines and the telephone. There is a constant gap that is deeply rooted in socio-economic conditions and obstacles and cannot be bridged by simple technical training.

Yet due to the complexity of the internet and the variety of applications, Norris also points out that online inequalities should be assessed not only in terms of access, but also in terms of information skills. The interactive and complex properties of the internet enable those who possess better skills, education and multimedia literacy to retrieve more relevant and useful information which can be translated into social, economic and political advantages. Thus, when the internet is compared with other media (such as the press or television), DiMaggio et al. (2004) suggest that inequalities are greater on the internet. Being so diverse in terms of content and methods, inequality on the internet depends more than other media on information skills. In particular, their study indicates greater socio-economic differences on the internet when users search for health, politics and employment-related information. Drawing data from this and similar studies, they concluded that information would be more unequally distributed in a world dominated by the internet.

Similarly, Bonfadelli (2002) suggests that the relative heterogeneity and depth of coverage on the internet compared with that of newspapers and television is more likely to exacerbate information inequalities. The digital divide in Bonfadelli's view should be assessed in terms of information uses, in particular the ability of skilled information users to employ the internet to retrieve deeper and more valuable information. Thus, such users can retrieve a relatively high volume and variety of information and, at the same time, customise, exploit and control it successfully. To this end, search engines have an increasingly important role in empowering skilled users, as they also aim to cover an extensive amount of information (highest volume), and to enable online users to search, organise, customise and retrieve the most desirable and relevant information (highest control).[3]

The idea to examine the digital divide in terms of volume and control was also applied in a study by Ciolek (2003). He analysed the digital divide between states in East Asia as a result of different demands for online information, different redundancies of online resources (high volume) and different distribution of information skills (high control). His study indicates that developments in information and communication technologies and skills have established a new hierarchy of leaders across Eastern Asia, with Japan, Taiwan and South Korea being particularly dominant in hardware, software and information skills. Ciolek argues that this digital divide of skills in this region is expected to grow in the future. He distinguishes 'performer' societies and states from 'spectator' societies and states, where the former actively produce online information, and therefore have economic and political advantages over the latter.[4]

Thus, in order to address the problem of the digital divide it is important to look at both the unequal volume and the unequal control over information. As was previously argued, tackling the problem of volume alone through investments in ICT will not solve the problem. Warschauer (2004) gives various examples of unsuccessful governmental projects in India, Ireland and Egypt, which attempted to decrease the digital divide through massive investments in IT infrastructure. Rather than access, he suggests encouraging *meaningful* access, which also includes the use of content and language, literacy and education, and community and institutional structures. In terms of content and language, he indicates the unequal production of websites, which is concentrated mainly in the USA and Europe. Hence, even with cheaper hardware and greater access, online users in developing countries will find hardly any benefit in using the internet.

This division of online content is applicable at the international and also the national level. Lazarus and Mora (2000) indicate the digital divide of content within the USA itself, where most websites are developed to answer the needs of the country's wealthier online users, while the poor remain with incomplete online information. In order to solve this problem, Warschauer (2004) proposes assessing the needs of the local population and encouraging community involvement and production of local content and applications, particularly in the fields of economics, health, education and local news. Chapter 4 suggests focusing on similar topics while assessing the digital divide of information uses.

The problem of unequal control over information is therefore related to information skills as well as the variety and type of content being used. Towards the end of the 1990s, observers had already noted that some users tend to use the internet more than others, and that these users are often more educated and receive higher salaries (Benton Foundation, 1998; Hoffman and Novak, 1998; 1999; Strover, 1999; Bucy, 2000). Clearly, there is a certain connection between information skills and uses. Howard et al. (2001) studied the digital divide of information uses by looking at the length of users' experience and the frequency of their logging on from home. They subsequently constructed four categories of internet users: netizens (heavy and enthusiastic users), utilitarians (functional users), experimenters (use the internet mostly as an information retrieval tool) and newcomers. Their study indicates that netizens use the internet more than others for economic and political purposes (e.g. financial activities, getting the news, and education). Additionally, they found differences between the information uses of men and women: the former are more likely to seek news, finance, sports and shop online, while the latter are more likely to search for health-related information, religion, new jobs and online games. In terms of age, the different information uses are even more prominent: younger users are more likely to use chat rooms and instant messaging, download music and pursue other entertainment-related activities. In short, their findings suggest that different uses of online information stem from various demographic and socio-economic factors as well as experience and long exposure to the internet.

DiMaggio et al. (2004) further expanded the concept of the digital divide. They identified five forms of information inequality: inequality of technical means (e.g. hardware, software and connection), the extent of autonomy in using the web (e.g. monitored or limited use), inequality of information skills (knowledge of the interface, software and hardware), inequality of social support and, finally, the different purposes of information uses. Their study suggests that these differences shape the online experience of users and their political and economic advantages.

Looking at the different information uses and purposes, Robinson, DiMaggio and Hargittai (2003) indicate that college-educated online users possess clear advantages over high-school educated online users. They suggest that the former use the internet much more to search for jobs, health, education and other economic and political benefits. Subsequently, their study concludes by suggesting that the digital divide is further widened by different uses of online information and particularly by political and economic uses.

The digital divide has important implications for the structures and hierarchies of the information society. While the internet was initially thought to provide equal opportunities and freedom of information for all (Rheingold, 1993; Negroponte, 1995), it also appears to empower certain online users with more resources and information skills (Resnik, 1998;

Hargittai, 2000, 2003; Norris, 2001; DiMaggio et al., 2001; Ciolek, 2003; Castells, 2004; R. Rogers, 2004). While it was expected to be open and encourage a plurality of expressions and views (Shapiro and Varian, 1999; Caves, 2000), it also appears to commodify information and promote dominant paradigms through gatekeeping mechanisms (Waxman, 2000; Webster and Lin, 2002; Barzilai-Nahon, 2006b). This book focuses mainly on what Norris (2001) calls the 'democratic divide' worldwide, looking at the different applications of online information in different states. It deals less with the inequality of access and more with the inequality of uses and skills. Various examples will suggest that the production of information and its uses play a vital role in the emergence of the digital divide. This depends on the content, i.e. *which* kind of information is produced and retrieved, as well as the context, i.e. *how* this information is acquired and used. Search engines, which prioritise, organise and customise online information, are therefore very important agents in this context. As indicated in the following chapters, the ability of online users to obtain and extract relevant information depends greatly on their organisation of online information based on their technologies, search mechanisms and other corporate considerations.

The online knowledge/power nexus

The growing consumption of and dependence on online information is closely linked to the online knowledge/power nexus. Knowledge can be understood in this context as the production and use of information. It is a higher evolutionary form that requires abilities to recognise patterns within information and therefore involves awareness, understanding and learning of information (Roberts, 2000). New knowledge can lead to the production of innovative technology (Feldman, 2002), which has the potential to benefit and empower its users.

Lundvall and Johnson (1994) have divided knowledge into four types: *know-what*, *know-why*, *know-how* and *know-who*. *Know-what* refers to any kind of fact; *know-why* refers to scientific knowledge of the laws of nature; *know-how* refers to skills; and *know-who* refers to a specific social relation. While the first two types of knowledge are more explicit, and can therefore be easily coded for information and transferred online, the last two types of knowledge are more tacit, and are therefore embedded in local, social and cultural contexts and are not easily transferred online.

This taxonomy of knowledge is problematic particularly as tacit and explicit forms of knowledge are strongly interrelated. Even the very explicit knowledge of *know-what* that is easily coded and transferred, can be eventually decoded and understood only in specific social and cultural contexts (Roberts, 2000). Moreover, the knowledge of *know-who* gradually becomes more explicit in its online form and can be easily transferred through special interfaces such as chat rooms, forums and social network services. People not only communicate but also shape their online identities, add their photos and videos, share their thoughts and interact with other online users. Identities are therefore increasingly shaped by information production and consumption habits. Similarly, when it comes to information skills, *know-how* can be explicit and transferable. Online users can learn from each other how to write code, how to design websites, and how to retrieve relevant information. They further encourage one another to use similar interfaces in order to communicate, share files and transfer information skills.

Despite the complexity of online knowledge, dividing it into four types can be helpful. The knowledge of *know-what* and *know-why* are still relatively more explicit and clear, and can therefore be easily produced and distributed through online networks. Indeed, online information can be used in various ways depending on the information skills of users (*know-how*), and their characteristics and social networks (*know-who*). This kind of knowledge is still relatively more tacit, and can therefore be implied indirectly through the study of *know-what*. By observing what sort of information people search, one can learn also about their skills and methods. Chapter 4, for example, tries to assess the different information skills of users (*know-how*) by analysing the variety and specificity of their search queries in Google (*know-what*).

Another aspect of the *know-how* knowledge is examined through the operation of dominant online actors such as popular search engines that employ strategies and tactics of manipulation of online information. Again, the knowledge of how, i.e. search engine strategies and methods, could be derived from the information and services that they produce and provide (*know-what*). A major challenge of internet researchers in general and this book in particular is to look at the various aspects of online information and the way it evolves to become different types of knowledge and ultimately an instrument of power. Knowledge in this sense is perceived as a means of gaining competitive advantages and maintaining certain social hierarchies. This view is directly linked to the historical struggles over knowledge and power that were discussed earlier.

The emergence of the information society

The digital divide and the particular role of search engines are part of a broader discourse on the information society. Mattelart (2003) reminds us that most of this discourse tends to focus on recent ICT developments, without taking into account the historical perspective and the origins of the concepts of 'information' and 'network'. These roots can be traced back to the development of statistics and data collection in the seventeenth century. Later, together with the growing popularity of positivist theories, scientists started perceiving society as a functional industry that should be constantly measured and assessed.

The information society as a concept was popularised by the economist Fritz Machlup (1973), who studied the production, distribution and consumption of information in the USA. Like many other communication theorists, he understood the significance of the political economy of knowledge in the society of the time. Machlup was especially interested in the uses of information in the economic sphere. Subsequently, together with the rapid spread of ICTs and their integration in almost every aspect of life, the information society became a subject of study in a wide range of disciplines.

Some scholars believe that the information society is a culmination of the industrial society (Hardt and Negri, 2000; Kellerman, 2002). They use terms such as 'immaterial labour', 'mass intellectuality' and 'creative class' (Florida, 2002) or refer to 'informational labour' that is highly educated and capable of 'self-programming' (Castells, 1996) in order to describe the growing information skills required from labour (e.g. engineers, scientists, technicians and researchers). This view perceives information as a commodity and therefore also as a main source of economic power, particularly for global communication corporations which are capable, often more so than others, of controlling the production, distribution and exchange of information (Mosco, 1996). In this context, the digital divide therefore appears as the different information skills and companies' abilities to customise information for specific needs and manipulate and control appropriate information.

A study by Virni and Hardt (1996) analysed the current transformation of productive labour. It found a growing tendency for immaterialism. Intellectual, immaterial and communicative labour has gradually come to dominate the social scene, especially in post-industrial countries. Manufacturing and production increasingly depend on integrating and processing ICTs, but that does not necessarily mean that today's society produces more information products than before. It means, primarily, that the focus moves from the production of symbols to the circulation of symbols. Circulation and dissemination of symbols is exactly what search engines are about, which explains their increasingly important role in the emerging information economy and the inevitable digital divide of information uses.

Hardt and Negri (2000) suggest that inequalities and hierarchies in the information society are shaped by the dominant immaterial production, the increasing integration of ICTs and the operation of transnational corporations. Interestingly, they view this socio-economic, informational and communicational order as a new type of empire, which is different in many ways from the old empires. In most cases, dominant actors do not physically intervene in independent juridical territories, but rather try to unify the world and construct the moral, normative and institutional order of an empire by controlling the processes and structures of production and communication.

The importance of internet companies (and, to that end, also search engines) to the emerging information society receives further support in the work of Castells (1996). He believes that the global economic, social, political and cultural changes in the last few decades correspond with technological developments, some of which originate in Silicon Valley. These technologies were initially designed by small groups of innovators to address the crisis of company profitability, and to increase productivity dramatically. Although assessing the contribution of information systems to productivity is relatively complicated even at the micro-organisational level (Garnham, 2001), they have certainly contributed to the development of a new industry of knowledge. Here again, search engines and their ability to increase the popularity of certain online businesses as well as to retrieve business-related information have become an essential source of production and power and thus provide an important field of investigation.

The power of interfaces

While the digital divide is concerned with various information uses and skills, there is also much significance in the way in which technology is designed and shaped. People acquire online information and translate it into knowledge using various interfaces. However, some online interfaces (e.g. the Google homepage) are more dominant than others. One may argue that on the internet people can choose to obtain varied online content and enjoy freedom of expression, but in fact their choices are very often limited to popular and standardised interfaces, browsers and operating systems. Like the internet, the telephone is characterised by a standard method of communication, while the content remains varied and free. With the telephone, people can communicate across geographical boundaries, and are free to choose the language and the content of the conversation. Television also provides a standard method and form of transferring a diversity of mass communication content to individuals. Here, too, there is a trend towards an increasing choice of channels and narrowcasting capabilities.

The internet, which combines individual as well as mass communications, has similar traits. However, when compared with older technologies that had a rather primitive interface and simple embedded software, the use of computer-mediated communication (CMC)[5] opens a completely new dimension of methods to communicate and acquire information. For example, the experience of reading online news (as opposed to reading newspapers) provides users with immediate and free access to a great variety of online sources. Most of these sources enable further searching and customisation of the news for the specific interests of each reader. Moreover, online news increasingly combines video and sound files as well as interactive abilities (such as talk-backs and sending articles to friends). The variety of software and advanced interfaces provides CMC in general and the internet in particular with new ways of doing things. Hence, the role of the code and the method of communication, i.e. how information is retrieved, has become a much more significant aspect of media and social studies.

Yet, together with more ways for doing things online, the following chapters will indicate that certain interfaces (particularly Google Search and its specific channels) increasingly dominate the online landscape and reinforce – through their code and automatic algorithms – common standards and online practices. Chapter 5, for example, examines Google News, an increasingly popular interface that aggregates various online news sources. It shows that together with new opportunities to read various news sources, there is also a clear preference (embedded in the automatic search algorithm) for the bigger and more popular English news sources, which, in return, shape a certain understanding of the world.

This suggests that behind the interface lie various economic and political considerations. Being the mediator between hardware and people, interfaces are deeply embedded within the infrastructure of the network: telecommunication lines, electrical power, computing technology, information resources, organisational arrangements and users' practices (Star and Ruhleder, 1996; Borgman, 2000). Yet they are also embedded in ideology, culture, ethnicity, class, gender, age and the physical limitations of their users. Similar to stone, metal, fire and other tools, interfaces do not have pre-assigned properties that are detached from time, space and context (Grabill, 2003). On the contrary, the different ways in which people adapt and operate interfaces constantly shape new meanings to them. They provide a continuous dialogue, i.e. a relationship between infrastructural interfaces and their users, tools and people, technology and society. As such, the interfaces of Google and other popular websites are being shaped through a constant dialogue between the needs of online users, the companies' commercial considerations and the dominance of certain states.

'Informational politics' online

There is no doubt that the growing popularity and dependence on online interfaces have certain implications also for the political sphere (Castells, 1997; May, 2002; Mattelart, 2003; Barney, 2004; van Dijk, 2005). The online infrastructure extends the traditional public forum, as it allows for the formation of communities and political agents, representing interests and ideas that gradually become more specific and specialised (Nguyen and Alexander 1996). Norris (2001) has indicated that the internet increases the chances of smaller and single idea-oriented parties to reach audiences and publicise campaigns. Hill and Hughes (1998) found that the internet often serves as an anti-government or alternative channel to express marginal and non-canonical ideas. It supports the operation of marginal groups and subcultures, some of which might be extremist (Bell, 2001) and revolutionary, as it broadens the abilities of online users to spread ideas and recruit people on a global scale. The favourite example among scholars is that of the Zapatistas, a Mexican revolutionary movement, which exploited the internet very effectively to get international support and promote indigenous rights in the Chiapas region (Cleaver, 1998; Ronfeldt et al., 1998). Since then, the world has seen several successful and less-successful attempts to use the internet to promote the interests of the Association of Women of Afghanistan, the 'patriotic' right-wing militias in the USA and the aboriginal people in Canada. These marginal groups not only publish online information, but also recruit members, raise funds, maintain communication, coordinate political actions and events, establish links with other organisations, maintain political forums and online debates, and, finally, promote political goals through mass e-mail campaigns, parody sites and denial of service attacks (Barney, 2004).

Apart from an alternative channel for marginal groups, the internet also serves as a supportive communication infrastructure for a growing number of international political networks such as those of environmentalists and human rights activists. An empirical study by R. Rogers (2004) suggests that such online networks tend very often to depart from the national institutional framework. In this way, the internet and its online community challenge the national structure and enhance re-territorialisation processes. Online communications may therefore instigate decentralisation of the political map. Additionally, Bohman (2004) argues that the internet provides a more open public sphere because of the relative difficulties of governments to enforce censorship. The online network allows opportunities to express and share public ideas and therefore some argue that it is the ultimate medium to exercise freedom of speech (Rheingold, 1993; Negroponte, 1995; T. B. Riley, 2001).

However, the fact that individuals can express themselves spontaneously, randomly and often anonymously has political drawbacks. Anonymous online users can be easily tempted to take no responsibility for what they say or write. This is also why Bohman (2004) perceives the internet as a relatively 'weak' public sphere where the political forum is still unable to exercise direct influence through institutionalised decision procedures. Moreover, Schenk (1997) argues that the flood of information (or disinformation) misleads online users and obscures any sensible political dialogue, reducing the possibility of developing deep and meaningful arguments. This makes the internet a useful political instrument to reinforce dispositions and mobilisation, rather than to listen and debate.

Thus, when politics goes online it has to play by the network's rules. On the internet, individuals, organisations and governments compete to be found through search engines and to be associated with certain keywords. This has also been described as the 'politics behind information retrieval, or back-end information politics' (R. Rogers, 2004: 4). The media-saturated society, the competitive capitalist environment and the increasing density of information are factors that encourage political parties to provide information in easily accessible form, and to 'brand' their politics (Downs, 1957). Castells (1997) goes on to call it 'informational politics', suggesting that current politics can exist mostly through media channels, which politicians must manipulate constantly in order to gain or retain their power. First, politicians are required to deliver simple yet ambiguous messages in order to attract heterogeneous audiences with diverse views. Second, they increasingly employ 'destructive politics', i.e. directly or indirectly revealing the personal scandals and professional mistakes of their competitors, which can be easily exposed and rapidly disseminated in the global network. As a result, informational politics can bring about scepticism, governmental mistrust, and a 'crisis of democracy in the information age' (Castells, 1996: 302). Although the decentralised network may, in theory, provide more political opportunities, there is also a certain competition, and, as will be suggested, search engines play a central role in channelling the attention of online users to the bigger and more popular political actors.

Apart from popularisation, 'informational politics' is shaped by the principle of customisation.[6] It is important to note that the internet has various applications, and some online channels offer a growing number of opportunities to develop deeper and more comprehensive debates, publish papers in e-journals, reflect thoughts in weblogs, and carry out similar activities. Thus, in order to understand the political implications of the various online communication channels, one must also explore the specific ways in which they are used. This is particularly crucial as unlike television, radio or newspapers (at least in their previous non-interactive form), the internet enables users to choose their content and to 'compose' their story rather than to receive the ready-made edited and interpreted story. Nonetheless, online customisation can also have a negative influence on the political discourse. While news and politics used to be the main part of the primetime content on television, on the internet it is only an option for those users who are interested in news. In many portals, politics and news are placed graphically and conceptually at the same level with other items such as sports or entertainment. Any kind of content that goes online may become no more than a customised information product with a special priority to commercial content. Today, news on television or radio is broadcast by a common preference order of significance: for example, international news about war and peace, national news, economic affairs and, only at the very end, sports and entertainments. Similarly, in the press, politics usually appears on the front page, while sports and entertainment usually appear at the end. On the internet, users have greater freedom to choose what information to obtain from the very beginning, and then edit the length, the depth and the sequence of the stories according to their own interests. Based on hypertext, the internet offers a perfect customisation of information for individuals, thus contributing to the emergence of a fragmented society with hardly any common preference in the order of significance (Sunstein, 2001). The signs of this trend can also be seen today in interactive television, where news is one of many information products – a branch of entertainment (Samson, 1996; Franklin, 1997; Tumber, 2001). National and international informational politics ends as a brand item, among many other information products that today's society produces and consumes.

Thus, customisation of information ultimately means a growing gap between the politically engaged and disengaged. Chapter 4 will examine the content of popular search queries, indicating that most searches (particularly in English-speaking countries) are about entertainment, while very few, if any, are about politics. This provides further support for the little interest of many online users worldwide in political matters, a trend which is only reinforced by the advanced customisation mechanisms of search engines and other new media (Sunstein, 2001; Introna and Nissenbaum, 2000).

Conclusion

> We live in an era of global communications. Scientists and technologists have achieved what militarists and statesmen down the ages have attempted to establish but without success – the global empire. (Saatchi & Saatchi, 1986)

This chapter examined the connection between the production and dissemination of information and the concept of the digital divide. It suggested viewing the internet and search engines in the light of the history of communication. Theorists such as Innis and Mattelart have provided a framework to understand the importance of communications in the productions of power.[7] Innis proposed that the stability of any social order requires a balance between time and space-biased media, while Mattelart argued that it could be effectively achieved by maintaining a plurality of expressions, in which the receiver can also transmit. It is therefore not surprising why the internet, which offers a variety of communication methods and can potentially provide a balance between time and space biases, has become a dominant medium in the information society. While allowing for heterogeneity of expressions, it also encourages the dominance of methods, standards and interfaces.

Innis's monopoly of knowledge could be practised today through the interaction of dominant actors (i.e. information-skilled users, popular search engines and other communication corporations and dominant governments) within the decentralised global online network. Although in theory the production and consumption of online information can be free and equal, it has been suggested and will be further shown that in practice economic imperatives play a significant role in the production of information inequalities. Despite the various initiatives of international organisations, it seems that US communication corporations and commercial practices often control the information flow and its content.

Both popularisation and customisation are described as the main commercial principles that shape the organisation of online information and thus also the digital divide. The principle of popularisation has been mentioned in this chapter in the context of the emerging 'informational politics' and the increasing competition for users' attention. As a result, the internet may allow plurality of expressions, but very few of them will reach a large audience. The page-ranking mechanism of search engines exhibits this practice. Similarly, the principle of customisation contributes to the digital divide of uses. It has been argued, for example, that unlike former mass media channels, the advanced abilities to customise information in new media immediately creates a certain divide between those who search for jobs, health, education and other economic and political benefits and those who search mainly for entertainment. This suggests that between the politically engaged and the disengaged there is an online gap which is broadened by advanced customisation mechanisms.

While this chapter focused mainly on the internet, the following chapters will demonstrate how these principles shape the production and consumption of information in search engines, and discuss their implications for information retrieval. The concept of the digital divide of information uses, which was introduced in this chapter, will be further examined through the growing ability of search engines to customise and popularise online information.

Notes

1. The duality of time and space-biased media and its current application will be elaborated later.
2. The popularity of information is another important factor in its lifecycle within the network. It is reasonable to believe that an mp3 of the Beatles, for example, will last in the network much longer than an unpopular song file. Network theory is a useful methodology to measure the critical point in the lifecycle of information.

3. The principle of volume and control of information uses is inspired by Lash's (2002) distinction between wild/tamed zones (i.e. different control over information) and life/dead zones (i.e. different volume of information). This principle will be applied in Chapter 4, while developing measurements to examine popular search queries in Google and Yahoo! worldwide.
4. A similar distinction was made by Castells (1996), who differentiated between the interacting and the interacted online population.
5. This trend is increasingly available in mobile phones and digital television.
6. See also the Preface for a detailed discussion on the principles of popularisation and customisation mechanisms and their application throughout this book.
7. Mainly the translation of symbolic power to economic and political power; see also Thompson's (1995) definition of power in the Preface.

2

The structure and power of search engines

Search engines increasingly serve as the main instrument to acquire online information (Hopkins, 2007). Several studies by the Pew Internet and American Life Project indicate that search engine use has become one of the most common online activities (Fallows, 2005, 2008). The growing popularity and power of search engines raises questions about their role in shaping the global information order.

While the first chapter provided a framework to contextualise the historical aspects of communication and the emergence of a global information network, this chapter and the next one focus on the operation of search engines in general and Google in particular. Search engines are perceived as agents that organise online information based on their code and their search mechanisms and therefore empower certain actors. But they can also be seen as mass media channels that continuously grow in terms of popularity, production and market share. To this end, as this chapter shows, they are often required to comply with local demands in order to gain and retain their competitive and at times dominant position.

A short history of information search

The word 'search' is commonly understood as the attempt to find something, whether it is known to exist or not. In most cases, the searcher already has an idea of what is being sought, and the object of the search, once found, may provide the searcher with certain advantages, e.g. the search for food, gold, valuable items, information, and so on. The history of information retrieval goes back to the invention of writing. Although retrieving information from papyrus scrolls was not always efficient, the Greeks and the Romans developed various methods, such as tables of content, hierarchical chapters or alphabetisation systems; these were used, for example, in the famous library of Alexandria (Skydsgaard, 1968). The term 'index' was used to refer to the little slip attached to the papyrus scroll in which the title and sometimes the name of the author were written. Later, the term was extended to refer to a list of titles. As long as information was stored in papyrus scrolls, it was difficult to indicate the exact position of the content within a scroll. Only with the advent of paper and then printing, where information was stored in identical book copies, was it possible to add page numbers to the index, thus greatly facilitating information search (Wellisch, 1991).

During the 1950s, the technical potential to store information in digital media encouraged scientists to develop automatic mechanisms of search and information retrieval based on the previous librarian model. In this model, the user who has some initial information needs, fashions a request as a query, and the system returns a list of relevant documents (Ramana, 2004). One of the greatest challenges of this model is that users must reduce their information needs to a search query, and search mechanisms are supposed to 'guess' their requirements from this query. Automatic search systems are required to build an index that links search queries with relevant documents and therefore extract, summarise, classify and eventually visualise content in friendly interfaces. In other words, they attempt to shorten some of the information retrieval procedures previously done with the help of professional librarians. However, despite the great benefits this system can offer, during this complex process it is always possible that users will translate their information needs into inadequate search queries, or that the system will omit very relevant documents from its index or its search results.

The first search engine, Archie, was developed in 1990, and was based on the idea of downloading the directory listings of all files located on anonymous public File Transfer Protocol (FTP) sites, thus creating a searchable database of filenames. A year later, Gopher was introduced, enabling online users to search within the content of plain-text files. In 1993, various crawl-based search engines, also known as 'robots' or 'crawlers', were developed (e.g. Wandex, WebCrawler and later commercial ones such as Lycos, Excite, Infoseek, Inktomi, Northern Light and AltaVista). The basic principle of those search engines, which is still common nowadays, is to follow hyperlinks from one website to another and retrieve their content, creating an index that connects keywords or search queries with URLs[1] (Sherman and Price, 2001; Battelle, 2005).

In an early analysis of the search engine market, Gandal (2001) noticed that the five big search engines, Yahoo!, Lycos, Excite, Infoseek and

AltaVista, could not maintain their dominance. In 1999, six late entrants (About, LookSmart, Snap, HotBot, GoTo and AskJeeves) grew steadily and reached a market share of 5–6 per cent each. This is to suggest that the power of a brand name alone did not help the big five search engines to retain their competitive position in the long term. Gandal reasoned that the big search engines could not keep up with the rapid growth of the web, and their indexing abilities declined from 20 per cent in 1997 to 16 per cent of the indexable web (Lawrence and Giles, 1998, 1999).[2] Moreover, the search results of the various search engines in the market were different from one another and hardly overlapped. Hence, it is not surprising that online users started using two search engines instead of one in order to get more comprehensive results.

Looking at search and information retrieval, it is particularly appealing to follow McLuhan's (1994) proposition and view electronic media as the extension of our nervous system. The process of remembering, especially in terms of episodic memory (Tulving, 1983), i.e. retrieving context-specific information from our memory, requires finding a *path* in our mind that leads to that information. If, for example, we want to know what we did last weekend, we may first think about the places and people with whom we are more likely to be on weekends, hoping that these memories may also provide a link to the events and activities associated with them. As the internet infrastructure is based on hyperlinks, the process of retrieving online information is very similar to the process of remembering. It also requires finding a certain path that links to an answer. Thus, the first query posed, i.e. the first node to which we connect, can determine the length of the path, including whether there is any existing path to the answer. From this perspective, the search engine is one of the most crucial actors in the network, as it serves as a central hub that links to the other less central nodes. Similar to the process of remembering, in the process of retrieving online information, one needs to ask the 'right' questions, i.e. to use the most relevant keywords. The main challenge of search engines, with a certain resemblance to our mind, is to process those keywords and produce the most relevant answer customised to the specific needs of each user.

Unlike human-mediated information search (e.g. librarian assistance), in automatic search systems the potential of users to find relevant and valuable information depends almost entirely on their information skills, and even more so on the classification and indexing algorithms. This suggests that the biases of knowledge increasingly stem from the technological, economic and political biases of search engine companies. These companies, which develop the code and are therefore responsible for the operation of the search mechanisms, are constantly required to enhance their indexing mechanisms, increase their information coverage and gather more personal information about their users in order to customise and enhance their search results. While trying to cover the most extensive volume of information, search engines face two main technical challenges: the challenge of the deep web and the challenge of the internet infrastructure.

The challenge of the deep web

Computer scientists have defined online information that cannot be accessed through search engines as the 'deep web'. For example, Google (with the greatest search power among popular search engines) can search more than 8 billion webpages, yet this is estimated to be only a small part of the entire web.[3] The index of search engines is created by robot programs called 'spiders' which automatically crawl the web by following links from one webpage to another. As such, search engines can mostly reach only static webpages that have incoming links from other webpages. It is more difficult for them to reach dynamic database webpages with no incoming links, which can be generated only by posing search queries within the database websites themselves. For example, in e-commerce websites or online library catalogues, whenever a person searches for a certain book by typing its name, a new result page is dynamically generated. This unique result page usually has no incoming links from other webpages. As such, it cannot be indexed by most search engines and cannot be accessed from their search results.

Most of the deep web consists of searchable databases such as e-commerce websites, library catalogues, phonebooks and law databases. Another kind of content that, technically, cannot be included in search engines is password-protected websites (e.g. e-journals or premium content that requires subscription). Finally, there is much information on the web in PDF, Flash, Microsoft Word, PowerPoint or image formats, rather than in HTML format, which is the basic web language. Some search engines choose to exclude this kind of information, because of the complexity in indexing it.

Google has been trying to provide deeper access to online information by enabling searching within useful databases such as people finders, patents and dictionary definitions. It also enables searching in various file formats such as PDF and Microsoft Word. Yet, despite all these developments, it can still cover only a small part of the online information available. A study conducted by Bergman (2001) indicates that the deep web has a surprisingly uniform distribution of content across various areas such as the news, technology, humanities, business and the media, most of which is stored in topical databases and is not password-protected. Significantly, it is suggested that the deep web offers much more valuable and relevant content to online users than the 'surface web', i.e. the online information that is indexed by search engines, something that underscores its importance as well as the (often forgotten) limitations of popular search engines.

Nevertheless, many homepages of searchable databases can be retrieved via directories and search engines. After finding the relevant homepages of a searchable database (e.g. the homepage of a library catalogue), it is possible to continue and search for the information in the deep web. In this way, users are required to operate a split-level search. If, for example, one searches for a new job as a scientist in Germany near Hamburg, one first has to locate a website containing searchable databases of vacancies in Germany. As there are many of them, one is required to search, make assessments and choose. This process, which starts with search engines and ends with certain websites of searchable databases, requires time, patience and information skills. In short, there is plenty of valuable information in the deep web, which requires users to exercise high information skills and constantly update and upgrade their findings, as new websites of searchable databases emerge online every day.

Apart from dynamically-generated webpages, many new static webpages that are not linked to the entire web cannot be included within search results. As the basic infrastructure of the world wide web is a network of hyperlinks,[4] for most of the time the search engine's spiders cannot 'see' even relatively big and relevant websites if they are not linked to another indexed webpage. Subsequently, there are always new clusters of websites with valuable information which are hidden from users if they are not linked. Similar to explorers, who used to search for 'new lands', search engine spiders are programmed to continue the quest for the constantly growing web spaces. Those unlinked websites may be doomed to be forgotten or rendered incommunicado, even though they could yield valuable information for online users.

Furthermore, one needs to remember that the internet is constantly growing. At the same time that search engines add new webpages to their index, there are many more new webpages added to the web. As the internet is currently growing much faster than the search engine index (Sherman and Price, 2001; Barabási, 2002), the deep web is also constantly growing. While search engines can cover only a small part of the entire web, they tend to emphasise the quality (rather than the quantity) of search results and the ability to customise online information. This trend makes search engines very useful in finding popular information. When one searches for information about a popular movie or a music band, instead of having billions of links without a preference order, search engines attempt to provide the most popular, comprehensive, 'authoritative' and up-to-date information in the first page of results. However, search engines are a less appropriate tool when it comes to finding very specific, relatively new or esoteric information, which may be found only in the deep web.

Together with the growing depth of the web, new search engines and searching tools emerge. Their aim is to integrate valuable and meaningful databases, and to provide cross-search services. Search engines such as Complete Planet, for example, perform cross-searches in more than 70,000 database websites. Similarly, there are a growing number of domain-specific 'vertical' search engines; one such example is GlobalSpec, which crawls only engineering websites and databases to provide comprehensive catalogue-based information about engineering parts (Battelle, 2005). Apart from specific 'vertical' search engines dedicated to deep web data-mining, popular 'horizontal' search engines such as Google and Yahoo! constantly develop their technology to include more searchable databases and to integrate into their search results more clusters of unlinked webpages, a process also known as federated search (Asadi and Jamali, 2004). Thus, Google has launched Google Scholar, Google News, product search, and parcel and patents tracking, all of which can search within specific databases. Similarly, in March 2004 Yahoo! launched its Content Acquisition Program, integrating more valuable content to its search results from databases of non-commercial sites such as the National Public Radio or UCLA's Cuneiform Digital Library Initiative (Sherman, 2004). Nonetheless, there is still no search engine today that can cover more than a small part of the entire web.

The problem of the deep web is in many ways related to the problem of the digital divide, as in order to reach online information without the help of search engines, users are often required to employ extra financial resources and information skills. They have to be aware of the existence of particular websites so that they can reach them directly, pay membership fees for password-restricted information (e.g. e-journals), use specific search engines that harvest the deep web (e.g. Complete Planet or GlobalSpec), or have an extensive knowledge of the code and the internet infrastructure (e.g. hackers). However, it is important to realise that indexing the deep web does not necessarily mean bridging the digital divide.

Even if most of the deep web becomes accessible through search engines, their strict and discriminating rules will still apply, through page-ranking mechanisms, money-based promotion deals and greater dependence.

The challenge of the internet infrastructure

The other technical challenge for search engines is the ability to retrieve not only information from the deep web, but also information from the entire internet. One should realise that both the surface web and the deep web are part of what is known as the world wide web, which is only yet another informational space within the online network, albeit a significant one. The internet, often mistakenly used as a synonym for the world wide web, includes e-mails, FTP and peer-to-peer protocols. All these spaces serve as resources from which to retrieve and produce online information. The idea behind the internet infrastructure is that when a computer is connected to the network, it can technically communicate with any other computer and exchange online information using a variety of methods. This means that, potentially, search engines can access and use the files and e-mails of any computer in the network.

The architecture of the internet and its code are the communication standards that regulate what people can and cannot do and how (Lessig, 1999). They determine, for example, whether users and their activities are anonymous or identifiable. Anonymity allows for privacy and liberty, while identification leads to surveillance and regulations. Identifiable structure and code are preferable for many governments, furnishing them with greater control and power, and for companies by offering them wider ability to authenticate and secure transactions and intellectual properties, as well as to collect personal information for customisation and marketing purposes (Barney, 2004). In contrast, individuals may prefer an anonymous network architecture and code to protect their privacy and thus encourage free exchange of ideas.

The world wide web space enables computers (clients) to retrieve online information from other computers (servers) using specific software also known as browsers (e.g. Internet Explorer or Mozilla Firefox). The peer-to-peer space enables any computer to exchange information with any other computer using common software such as Skype, Napster or Kazaa. In this way, every single private computer that connects to the internet to retrieve information also serves as an information provider. Similar to webmasters, who use servers to host their websites, with peer-to-peer software online users can choose to share information space in their private computer with all other online users. Like Google's robot that crawls and searches webpages through the world wide web space, the search engine of Napster searches for shared files within the shared informational spaces of its subscribers. Although the peer-to-peer technology exhibits a voluntary intention to share private information, in the online network various examples exhibit the opposite practice. Personal information is often gathered without being noticed and without previous permission. Using the appropriate software, any amateur hacker or advertiser can retrieve personal and private details from computers connected to the online network.

In Chapter 1 it was argued that the digital divide is not only about accessing online information and the technical gap, but also and more important, it involves the various aspects and practices of online information use. While the deep web refers mainly to the major part of the web that cannot be indexed by search engines, valuable online information is also stored in e-mails and shared files,[5] and is still far from being indexed by most search engines. Apart from technical difficulties in accessing this information, the growing need for privacy is one of the main reasons why search engines may face resistance while trying to increase their coverage and 'organise the world's information'. In order to satisfy customers' demands, search engines often engage in the opposite practice, i.e. providing tools for individuals and governments to filter undesirable information and enhance their exclusion mechanisms.

Information protection and digital 'islands'

In February 2006 Google launched Google Desktop 3, software that enables users to search for personal files and e-mails within their own computer and integrate them with the web's search results. A couple of weeks later, a leading US digital rights campaign group warned against using this software, as it posed a serious risk to privacy. Some features in the software enabled Google to store private files, e-mails, chats and web history on its servers. Marissa Mayer, Google's vice president of search products and user experience, admitted the problem but downplayed its seriousness, commenting: 'We think this will be a very useful tool, but you will have to give up some of your privacy. For many of us, that trade off will make a lot of sense' (BBC News, 2006a). Freedom of information is often in a conflict with privacy, and the trade-off or balance between the two is a major challenge for the information society. On the one hand, greater access to online information may provide opportunities and advantages to a variety of actors. On the other, it may pose a threat to privacy and therefore also to the broadly conceived security of individuals. Information protection concerns three different levels of analysis: individuals, corporations and states, where search engines play a significant role as information brokers between them.

As explained previously, while connected to the internet, private computers can also serve as information providers, offering files to the entire online community. With peer-to-peer software such as Napster or Kazaa, online users can control to what extent they wish to share files from their private computers. A study by Lyman and Varian (2003) found, for example, that 9 per cent of Kazaa's users shared their files with other users, while 91 per cent of the users only retrieved files from others. New operating systems and antivirus software automatically offer basic firewall and other security features to block access and protect personal data.

From the other side, many individuals are interested in filtering and excluding online information that may harm them or their family. Apart from filtering information that goes out from the private computer to the online network, software is also designed to filter information that goes into the private computer from the online network. Google, for example, by default filters out pornographic images from its image search.[6] Many broadband companies provide similar services, enabling online users to control and customise the information they want to retrieve (Figure 2.1).

Figure 2.1   Exclusion mechanisms

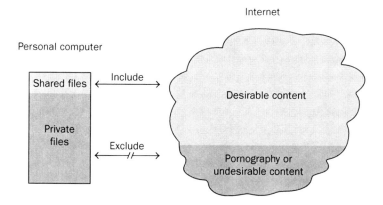

As a result of firewalls, filters and content moderation mechanisms, the online network and its computer 'islands' are actually viewed differently by different users. Moreover, for some online users, deep web content becomes more accessible, as they know where to find it. For example, the Right-to-Know Network (RTK Net) is one of the biggest deep web database websites, providing information on US corporations and their environmental damage.[7] Those who know the existence of particular database websites can actually access much more information in the online network. For other online users, who depend entirely on popular search engines to retrieve online information, the deep web databases are unreachable 'islands'. Hence, once again having information skills, such as navigating in the deep web or configuring firewalls, provides a significant advantage.

Corporations and organisations are responsible for generating the greatest deep web spaces. In a comprehensive analysis of the deep web, Bergman (2001) indicated that when combined, the largest 60 database websites contained more than 750 terabytes of data, representing 40 times the size of the surface web. US-based corporations and organisations such as the National Climatic Center, NASA, Amazon and eBay dominate the deep web.[8] Most of these corporations and organisations provide public information. In fact, Bergman found more than 97 per cent of the deep web to be free and available to the public without password restrictions.

Apart from online information, many companies and organisations have their own network (intranet), through which employees can exchange and share specific information. Similar to information produced by individuals, this type of information is mostly private and protected behind firewalls. However, unlike individuals, organisations have many more resources and capabilities to secure their non-public information. They can employ network engineers and invest in sophisticated firewalls and proxies in order to protect information and exclude users. These organisational firewalls work in both directions, blocking information from getting out and filtering undesirable information from getting in, especially information that may distract employees from work and therefore reduce productivity. Similarly, organisations have much greater power to produce online information and diffuse it through advertisements and other marketing mechanisms. Thus, for practical purposes, corporations and organisations have more control both over access to information and information protection.

Finally, at the national level, as demonstrated in Chapter 3, different countries exercise different exclusion mechanisms in order to enhance their national security and protect or marginalise specific groups. As search engines increasingly work to personalise and customise their services, they often keep records of the search history of their users. Using such data, governments can easily link certain search queries and websites (e.g. bomb-making, pornography, anti-governmental information) with particular users or machines. Thus, search history can be used to address criminal, terrorist or dissident activities. Each country employs different filters to focus on different 'threats' depending on the dominant norms of security, privacy and freedom of information and who the dominant actors may be.

Not surprisingly, states are also especially interested in making use of strong exclusion mechanisms to guard their military information. Military intranets and computers with sensitive military files are usually not connected to the internet, and therefore mostly invisible 'islands' for online users. However, like any other organisation, the army depends on the internet as well, and it is enough that one military computer has links to both internet and military intranet for it to become a gateway to unlimited military information. Thus, in May 2006, a British hacker was found guilty of hacking 97 computers of the US Army, Navy, Air Force and NASA (BBC News, 2006b). In a way, advanced information skills, probably even more than financial resources, provide the greatest advantage in retrieving online information not only from the deep web, but also from every single private computer connected to the internet. Moreover, with the emergence of popular tools such as Google Earth and Windows Live Local, it will be shown that many (but not all) governments have less control over the exclusion of sensitive information such as aerial images of military installations.

Interest/internet conflicts

Lewis Mumford (1964) suggested that technology serves various goals, and its nature ultimately depends on its use or misuse (what he called 'technics'). He distinguished between two opposite technics: authoritarian and democratic. 'Authoritarian technics' refers to the utilisation of technology to maintain top-down control over society. 'Democratic technics' refers to the use of technologies by local groups to produce innovation and maintain social interaction and bottom-up control. Over the years, the same technologies have served to exploit both authoritarian and democratic technics, and with the emergence of the internet they still coexist and constantly compete with each other (May, 2002).

The study of the deep web and the conflicts between privacy, security and freedom of information illustrate this idea, adding another dimension of complexity. There are three different levels to the information society: individuals, corporations and states, which compete to exploit ICTs to gain and restrict information. Apart from the need to find the balance between public and non-public information within each level, there are very often interest conflicts and clashes between the different levels (Figure 2.2).

Thus, individuals who produce websites or write weblogs might wish to keep their content confidential or limit its diffusion, while Google and other search engines might wish to index it and make it available for everyone. Many online users who wish to restrict their personal information or even delete it, find themselves struggling against popular search engines. Although webmasters and weblog owners may use Robot Exclusion Standards[9] in order to make their websites invisible to search engines, many search engines might ignore these standards and index their private websites anyway. Even when web owners physically delete their websites, search engines may keep a cache of their indexed information for a couple of months, and in theory forever.

Furthermore, as Google integrates various databases into its index, a Google search for personal names or telephone numbers can increasingly reveal other personal data such as home addresses, occupation, information that a person has posted in online forums – and even criminal convictions and news publications. Another conflict of interests emerged when Google

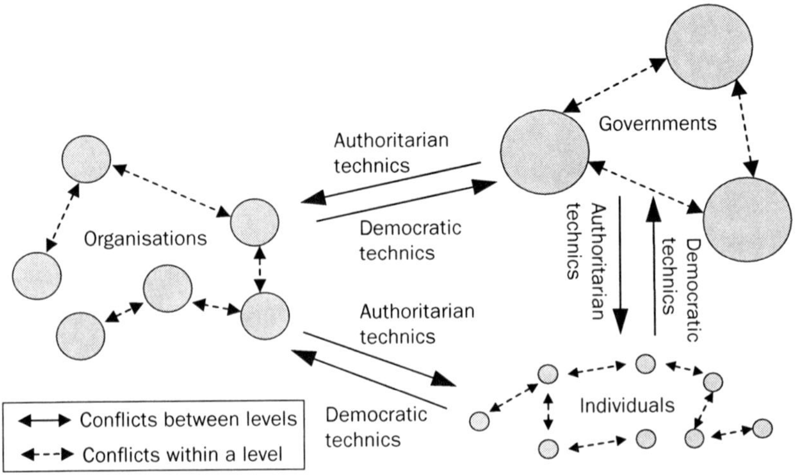

Figure 2.2   Interest conflicts within and between levels

introduced Gmail, a web-based e-mail service. Unlike Microsoft and Yahoo!, Google developed an automatic advertising mechanism that analyses the content of e-mails and offers appropriate advertisements. Thus, a person who receives a romantic e-mail may also receive an offer from Google's interface to purchase a romantic gift. Although in practice nobody actually reads the content of e-mails sent by Google's users, its new advertising mechanism has become controversial and rightly raised users' concern for their privacy (Battelle, 2005).

Subsequently, the introduction of Gmail was heavily criticised. In Massachusetts, anti-Gmail legislation was introduced, while in California, privacy activists organised protests and legislators worked to close down this service (Vise and Malseed, 2005). Walt Mossberg from the *Wall Street Journal* suggested that Google should 'offer Gmail accounts without the ads, and without the scanning, for a modest annual fee' (MacMillan, 2004). In a sense, with the introduction of Gmail in April 2004, many online users have realised for the first time how deeply search engines can penetrate into their private life.

From another angle, search engines and media companies may wish to safeguard their own intellectual properties and develop exclusion mechanisms to limit the diffusion of information and services to their paying customers. Premium content, online music, software and books are password-protected and their access is limited and controlled. However, given the ease in duplicating and diffusing information products, the internet and its open architecture often make it difficult to enforce intellectual property rights. Especially popular peer-to-peer file-sharing applications such as Napster and eMule, with which users can 'illegally' share copyrighted software and audio files, are considered as a real threat to software and media companies. As such, many companies have been fighting vigorously to protect their private properties through pressing for legislation on copyrights, filing lawsuits, developing technologies that disable unlicensed duplications, and cooperating with other companies to integrate software with hardware (Barney, 2004).

Individuals must also negotiate government policies in order to secure their freedom of information and human rights. Being in the middle between governments and individuals, search engines are often used by governments to track down unlawful users and to limit their freedom of information. The Chinese government, for example, used e-mails from Yahoo! to catch and imprison a local journalist (Nystedt and McCarthy, 2006). Similarly, the Brazilian and Indian police used Google to identify online users who posted illegal information in its social network service, Orkut, advocating violence, crime or human rights violations (Astor, 2006; Chowdhury, 2007).

Finally, as will be described in subsequent chapters, clashes may occur between governments and corporations, such as the dispute between Google and the US government over providing search queries (de Vries, 2006), the concern of governments about certain sensitive aerial images on Google Earth, or Taiwan's pressure on Google to change its labelling in Google Maps, where Taiwan appeared as a province of China (Gluck, 2005).

These examples suggest that freedom and privacy of information are constantly contested between and within the different levels. May (2002) has suggested that many individuals tend to give up their privacy in order to gain greater economic advantages (through companies' customisation of services and products) and better security (through government surveillance). With the continuous developments in ICTs, companies can gather a great volume of personal information about the consumption habits of their customers (through credit records) and even about their movements in space (through the records of mobile phone companies). Although the increasing capacity of companies to monitor users' personal lives can pose a threat to privacy, it is still relatively unrecognised and rarely perceived as problematic (May, 2002), as the benefits of improved services apparently outbalance the risks.

Similarly, people generally tend to give up their privacy and accept closed circuit television (CCTV) as a governmental means of surveillance, although in practice it has not been proven to be effective in reducing crime levels (Wilkin, 2001). Various examples indicate that in the clash between privacy and security, the balance still seems to lie with the latter. In the clash between freedom of information-sharing and property rights there is an increasing tendency to capitalise information as a property despite its potentially free availability (May, 2002).

Control over informational commons

Mattelart (2008) suggests that the struggle for the status of information products and cultural artefacts should not be separated from the struggle for other global commons. The information in the surface and deep web is potentially available to all through one global network. Whether online information is a free public resource or private property, and which aspects of it should be freely accessible or restricted, are matters of ongoing debate. Hess and Ostrom (2006), for example, perceive the internet as the ultimate medium for information sharing (or, as they call it, 'knowledge commons'), particularly due to its decentralised structure.

They suggest that online information flows from one node to the other, and any attempt to block, censor or control it can be easily circumvented.

Yet, the internet infrastructure and the web structure are not entirely flat, and could be best described as scale-free networks (Barabási, 2002), in which there are a few highly connected hubs (i.e. popular websites), while most other nodes have very few links and little popularity. Subsequently, Zook and Graham (2007) suggest that in theory, skilled users can circumnavigate some or even all the information they encounter, but most users, and even highly-skilled users, are more likely to use the hubs, e.g. search engines (which further reinforce this hierarchy by ordering and prioritising popular websites).

Search engines also play a significant role in drawing the line between private and public online information, and in developing mechanisms of information inclusion and exclusion. At the same time, they continuously exploit various strategies in order to index more parts of the deep web. Google, for example, has developed relations with publishers, aggregators and libraries in order to increase its share and control over online information through products such as Google Scholar and Google Books. As argued previously, covering more parts of the deep web does not necessarily mean bridging the digital divide of online information. While Google Scholar includes online articles in its search results, it also reinforces the page-ranking mechanism. Online articles cited by many other online articles get automatically higher ranking-scores and appear first in search results. In this way, popular articles become more popular, and less popular articles are further marginalised.[10] The continuous effort of search engines to unveil the deep web can therefore widen the digital divide of online information.

As part of the expansion race, Google is currently looking to capitalise on the growing online population in the Middle East and Africa. It has recently signed deals with East African countries to supply information and communication services, such as e-mail and word processing, to students and government workers (Auchard, 2007a). Similarly, it is setting up offices, hiring staff and translating its interfaces (e.g. Google News, Google Maps, Google Scholar and Gmail) into Arabic (Wallis, 2006). In June 2006, for example, Google launched an Arabic version of Google News. The ability to search within Arabic news resources is another quest to make the deep web accessible and searchable. However, similar to Google Scholar, indexing the deep web via Google News may further polarise the information society. Pulling information from various Arabic news sources,[11] Google News may undermine the significance of national and regional news sources, intensify more popular political trends, and further marginalise alternative views in the Arab world.

More than any other company, Microsoft has probably the greatest potential to 'conquer' more private spaces by exploiting its global monopoly of software. As 90 per cent of personal computers run Windows operating systems (W3Schools, 2008), Microsoft has the greatest potential power to determine the border between public and private, freedom of information and security. Similar to Google Desktop, in MSN Toolbar Microsoft has integrated web search with desktop search. Online users can simultaneously search for information from the surface web and within their own private computers. It is believed that the day is not far off when Microsoft will develop an operating system, in which users will be able to define folders in their own computers that will be part of the indexed accessible web, thus dramatically increasing the information available for online users as well as the dissemination of information by individuals and personal computers. Lessig (1999) has argued that control over code also means control over the operation of things. Microsoft has defeated Netscape in the competition for the browser market, and it may well defeat other companies in the competition over information search and provision by exploiting its advantage over the code and by unveiling new information frontiers.

The battle between global media and communication corporations over the informational commons has recently become even more intense with the lawsuit against Google. Viacom, a US media conglomerate which also owns the MTV network, has sued Google for allowing online users to upload copyrighted video clips, making them publicly available through its recently acquired video channel, YouTube. Similar lawsuits of copyright infringements have been filed against Google Books and Google News. As Google had already signed contracts with other media companies such as CBS and the BBC to deliver their content through YouTube, the Viacom lawsuit was perceived by some observers as a tactic to get better terms in a deal that both sides need (Fabrikant and Hansell, 2007).

As mentioned earlier, Napster and other online services that allow free information-sharing and distribution have posed similar threats to software and record companies. Like many other services, YouTube started as a platform for sharing personal and home videos, and gradually, together with Google's acquisition and the deals with other media companies, it became a global multimedia distribution network. Here, commercial content such as MTV video clips compete with individual production (based on the same principles of page-ranking mechanisms), and eventually undermine to some extent the role and position of most individuals and smaller actors in YouTube. The internet has followed similar stages of development, and it seems that many new innovations follow similar patterns. At the outset, the informational commons are used by information-skilled users who share their creations based on the free principles of the 'hacker ethic'.[12] As soon as companies enter the network and commercial interests are allowed to participate, the nature of the informational commons is transformed, driven by capitalist paradigms, regulations and copyrights. Hence, the recent battles for greater control over informational spaces provide a significant historical milestone on the way to regulate and order our global informational commons.

Global media corporations not only increasingly dominate the informational commons, but also gradually evolve and change their own nature. While previous media companies often produced their own content, new media companies (such as Google News and Google Video) aggregate their content from various local agents and distribute it globally through a single popular channel. While previous media companies depended on local distribution, new media companies increasingly use online networks and satellite technologies to distribute content worldwide. Finally, while previous media companies generated their revenues by selling their content, new media companies provide free content and sell informational spaces to advertisers. Their control over the informational commons is a direct result of their global reach and ability to customise their information based on the specific preferences of each and every individual.

The European answer

An interesting initiative was taken by the French and German governments to develop the next generation of search engines. The project, called Quaero, was conceived in April 2005 to challenge the dominance of US search engines in general and Google in particular, aiming to increase the European role in the production and distribution of online information. As the former French President, Jacques Chirac, put it: 'We must take up the challenge posed by the American giants, Google and Yahoo! For that, we will launch a European search engine, Quaero' (O'Brien, 2006).

One of the main ideas behind this half billion-euro project (Chrisafis, 2006) is to widen the search technology and also include multimedia search. It is meant to use techniques for recognising, transcribing, indexing and translating audiovisual documents in several languages. Later, online users will be able to find patterns, shapes and colours of images, as well as words and sounds from songs or movies. Moreover, Quaero claims to be able to provide greater control over copyrights, intellectual properties and cultural heritage. The Quaero project suggests that governments and political leaders have realised the tremendous impact of search engines on cultural, social and economic matters. In his speech, Chirac argued that 'culture is not merchandise and it cannot be left to the blind forces of the market. We must staunchly defend the world's diversity of cultures against the looming threat of uniformity' (Litterick, 2005).

The project was criticised as being very small in terms of budget and technological capacity compared with similar projects by Microsoft or Google. Some search experts called it 'a blatant case of misguided and unnecessary nationalism' and warned that by the time Quaero is developed, the market will have moved on (Chrisafis, 2006). Finally, there were fundamental disagreements between France and Germany regarding the use and technical aspects of this search engine. While France favoured a multimedia search engine, Germany favoured a text-based search engine. As a result, many German engineers refused to be associated with what they thought was becoming an anti-Google project, rather than an innovative and independent project. In December 2006, the German government withdrew from the project to focus on its own domestic search engine, called Theseus (O'Brien and Crampton, 2007). Similar projects for multimedia search are being currently developed by other governments (e.g. the Norwegian Pharos) and backed by funds from the EU, which has recognised the increasing importance of search engines.

Van Eijk (2004) presents another example of a German project (called 'SuMa-eV') that was established to develop search engine technology that promotes free access, versatility and non-monopolistic practices. He believes that search engine mechanisms have a strong influence on the freedom of information, and therefore it is important to work on local legislations that encourage transparency in their operation. In addition, he suggests that governments should offer an alternative to the commercially available information services.

Nonetheless, the economy of scale is a very important factor in the growth and success of search engines. Similar to other initiatives taken by international organisations such as UNESCO, International Telecommunication Union (ITU) and United Cities and Local Governments (UCLG) to tackle information inequalities and prevent US dominance (which were limited in success and often overshadowed by commercial forces), it is more likely that a new rising search engine will either be acquired by one of the larger US hubs or become commercialised in order to support its competitive position. Consequently, it will not be able to sustain information equality and diversity of alternative views, and will mainly represent the views of the richer and more popular nodes. This, in practice, will be another example of intensifying the digital divide.

The long tail of search engines

Together with the five big US corporations (Google, Yahoo!, MSN, AOL and Ask.com) that control more than 90 per cent of the search engine market (see also Appendix A), there are many small search engines that provide alternative means of information retrieval.[13] The long-tail theory, which shows empirically that profit lies behind the economics of abundance (C. Anderson, 2006), stresses the importance of the accumulative power of those products which are in less demand. When applied to the search engine market, it can be argued that although the many small search engines are not as popular and influential as the five big ones, together they may still provide a large volume of information to a decent number of users. Moreover, in order to survive, they are required to offer innovative and useful alternatives for information retrieval that cannot be found in the bigger search engines. Consequently, they may develop important and useful technologies that could later rival the conventional search technologies or be acquired by one of the popular search engines and become a dominant search method. As such, it is important to study the various alternatives that are currently available on the margins of the search engine market.

C. S. Knight (2007) has described some of the recent developments in alternative search engines. He provides the example of Microsoft's Ms Dewey, which represented an attempt to challenge the 'clean' and simple interface of Google by providing a more appealing visual of a person that could interact with users and conduct their searches. An interesting approach in the field of information retrieval is the application of natural language processing technologies. Such technologies aim to 'humanise' the interface and the interaction between users and search engines, enabling them to ask questions and get answers in their own language. Ask Jeeves was one of the first commercial search engines to implement artificial intelligence technologies to recognise questions in natural language. Hakia, is a more recent search engine that makes use of semantic analysis and categorises information by meanings and subjects. Other search engines (e.g. Google Answers and ChaCha) introduced a human mediated search, where online users could ask questions in their own language and other users helped them to retrieve their answers.

Another interesting direction of development is the visual presentation of search results. While conventional search engines display results in a long one-dimensional list, some search engines (e.g. KartOO and Quintura) display a two or three-dimensional map of interconnected websites. They cluster search results into topics, enabling online users to navigate through the map in search of the most relevant answers. For example, a search in KartOO for the word 'empire' provides a two-dimensional map that clusters websites related to politics, education, shopping and entertainment, enabling users to 'zoom in' and focus on their desired content.

Some alternative search engines elaborate the multi-dimensional display of search results by recommending other related information. When users search for certain artists, music or films, these search engines (e.g. Music Map and Live Plasma) automatically recommend other related titles. This mechanism, which was popularised by Amazon[14] and is increasingly used by e-commerce websites, has important implications regarding the diversity of content and the increasing long tail of information production and consumption.

Finally, some alternative search engines such as Dogpile, also known as meta-search engines, developed the capacity to aggregate search results from all popular search engines and from some other specific vertical search engines, attempting to cover the highest volume of the deep web. One should note that while using the search mechanisms of popular search engines, they also contribute to their traffic and do not fundamentally change the information order or the information retrieval processes.

Apart from commercial search engines, there are hundreds of open source engines developed by the online community (Battelle, 2003). These applications are not owned by private commercial companies, and thus enable anyone to use, modify and even profit from them as long as they contribute to the project. The main difference between commercial and open source search engines is that the latter are transparent, i.e. online users can look at their indexing and page-ranking mechanisms. Another important difference is that there are more skilled programmers who can potentially contribute to the development of an open source search engine than programmers employed in any commercial search engine. Wikia Search is a recent example of a non-commercial search engine promoted and supported by Wikia Inc. The four principles that currently guide its development and exemplify the search for alternative solutions are transparency (i.e. openness of the system and its algorithms), community (i.e. everyone can contribute and take part in the evolving enterprise), quality (i.e. improvement of search results based on relevancy and not commercial considerations) and privacy (i.e. not storing any identifiable data on the users and their information preferences).[15] Nonetheless, it has been argued that the economy of scale plays an important role in the search engine market. As long as indexing technologies require a massive amount of storage,[16] there is an obvious advantage to the commercial model of search engines. Only if a new technology enables private computers to voluntarily serve as a shared resource for global storage through the internet, then open source search engines may have a case to challenge commercial ones.

Although there is an interesting and diverse market of alternative search engines, statistics indicate that the long tail of search engines is getting smaller, i.e. the most popular search engines continuously increase their share, while alternative search engines get fewer visitors.[17] Moreover, the popularity of alternative search engines and their traffic ultimately depend on their ranking in the bigger search engines and particularly Google. Mowshowitz and Kawaguchi have summarised the possible implications of the search engine oligopoly:

> The only real way to counter the ill effects of search engine bias on the ever expanding web is to make sure a number of alternative search engines are available. Elimination of competition in the search engine business is just as problematic for a democratic society as consolidation in the news media. Both search engine companies and news media firms act as intermediaries between information sources and information seekers. (Mowshowitz and Kawaguchi, 2002: 60)

As with other media channels, on the internet there is a general tendency to increase the diversity of content, while decreasing the diversity of forms and standards as a result of monopolisation processes. While the number and variety of television channels are growing, the number of media conglomerates is becoming smaller. While the variety of search queries increases, the number of search engines that control the online information market decreases. While the long tail of search *queries* becomes a significant economic factor, the long tail of search *engines* gradually atrophies.

Conclusion

This chapter has argued that search engines provide one of the most crucial services in the contemporary world – the organisation of information. While doing so they are required to constantly develop and refine their search mechanisms to provide more relevant and qualitative information (greater control) on the one hand and, on the other, to expand their coverage of information (greater volume). The latter requires addressing two main challenges: the challenge of the deep web and the challenge of the internet infrastructure.

Ultimately, the web and other internet protocols (e-mails, FTP and P2P) serve as fundamental informational spaces. Individuals, organisations and states compete for access and introduce restriction to specific information. In this battle, search engines and large internet companies are located in a strategic position as they own the code and the navigation tools that allow online information diffusion and retrieval. Moreover, in a neo-liberal global economy, open access and freedom of information are constantly confined by property right regulations. Hence, internet companies in general and search engines in particular benefit greatly from this economic order as it allows them to design the code, organise and capitalise online information.

While expanding and deepening their control over more informational commons, search engines impose their own rules and standards, such as the page-ranking mechanisms, promotion deals and greater dependence on their services, all of which will be examined in the following chapters looking at the practices of Google. In order to attain and retain popularity, search engines are also required to comply with the various needs of their users for privacy as well as the various needs and demands of national governments, constantly negotiating the balance between different and often conflicting interests. In some cases, search engine databases are used by certain states (as has happened both in the USA and China)[18] in order to learn about the information production and consumption habits of their citizens, track down dissidents and limit or exclude undesired content. On the other hand, search engines increasingly disseminate sensitive information (e.g. images and maps of military installations) free of charge, and thus threaten national security. Subsequently, some governments start cooperating with search engines in order to increase their control over local and global informational commons.

The growing popularity of US and commercial search engines has further raised the concern of some European countries. Subsequently, new projects such as the French Quaero and the German Theseus were introduced mainly to challenge the dominance of US search engines. This suggests that search engines are already recognised as global actors with the power to disseminate US views and commercial practices online. The idea behind these projects and other open source initiatives is to develop more transparent methods to organise information, which are constantly subject to public review and can offer alternatives to the commercially available information services. Nonetheless, it has been argued that the economic and technological capabilities of individual governments and international organisations are limited, and the dominance of capitalist systems supports the growth and strengthening of the popular commercial and US search engines, which still provide the most comprehensive, accurate and relevant search results along with increasingly customised and relevant advertisements.

Notes

1. See Chapter 3 for a more detailed review of online search mechanisms in general and the search mechanism of Google in particular.
2. See also the section on the deep web in this chapter for the explanation about the 'indexable' or 'surface' web.
3. Bergman (2001) estimated the deep web to be 550 times larger than the searchable web. More recent studies, however, have questioned his methods and measurements, suggesting that his size estimates are far too high (Lewandowski and Mayr, 2007). Still, although there is no consensus regarding the accurate size of the deep web, most researchers agree that modern search engines can cover only a minor part of the deep web (He et al., 2007).
4. See also the next section on the structure of the internet.
5. According to Lyman and Varian (2003), the surface web contains 167 terabytes of information, while the deep web contains 91,850 terabytes. The study also suggests that each year, e-mails account for 440,606 terabytes of information, instant messaging for 274 terabytes, and that users on Kazaa alone share almost 5,000 terabytes of information. Further study is currently in progress.
6. In order to include pornographic content in Google Images, one must modify the Safe Search preferences in the advanced search options.
7. Bergman (2001) described the RTK Net database as containing more than 14 terabytes of information.
8. Of the 60 largest database-driven websites, 54 were US corporations and organisations, and accounted for 99.91 per cent of the deep web space (Bergman, 2001).
9. Robot Exclusion Standards are conventions to prevent web spiders from indexing a part of or a whole website. As there is no official standard body, these protocols are purely advisory, and some search engines can choose to ignore them (Vise and Malseed, 2006).
10. The centrality and implications of search engine popularisation mechanisms have been also indicated by Cho and Roy (2004) and Hindman et al. (2003). See Chapter 3 for a detailed review of Google's page-ranking mechanism and its implications.
11. In June 2006, the Google News website claimed to integrate 150 Arabic news sources, while some news agencies claim that Google News actually integrates more than 500 Arabic news sources (Chapman, 2006).

12. Himanen (2001) and Castells (2004) suggest that the real potential of the internet is in the emergence of a culture of sharing based on open source, or what they also call the 'hacker ethic', which was practised by the network of innovators who created the internet. As opposed to the practice of capitalists who constantly attempt to protect their property rights, the hacker ethic is the passion for creation and innovation for its own sake and the culture of sharing the joy of creation with others.

13. Some meta-search engines such as GoshMe indicate that there are more than half a million search engines on the web.

14. A process known as collaborative filtering, where companies can compare the buying patterns of their customers and recommend relevant products (Broersma, 2001).

15. See also: http://search.wikia.com/wiki/Search_Wikia (accessed May 2009).

16. The Google Grid, for example, stores its index on more than 450,000 servers (Markoff and Hansell, 2006).

17. The increasing share of the bigger search engines and the decreasing share of the smaller ones could be displayed when comparing recent statistics (see Appendix A) versus previous data such as Search Engine Watch (2006) and Gandal (2001).

18. See also Chapter 3.

3

Google and the politics of online searching

In the world of the Web, esse est indicato in Google: to exist is to be indexed on Google. (Hinman, 2005: 21)

There is no doubt that Google is the most popular search engine today worldwide. Google provides information to more than 775 million different users every month (Sullivan, 2006; Kopytoff, 2007a; comScore, 2009a), which is about half of the entire online population (Internet World Stats, 2009). It has also been estimated that 74 per cent of users turn first to Google when they search for information on the web (Hinman, 2005). This chapter investigates Google's operation and information strategies, looking at their implications with respect to the digital divide.

The first sections of the chapter examine the ideology of the corporation, the various information products and internet tools that it introduces, and its global popularity. The later sections look more specifically at the politics behind information search, e.g. Google's global strategies and its organisation of online information. While Google provides information services worldwide, it is often required to deal with local authorities and governments. Various examples will demonstrate that being a commercial company, Google tries to maximise its profits and information market, while minimising its damage. By doing so, it often also shapes the boundaries between private and public, local and global control over information, inevitably forming certain inequalities and biases. Finally, this chapter demonstrates how Google increases its users' dependence, encourages allegiance, and 'punishes' or excludes actors from the global network, and thus maintains its control and perpetuates the commercialisation of online information.

Google's big idea

In January 1996, two students at Stanford University, Larry Page and Sergey Brin, were working together on a project to develop a search engine mechanism that could analyse the 'back-links', i.e. the number of links pointing to a given website. In the same year, they started searching for a company to buy their idea, but none were particularly interested (Vise and Malseed, 2005; Google, 2007a).

In 1998, they decided to run their own business, using the name Google. The name was a variation of the term 'googol', coined by the nephew of US mathematician Edward Kasner. It refers to the number represented by the numeral 1 followed by 100 zeros. The term was branded and popularised to reflect the seemingly infinite amount of information available on the web, which Google aimed to organise.

Page and Brin raised an initial investment and operated a small but constantly growing business. Eventually, the more people used Google for searching the web, the more other companies became interested in cooperating with Google. When it reached the point of answering 10,000 search queries each day, the local press began to take notice and published articles extolling the enterprise. When it was answering more than 500,000 queries per day, interest in the company had grown considerably, and companies such as Red Hat became its first commercial search customer. Later, AOL/Netscape selected Google as its web search service and increased the queries in Google to 3 million searches per day.

Gandal (2001) studied the evolution and competition of the search engine market, indicating that while early entrants (e.g. Yahoo!, Lycos, Excite, Infoseek and AltaVista) had some advantage, those that eventually managed to survive were constantly offering innovations and updates as well as superior products and services. This can explain why Google, which entered the market relatively late, could still break through by offering its new search technology. Rather than counting the frequency of queries on the webpage to determine its relevancy, it counted the number of back-links a webpage had from other webpages, and thus provided superior results. Unlike other search engines, Google's new approach also avoided webpage spamming, which during the late 1990s was based on filling webpages with irrelevant words in order to appear in the top search results.

Thus, Google grew and established a dominant online position by offering an innovative and much demanded technology and service, and by continuously increasing the number of its users. Originating in the Silicon Valley and collaborating with other global communication corporations have certainly helped Google build up its dominant position.[1] Subsequently, the company expanded to Europe and signed contracts with the Italian portal Virgilio and with the British Virgin Net, the UK's leading online entertainment guide. Together with its global expansion, Google introduced multilingual interfaces and developed its search facilities to support other languages.

After achieving worldwide popularity and reputation, Google started charging fees for additional and premium services. For example, since 2000, Google has had a growing number of clients sign up to use its search technology on their own sites; in addition, it has also launched its keyword-targeted advertising programme, 'AdWords' (Google, 2007a). Through AdWords, Google users can open accounts and bid for certain keywords to be associated with their websites. This automatically places the user's website in the sponsored links at the top of the search results for any desired keyword. Of course, some keywords, such as 'books', 'flowers' or 'hotels', are in greater demand than others. As such, the price to appear at the top of the search results always depends on the popularity and demand for keywords. For example, appearing at the top of Google's results with the query 'hotel' costs around $3.50 per click, which is 35 times as much as appearing at the top with the query 'Japanese Origami' (about 10 cents per click).[2] Google uses a system of cost-per-click (CPC) rather than cost-per-impression. This means that the website owner only has to pay if somebody actually clicks on a sponsored link in Google's search result. To this end, Google's classification of information is hierarchical and based on commercial considerations.

In addition, Google has developed a reselling plan called 'AdSense'. Website owners can provide Google with a space on their website to promote Google's advertisers. For example, online newspapers can display customised advertisements from Google on any subject. Similarly, political parties can promote on their websites relevant organisations and companies that advertise with Google. Significantly, clients signing up to be resellers can choose the kind of content to be promoted on their website, and filter out links to competitors or any other undesirable content. Ultimately, Google shares its advertising revenues with its resellers, i.e. if somebody clicks on Google's sponsored links in the reseller's website, Google credits the reseller's account. This filtering mechanism, combined with the capacity of Google to categorise, package and sell information through its own results as well as through resellers' websites clearly illustrates the economic and social subtext behind the apparent neutral provision and organisation of information. Whereas there might be a variety of reasons why certain information is excluded (e.g. not a relevant or popular website), it is quite obvious that

Google also practises exclusion and marginalisation on payment through creating a hierarchy of search results.

Following the huge success of the AdWords programme, Ask Jeeves, a search engine company in decline, signed a partnership agreement with Google in 2001. In this way, people who used Ask Jeeves got customised advertisements from Google and the revenue was divided between the two (Vise and Malseed, 2005). More than saving Ask Jeeves from bankruptcy, this deal has defined Google as a dominant online advertising agency.

Aside from new technology, there are several other explanations for Google's growth and success. Shillingsburg (2006) gives three such reasons, likening the innovative contribution of Google Search to that of Gutenberg. First, while the press 'democratised' books and other texts, giving less wealthy people access to literature, the world wide web 'democratises' information, and Google has become one of its main gateways. Second, Google has carefully separated commercial information and advertisements from the main results, giving its information greater integrity and seriousness. Finally, it has popularised a new business model based on pay-per-click, which is significantly different from the business model of traditional publishers. In short, its technological, informational and economic services and methods have been both innovative and influential, contributing to its popularity and rapid growth.

But what are the implications of this dominance on the production of information inequalities? While it is clear that the promotion of paying websites increases the gap between rich and poor, it is less obvious that the automatic organisation of information in Google Search and its various channels is also problematic, despite its repeated claims for neutrality and online 'democracy'.[3]

Google's search engine mechanism

The most important service provided by Google and similar search engines is the list of results to a search query. In offering this service, search engines constantly organise, prioritise, include and exclude websites. There are two major approaches to operate this process technically: the 'voluntaristic' approach and the 'non-voluntaristic' approach (R. Rogers, 2004). Both have implications for the organisation of online information.

The 'voluntaristic' approach requires self-reporting. Once a website is ready to be accessed, website owners actively add it to certain search engines and directories. To do this, they are required to fill in an online form indicating the domain name of their website, its relevant keywords, a short description of its content and a suggested topical classification. Search engine companies employ editors who review and filter the different individual requests, using their expert knowledge and the search engine guidelines. Ultimately, it depends upon the editor to decide whether to include or exclude websites from search results. This is the way it works in web directories such as Yahoo! Directory, Yellow Pages and the Open Directory Project (dmoz.org), which will be discussed further in Chapter 4.

In the 'non-voluntaristic' approach, the search engine must actively crawl the web and add new webpages to its index. The index comprises enormous databases that link page content[4] to keywords and to URLs (Introna and Nissenbaum, 2000). Each website is automatically evaluated to determine its popularity, size and importance, mainly by counting the large quantity of outgoing links it has to other websites, and the back-links it gets from other websites. As was previously argued, the popularity of one particular website among others determines its place within the search results; the more popular, the higher it appears (Cho and Roy, 2004). Google, Yahoo! Search, MSN and Ask.com currently use robots to crawl the web, organise and prioritise online information, and to systematically include 'desirable' and exclude 'undesirable' content.

Not only does the number of back-links determine the ranking of a website in the search results, but so do the 'importance' and ranking of its referrer websites, i.e. the websites that link to it. Thus, for example, a link from Intel's official website to IBM's website is considered more valuable than a link from a small personal webpage to IBM's website. The value of back-links is defined by the popularity and ranking of the referrer websites, i.e. the number of their own back-links (Battelle, 2005). Figure 3.1 illustrates the basic principles of the page-ranking mechanism in Google (also known as 'PageRank'), which has become a common practice in many 'non-voluntaristic' search engines.

Figure 3.1 The basic principles of page ranking

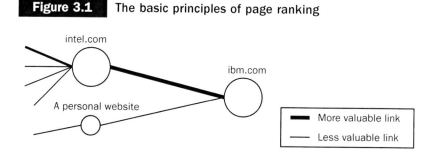

Apart from analysing back-links, Google's page-ranking system also examines the actual position of the words from the search query within the webpage, the font size and whether they are written in upper or lower case. One should take into account the huge trade-off between the many factors in the page-ranking mechanism as well as the computing and processing time and power required (Vise and Malseed, 2005). In general, the page-ranking mechanism takes a user-centric approach; it tries to assess and analyse users' experience and needs, translating this information into automatic technologies and scripts.

One of the significant points noted in comparing the human-mediated or 'voluntaristic' and the automatic or 'non-voluntaristic' approach is that their search results often differ. While Google's search results are automatic and based on 'intelligent' algorithms, those of Yahoo! integrate human-edited directories and make possible content classifications by topic. An example would be a search query for 'apple' – using Google, the first ten pages of results only contain information about Apple Inc., as the computer company is much more 'authoritative' and has many more back-links than the fruit with which it shares a name.[5] Although Yahoo! provides similar results, it also suggests an alternative search based on other topical categories that include the word 'apple', such as 'apple pie recipe' or 'apple cider vinegar'. In this way, the combination of the manual and automatic approaches to search can often yield more heterogeneous, qualitative and relevant results.[6] In contrast, the purely automatic organisation of information primarily promotes popular, bigger and more commercial actors. It thus perpetuates certain information inequalities and biased perceptions (as will be shown, for example, in Chapter 5 in the study of Google News).

Search engines can be divided not only by their different search mechanisms but also by their different marketing strategies. Van Couvering (2004) suggests that all search engines conform to a similar business model known as the 'dual product' market. On the one hand, they produce customised information products and services for individuals, and on the other, they produce advertisements. Different search engines exploit different aspects of production. MSN, for example, gets 29 per cent of its revenue from advertisements, while Yahoo! gets 82 per cent and Google gets 95 per cent of its revenue from advertisements. These different business strategies may also suggest that MSN benefits more from direct subscription and from customised information products, while Yahoo! and, even more so, Google rely heavily on advertisements. While MSN tends to concentrate more on strengthening the affiliation with individuals by understanding their needs and tailoring specific information services, Yahoo! and Google tend to focus on strengthening their affiliation with companies and website owners by tailoring sophisticated advertisement solutions. One of the first indications of those different strategies can be observed through the interface. While Google's local homepages (e.g. google.co.uk or google.co.jp) are similar in form and content, MSN local homepages are very different from one another both in content and form (Segev et al., 2007). Nonetheless, in all cases, the development of advanced search customisation mechanisms is driven not only by the search engines' need to improve the relevancy of their results, but also, and probably more significantly, by their need to tailor specific advertisements and increase profitability.

Unlike other search engines, Google has integrated the PageRank mechanism in its sponsored links (i.e. the search results promoted by AdWords). So, for example, if a popular company is ready to pay $1 per click for the query 'flowers', while a less popular company is ready to pay $1.50, Google's sponsored links would give priority to the more popular company rather than the one which pays more per click. Through this practice, Google has gained both press and industry support, and has been praised for being 'less evil' and more 'objective' than other search engines.[7] Of course, giving priority to popular websites in the sponsored links has also increased Google's profits, suggesting that its decision was primarily economic. Various examples in this study will further indicate that Google's motto 'Don't be evil' is more than anything else an exercise in public relations, and economic considerations often predominate over moral ones.

Google's customised search

Google's homepage displays a standard design in all languages, representing the company's principles of 'simplicity' and 'focused search'. However, in order to customise results to the specific needs of its users, Google also provides personalised search and specialised search channels. It is through these mechanisms that Google is able to exercise even more control over its users and at the same time empower them in return.

With personalised search, Google stores the search history of its users (through their personal accounts), and thus can constantly refine the results to be more accurate, relevant and specific. If, for example, one is interested in politics and current affairs, Google may analyse one's search history to offer news and politically-related information first in the search results. Moreover, users can view, manage and organise their search history according to their preferences. With the Google personalised homepage (also known as iGoogle), users can customise their homepage to display certain information such as search results of any predefined query, calendar, e-mail, weather information and news. Finally, with Google Alerts, users can receive information updates directly to their e-mails, so that instead of searching for information, information comes after them.

Some specialised search channels such as image search, news search and local search (Google Maps) also appear on Google's homepage. Other specific search facilities appear on the inner pages of Google and require more online experience and information skills.[8] Such facilities include book search, online articles (Google Scholar), newsgroups, product search, catalogues, currency conversion, word definitions, file search, videos, local movies, phones and addresses, number search (including package tracking and US patents), site search (restricting search to a specific site), safe search (filtering pornographic content), stock search and weather search. These specialised channels can actually provide considerable, if not invaluable, assistance to the users who are able to master them. Google's Product Search, for example, provides an opportunity for users to search within e-commerce websites for particular products and compare their prices.

Book search is another example of customised service, in which users can search for the full text of books. Google has been scanning and digitising all books from its partner libraries at Michigan, Stanford, Oxford and Harvard universities as well as from the New York Public Library. For legal reasons, people are still restricted from reading the entire content of copyrighted books online. However, users can search for books, read their abstracts and tables of contents, and ultimately order them online. Out-of-copyright classics such as the works of Shakespeare or Dante are available to download and print free of charge (Blakely, 2006). In this way, Google brings a massive (and growing) volume of offline content to the reach of its users. It therefore 'Googlises' offline information and enhances its ambition to 'organise the world's information'.

It is true that much of the information found through the specialised search channels, can also be found through the general search. For example, it is possible to find an illustration of the EU flag by typing 'EU flag' in Google's general search interface (google.com). However, it would be quicker to type 'EU flag' in Google Images (images.google.com), as the flag immediately appears in the search results. As another example, if one wants the latest news from South Korea, one can type the query 'South Korea latest news' into Google's general search interface, however, the top search results would be links to popular news portals such as CNN, CBC or Yahoo! News, in which one is required to continue searching. Alternatively, one can click on Google News and choose Korea as a region, thereby getting the latest news from the leading Korean online newspapers, already in the Korean language.

The growing number of specific search channels highlights the increasing demand for customised information services. A person who knows about the possibilities of focused search, such as image search, product search or news search, can retrieve much more accurate and immediate information than one who does not. Moreover, with the growing customisation in Google and other information agents, users increasingly design their 'daily me' newspapers and are no longer exposed to the same information, a trend that enhances social fragmentation (Sunstein, 2001), and can therefore contribute to the emerging digital divide of information uses (DiMaggio et al., 2004). The analysis of popular search queries in Chapter 4, for example, indicates that many users search for entertainment rather than for political and economic-related information. This is to suggest that unlike previous mass media channels, search engines have become an important customisation tool, enabling users to focus on specific interests and avoid exposure to other issues (in this case political and economic issues), and thus effectively contribute to this divide.[9]

Google's additional services

Apart from direct information search, Google continuously develops indirect information products. Sergey Brin, the co-founder of Google, has introduced the 70-20-10 three circle formula (Battelle, 2005). The inner circle represents the company's core business (information search and search-related advertisements), on which it focuses 70 per cent of its efforts. The remaining 30 per cent is dedicated to related products such as e-mail services and weblogs (divided into the two outer circles of 20 and 10 per cent as will be described below). These additional information products and services help Google strengthen and maintain its position and clientele.

Google Answers represented an interesting additional service. This service (which was closed down during 2006) enabled users to ask open questions (i.e. without the need to type specific search queries), which would be answered by one of Google's qualified researchers. In this way, Google provided a human intermediary between its users and the search engine. While users were required to pay for their answers, this service demonstrated the importance of information skills and search engine technology, which could benefit both non-skilled users and those with limited time and resources, such as business professionals and academics.

Other services that Google offers which are not related to online search include Google Desktop, which enables users to search information within their own personal computer, and Google Earth, which enables users to view aerial images captured by satellites, search for schools, parks, restaurants and hotels, and get travel directions. Those services are not part of Google's 70 per cent core activity, but of the 20 per cent search-related activity of the first outer circle. Another important service that integrates very well with online search is the Google Toolbar, which offers online translation services and pop-up blockers to enhance the surfing experience. Skilled users can download and install Google Toolbar, and enjoy an online translation of webpages at the click of a button. On the one hand, Google technology may help diminish the language divide by offering access to a wider variety of information. On the other, it increases the online gap between those who possess information skills and control of new interfaces and those who do not.

Finally, Google offers a growing variety of additional services that are not directly related to information search, e.g. e-mail (Gmail), an online word processor and spreadsheet, a weblog service (Blogger), communication (Google Talk) and an online community service (Orkut). These are all part of the 10 per cent activities of the second outer circle and have one important feature in common: they increase online users' affiliation with Google, and therefore maintain and nurture a stable clientele. Gmail and Google Talk allow Google-registered users to communicate. The weblog service allows people to manage a personal diary online, which can be shared with others. In this way, every user can be a website owner, and not only consume but also produce online information. To this end, online community services, such as social network services (SNS), are probably the most interesting and developed of all. They allow registered users not only to build their own website and produce their personal content, but also to establish an entire online community based on common interests and traits. The main principle of SNS is that an initial number of users can send invitations to their friends, acquaintances and colleagues to join the online community of specific groups. Without an invitation, people cannot join the online community in some SNS; thus their network can also maintain a prestige of exclusivity and trust.

The growing popularity of online SNS is attracting the attention of sociologists, who are attempting to apply relevant theories and methods to explore online structures and relationships (Cardon and Granjon, 2005; Licoppe and Smoreda, 2005; Boyd and Ellison, 2007). Network theory is particularly useful for studying this emerging phenomenon, as it emphasises the significance of social ties between people, analysing their complex structures and assessing their role in constructing meanings and identities (Barabási, 2002). Moreover, many contemporary scholars have demonstrated empirically that network theory is an effective methodology to evaluate the performance of individuals and groups as well as their social status (Cross et al., 2002).

Advanced engagement in SNS can therefore be even more beneficial and competitive than simply acquiring online information or communicating with others. While e-mail and instant messaging software enable mostly one-to-one communication, and online chat and forums are restricted to specific topics and to the final decisions of website owners, the increasing number of weblogs and online community services opens a whole new dimension of social interaction and power dissemination. People can form their own communities through easy-to-use interfaces, and further decide which information to share and with whom. In very popular online groups, certain users can become opinion leaders, i.e. well-connected hubs that serve as editors of new mass media channels. Weblogs and SNS empower users with information skills and expression abilities, providing them with a wider range of opportunities to reach and influence audiences. The website of Markos Moulitsas Zúniga (*http://www.dailykos.com*), for example, which helped to raise funds for democratic candidates in the 2004 US elections, once boasted getting more than 500,000 different visitors every day. The weblog of Salam Pax, also known as the 'Baghdad blogger', is another example of an online user who became a popular news source, covering the war in Iraq (McNair, 2005). In some states, weblog owners are under constant supervision by local authorities and occasionally prosecuted for posting dissident or anti-governmental information (BBC News, 2007a). Being influential and popular agents, some weblog and social network users get paid by internet companies for increasing their traffic and maintaining their clientele. In return, their success in bringing together a growing dedicated community of readers and commentators increases the popularity of the search engines that host their websites and provide the tools, interfaces and technical infrastructure.

Additional services that enable users to communicate and maintain social relationships are not always directly related to online search, but are gradually being adopted by many search engines.[10] In fact, users who become political or social hubs in those networks help the corporations to gain greater traffic and audiences for their advertisement channels. As such, these additional services play an important role in increasing and maintaining the popularity, profitability and position of search engines.

Google Scholar

While attracting more academics, Google Scholar has had a tremendous impact on the acquisition and organisation of scientific knowledge.[11] Several studies have attempted to assess the information provided by Google Scholar and compare it with other scholarly search tools. According to Neuhaus et al. (2006), Google Scholar is stronger in natural sciences but provides less relevant results in social sciences and humanities. Similarly, Callicott and Vaughn (2006) find that Google Scholar does not match the quality and relevancy of results from subscription databases and library catalogues, although it is potentially useful as supplementary research tool.

One of the main reasons for the differences between these tools is their different approach for indexing and ranking academic articles. The 'About Google Scholar' section (Google, 2009a) explains that Google considers various factors in its ranking, including the full text of the articles, the author and the publication, and how often it has been cited by others. In other words, together with the actual fit between the search query and the content of the publication, Google applies the principles of PageRank in order to automatically determine the relevancy of academic papers.

As most evaluation studies on Google Scholar focus on the question of relevancy and quality of data compared with other scholarly search tools, they often do not fully take into consideration the influential power of Google's PageRank mechanism, which reappears in all of its services and fundamentally differentiates its search results from designated library catalogues. Jacso (2005, 2008) provides important evidence for those differences in his longitudinal studies. He suggests that traditional library catalogues base their search algorithms on tags and metadata, and often involve manual classification of content. The automatic organisation of results in Google Scholar relies mostly on the link and citation structure of articles. In this way, heavily cited articles will tend to appear in the first page of results and overshadow less popular articles that might be more relevant and of higher quality.

Obviously, the growing amount of publications makes manual and human classification methods less effective, and the current automatic ranking method of Google Scholar is very useful in making initial sense of the enormous information available online. It can therefore provide a more general notion of the field of study. However, more specific tools and search strategies should be employed in order to acquire deeper and more specific knowledge that is not always found in the most popular publications.

Over-reliance on Google Scholar in order to find publications or to be found by others has interesting implications for both readers and authors. Being acknowledged by the number of citations and links from other papers, authors are encouraged to form dense co-authorship networks, where they excessively collaborate and cite each others' work. Cronin (2001) describes this phenomenon as a 'hyperauthorship' perversion, suggesting that among all types of academic collaboration, co-authorship has become the most rewarding.

As a result of developments in writing practices and the organisation of online knowledge, there are very crucial changes in the practices and perceptions of readers. Most important is the widening gap between popular academic papers and less popular ones. This popularity or online visibility can be practised in various ways, some of which are familiar from the offline era, but are further intensified by automatic ranking mechanisms. First, from the economic perspective, more weight is given to bigger academic projects that enjoy larger research budgets and involve a greater network of scholars. Those projects therefore have greater opportunities to be cited by more scholars who are directly or indirectly involved in them. Second, from the cultural perspective, there is a higher preference for cultural and academic hubs such as well-known institutes in the USA and the UK. While papers from respectable institutes have always been more popular among scholars and therefore highly cited, page-ranking mechanisms further strengthen their position and online prominence. Finally, from a technological perspective, page-ranking mechanisms empower those who have greater information skills and know better than others how to manipulate and exploit links and citation structures. To this end, it is not impossible that certain academic individuals or institutes will in the near future employ professional technicians to promote the online prominence of their academic work. In short, automatic organisation and retrieval mechanisms intensify the tendency of the rich to get richer when it comes to academic knowledge.

Google Translate

While information inequalities emerge as a result of the language divide, Google Translate enables translating text and entire webpages in more than 40 languages. In addition, it enables searching across languages, i.e. using search queries and getting search results in one language from websites written in other languages. Unlike online services that use a dictionary translation,[12] Google also uses statistical machine translation, which generates translation by using statistical methods based on bilingual text corpora, such as United Nations documents, or the English-French record of the Canadian Parliament. First the system finds patterns within the human-translated bilingual text, and then it builds rules to translate any given text (Google, 2006a). Using this innovative approach, Google has achieved impressive results in translating online texts from Arabic, Japanese, Korean and Chinese. While this service is not directly related to information search, it definitely follows the line of Google's ambition to make the world's information available for all. It also has further implications for the problem of the digital divide.

Google Toolbar makes this service even more accessible as it enables the translation of webpages at the click of a button and therefore, on the surface, addresses the language divide, particularly by enabling non-English speakers to read online information in English. An interesting government response in this context was the blocking of Google Translate by the regime in Sudan in order to limit the ability of Arabic speakers to read English news online (Mathaba, 2006). This suggests that the political significance of online translation tools to diffuse Western views has been recognised.

Nonetheless, despite the promising ability to mediate and understand different views, it seems unlikely that most English-speaking users will suddenly start comparing resources and views as this requires extra time and skills. As most online information is in English, it is more likely that Google Translate will be used by non-English speakers to translate English documents into other languages. The analysis of information trends in Chapter 4 supports this assumption, where 34 per cent of popular searches for translation tools came from Japan, and 23 per cent of searches came from Sweden. During 2004 and 2005, there was not a single popular search for translation tools coming from the USA, Canada, Australia or New Zealand. This suggests that non-English speakers are in greater need of translation tools than are English-speakers. By providing translation *from* English rather than *to* English, online translation tools may empower non-English speakers but, at the same time, reinforce the dominance of English content online.

Furthermore, it is important to mention that as with other additional services provided by Google,[13] Google Translate provides only a limited solution towards a more open information society. There are still many Asian and African languages, such as Bengali and Swahili, that are not currently included in popular online translation tools. There may be a smaller online demand for African and Asian languages (Internet World Stats, 2009), meaning that companies find it less profitable to provide such a service. Clearly, however, the dominance of economic interests further empowers certain actors and thus polarises the information society. Even when online tools such as Google Maps and Google Translate add customised information services for online minorities, they also develop much deeper and more developed information services for the English-speaking majority, and the digital gap therefore continues to grow.

Google's global control by local use

Google provides global and local online information in more than 100 different languages. Together with technical adjustments, international agreements have helped Google expand its information services all over the world. In June 2000, Google signed a partnership contract with China's leading portal NetEase and NEC's BIGLOBE portal in Japan. Both portals added Google search to their websites, meaning that Google increased its global audience and expanded control over online information. A year later, an agreement with Lycos Korea brought Google search to a new group of Asian online users. In October 2001, a partnership with Universo Online made Google Latin America's premier search engine (Google, 2007a).

Together with new international alliances, Google has continuously developed its search engine to support multilingual interfaces that enable users to limit searches to websites written in Arabic, Turkish and many other languages. In 2004, Google introduced local search service to help its users find services and products within a 'walking distance'. Its technology has also enabled the customisation of advertising to local markets. Google Local has been integrated with Google Maps to provide maps and aerial images together with local information. Chapter 6 examines the information produced through this channel as well as its biases and implications regarding the digital divide.

The global reach of Google, as can be displayed by its growing worldwide presence in Figure 3.2, and particularly the open access to information that it provides, have often been at odds with national policies. Thus, global information inequalities can also result from Google's need to comply with local laws and practices. One of the better-known conflicts has been that between Google and the Chinese government. It started rather contingently in 2002, just before the 16th National Congress of the Communist Party of China, when Jiang Mianheng, the son of the former President Jiang Zemin, visited the No. 502 Research Institute of the Ministry of Information Industry, attending a demonstration of the second-generation broadband internet and its high-speed search facilities. In order to please him, an engineer typed the name of his father 'Jiang Zemin' in the Google search engine, and surprisingly, one of the first results was titled: 'Evil Jiang Zemin'. Jiang Mianheng immediately ordered the blocking of Google's website in China (Tianliang, 2005).

However, two weeks later on 13 September 2002, due to public pressure from the 30 million Chinese Google users at that time, China ended the ban and Google was available again in China. Yet users reported broken links in Google's results when they searched for sensitive information such as that on Tibet, Taiwan, President Jiang Zemin, Falun Gong and the Tiananmen Square revolts. The Chinese government has

Figure 3.2   Google's international offices

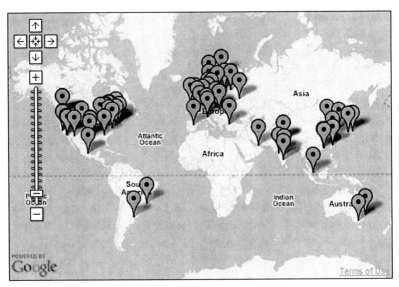

Source: http://www.google.com/corporate/address.html, accessed in April 2008

never publicly announced its intention to ban Google and other popular search engines (such as AltaVista), or to re-open access to some of them. In other words, the lack of governmental transparency makes it difficult to assess what information is censored in China and why (Deans, 2002). According to the Berkman Center for Internet and Society (2002), Google was often censored in China during 2002, and users who tried to reach it were automatically diverted to alternative local search engines such as Globepage, chinaren.com, search.online.sh.cn, and fm365.com, as these could be easily manipulated and controlled by the Chinese government.

In 2004, Google launched Google News, and automatically filtered government-banned websites such as the BBC News site, if search requests were made from computers in China. The same search, if conducted outside of China, would provide a full list of news articles. In response to its censorship efforts, Google issued a statement:

> there has been controversy about our new Google News China edition, specifically regarding which news sources we include. For users inside the People's Republic of China, we have chosen not to include sources that are inaccessible from within that country. (Hinman, 2005: 24–5)

Thus, Google justified the decision on the grounds that those websites were already inaccessible from China. Google's self-censorship was presented as a necessary evil, a price that had to be paid for enhancing the Chinese online experience (W. Knight, 2004).

Similarly, Yahoo! China excludes search results of a dissident nature and even information about the democratic system in general. A person located in China who types search queries such as 'Tiananmen massacre' or 'Falun Gong' (in Chinese or in English) in both Google and Yahoo! may find only the few results approved by the Chinese government. Until 2006, if one had searched for these queries outside of China, one might have found many results in Google China (*www.google.cn*), but still no results in Yahoo! China (*www.yahoo.com.cn*). This is to say that while Google used to omit results that were unavailable in China anyway, Yahoo! actively cooperated with the Chinese government and filtered undesirable and politically sensitive information within its own services. Moreover, if one attempts to search for politically sensitive information with Yahoo! China, one's IP address may be blocked for further access to Yahoo! China.[14] This means that it is difficult for Chinese users who cannot read English to use Yahoo! China to find information about the Tiananmen massacre or any other politically sensitive issues, even if they live in the USA or anywhere else outside of China (Mackinnon, 2005). What is more disturbing and revealing of online power abuse is that once these users try to obtain this information and are rejected, they are punished and excluded from further attempts to use Yahoo! China.

Following the strengthening of the position of Yahoo! China and Baidu.com, Google realised that the system of omitting search results that were already banned was slowing the surfing experience. As the Chinese government uses firewalls to filter certain information coming from outside the country, the US-based Google China was operating very slowly within China. To speed up the search experience and compete with other providers in China, Google launched a new version of its search engine in January 2006. Like the search engines of its main rivals, Google's new offering operated from within China. This time, Google cooperated with the Chinese government and actively filtered sensitive search results (Nystedt and McCarthy, 2006). This is to say that those who use Google China today cannot find any 'undesirable' information, even if they try to search outside of the country – just like Yahoo! China.

In June 2006, using *www.google.cn* to conduct a search for the query 'Falun Gong' yielded only official government information, which was obviously biased and highly controlled. The first result, for example, was from the *People's Daily*, a popular mainstream newspaper in China. The article explained the 'mental danger' of being involved with the Falun-Gong cult, and the vicious rumours that the Falung-Gong members spread against the government. The title of the article was 'Extreme exposure to Falungong' and the photograph attached was labelled 'Falungong addict is treated in the health care centre'.[15]

The same search at *www.google.com* yielded totally different results, where the first result was the official website of the Falun-Gong, claiming to be a peaceful organisation that is meant to enhance one's health based on the principles of truthfulness, benevolence and forbearance, with no political, religious or commercial affiliation (*http://www.falundafa.org/en*). The second result was from Wikipedia, which similarly explains that the Falun-Gong is a very popular system of mind and body cultivation. These examples demonstrate not only the significance of language skills (especially English) and the subsequent digital divide of information by language, but also the commercial and political considerations behind the production of information in search engines and the extent of government control even beyond national borders.

Information exclusion as a national policy in China is not limited to search engines. Harri Wu, a human rights activist, stated in a hearing in 2004 that many US-based high-tech companies such as Cisco and Symantec often cooperate with the police in China and censor anti-governmental information in order to increase their market share (Tianliang, 2005). Similarly, in order to enter the Chinese market, Skype signed an agreement with China to block certain keywords (Pain, 2007). These efforts often include voice recognition systems for telephone and voice-over IP (VoIP) conversations, as well as very sophisticated and advanced exclusion mechanisms, which make possible the filtering of content by keywords and the tracking of individual users. Cyber-cafés, which provide internet access to many Chinese, are required by law to maintain a detailed log-file of their clients. Similarly, internet content providers are required by law to control the access and use of bulletin board services, chats and forums. They are required to report and remove immediately any inappropriate or illegal postings. Similar to the situation in China, extensive online censorship occurs in Burma, Iran, North Korea, Saudi Arabia and the United Arab Emirates (ONI, 2005). This systematic exclusion targets sensitive governmental information, as well as matters relating to human rights, democracy, homosexuality and pornography. In all cases, online censorship lacks transparency, as governments never admit their filtering efforts nor publish lists of banned websites.

Censorship and government control is not restricted to non-Western states. For example, in January 2006, the US government required the biggest US search engines to provide a list of all search queries conducted over a one-week period, as well as a random list of 1 million websites that appeared in their search results. The government claimed it needed this information in order to revive the Child Online Protection Act 1998. Yahoo!, America Online and Microsoft immediately complied with the request. Only Google initially refused to provide the data, claiming it would violate the privacy of its users and reveal company trade secrets (L. Walker, 2006; de Vries, 2006). Three months later, a federal judge ordered Google to turn over some of the records demanded by the government, which it did (Schmidt, 2006).

Yet Google's concern with the privacy of its users is only a smokescreen. Although Google refused to share its clients' information with the US government until ordered by the court, at the same time it introduced Google Desktop 3, a product that enables users to search for information in their personal computer as well as transfer their private files to Google's servers. This means that Google can have access and store not only their personal interests through search queries, but also their personal letters, business records, financial and medical files (BBC News, 2006a). Similarly, the privacy policies of Google Toolbar and Gmail explicitly state that Google collects data about the websites visited by its users, and stores the e-mails that they send and receive (Google, 2006b, 2006c). Hence, this enormous and constantly growing database of private search queries, files and e-mails can theoretically reach the hands of the US government, as has happened before in relatively peaceful circumstances – not to mention in cases of emergency or war.

As a response to the growing concern of worldwide users and regulators (particularly in Europe), Google recently adopted a policy of periodically (after 18–24 months) removing the part of the IP address that identifies its users and links them with their search requests (Liedtke, 2007). It is believed that these privacy measures will not reduce Google's ability to customise its search results but will rather improve its image as a more 'secure service' among its users.[16] For similar reasons, Google's founders publicly expressed their regret for having to comply with Chinese censorship, admitting that this decision damaged their reputation among their US and European users (Martinson, 2007). At the same time, however, Google introduced a censored version of Google Maps in China (see Chapter 6) and deepened its grasp on the Chinese market, attempting to rival Baidu by scanning Chinese books and integrating them into its Google Books database (S. Taylor, 2007). In short, Google continues to make headlines on users' privacy, intellectual property and national censorship, trying to negotiate access to more information and maintain a balance among conflicting groups. Nonetheless, it is obvious that its operation is primarily driven by commercial motivations, and its recent efforts to improve its image as a 'non-evil', 'secure' yet free and equal service are, in most cases, examples of public relations rather than a dominant corporate strategy.[17]

Reinforcing online allegiance

Along with global expansion and international competition, search engines are required to develop certain mechanisms to maintain and, ideally, enhance the affiliation with their users. A survey conducted by the search engine marketing firm iProspect (2004) revealed that about 60 per cent of users use the same search engine when looking for information, while another 30 per cent use a few specific search engines regularly. The survey also indicated that the loyalty of users to one search engine differs among search engines, where Google's loyalty rate was 66 per cent versus 55 per cent for Yahoo! and MSN. More recent surveys support these figures, indicating that Google's loyalty rate has steadily increased in the last five years, while the loyalty rates of Yahoo! and MSN have decreased (comScore, 2009b; ZDNet, 2006).

Still, Google, Yahoo! and MSN dominate the information search market worldwide, allowing almost no room for alternative search engines to enter the competition. Perhaps the most important reason for this monopolisation of the search market is the inability of new entrants to invest hugely in hardware, software and connection capacity. Companies wishing to enter this market should not only provide information free of charge, but also do so better than others, i.e. provide more information, more quickly and more accurately; the information must also be relevant and more customised. Hence, unless they are very specialised, small search engine companies are effectively driven out of the market from the very outset; meanwhile, the popular search engine companies work constantly to develop and increase the variety of information and services.

Trying to maintain its competitive position in the market, Google has invested in research and development, and encouraged creativity among its employees. Nevertheless, there is no way it could compete with the mass of innovation and creativity outside its organisational boundaries. Once new and better search technology is introduced, online users might simply change their homepage and start using it.[18] Google has recognised this threat; thus it constantly and obsessively tries to provide its users with additional services that are not part of the core search service. This is also the main reason that 30 per cent of Google's work is related only indirectly to web search (Levy, 2005). Apart from maintaining creativity and innovation, services such as Google Toolbar, customised news, office tools, e-mail, weblogs and SNS seek to provide online users with a holistic solution for their online activities, and bind them to the information provider. This 'locking mechanism' is very important because it increases the dependence of users on specific services as well as the costs and effort involved in moving to competitors.

Similarly, the ability of search engines to customise content may also have a bonding effect. Google and other search engines provide organised and customised content in directories and online news services as well as marketing and stock services. Appropriate content may attract new users, deletion of content may prevent unwanted users from reaching them, and addition and updates of content may lock users to the gatekeeper (Barzilai-Nahon, 2006a). As previously mentioned, with Google Alerts users can decide what kind of content they wish to receive in their e-mail, and with iGoogle they can further design their customised Google homepage to display only 'desired' information (including e-mails, calendar and news). Hence, after investing time and effort on customising their homepage to fit their preferences, users are less likely to change their gatekeeper and information provider so readily.

The 'locking mechanism' can therefore be perceived as the power that search engines exercise in order to prevent users from changing their information provider. It is the same mechanism that Microsoft used when it introduced Internet Explorer as a free built-in browser and an integral part of the Windows operating system, marginalising Netscape Navigator, which previously dominated the browser market. By offering online word processing and spreadsheets, e-mail and weblog services, which are definitely not part of information search, Google not only creates a stronger affinity with its current users, but also penetrates into the commercial and informational territories of other internet companies. In short, one can see the expansion of information services ultimately as a means to expand and strengthen control over informational commons and their users. Thus, the various trends of inequality and information biases (which will be further examined and displayed) may become even more prominent and influential with the ever-growing control of search engines over their users.

Online manipulation and punishment

Information inequalities are not only a result of the organisation of information based on commercial considerations, but also of inclusion and exclusion mechanisms. Online manipulation and punishment refer to the different search engine mechanisms that prioritise or exclude websites and their owners from search results. A punishment of exclusion from the network, i.e. removal from the list of results, occurs if website owners break the local law, or try to hack and manipulate the search mechanism. As laws differ in different countries, Google employs a team of international lawyers that can advise on matters of human rights or copyright abuse on a case-by-case basis. The punishment is enforced locally; thus, for example, according to a report from the Berkman Center at Harvard University, Google France and Google Germany exclude websites that are anti-Semitic, pro-Nazi or related to white supremacy (McCullagh, 2002). Although such websites are not listed in the search results of Google France and Google Germany, they are still listed in the main domain, *www.google.com*, and any other international domain of Google, which means that, in this case, national laws are only partly observed.

Similarly, some countries, especially China and Iran, employ sophisticated and extensive censorship mechanisms for anti-government content, which affect the results in Google and Yahoo! local search engines. Online laws and their enforcement are not always clear and mostly subject to a local rather than global sovereignty. However, the global reach of the internet and its ability to bypass national boundaries has led to the emergence of global norms (e.g. assigning domain names by one authorised organisation) and, increasingly, transnational social and technological standards (e.g. freedom of expression, data protection, digital signature and even some laws against online crime in the EU) (Perri 6, 2002; Van Dijk, 2005).

While online crimes are still subject to national laws, the new dynamic of the internet has brought about new forms of cyber-crimes. Knowing the basic principles of page-ranking in Google, some website owners attempt to increase the number of links to their websites by artificial means in order to appear first in the search results. Walker (2002) suggests that web links have become a common unit to estimate online popularity and value; and therefore many try to manipulate search results and increase their website value by link exchange with other websites. Some have developed 'link farms', i.e. networks of websites with no content at all, but a massive amount of links. Website owners can purchase links from a link farm owner, and thus increase their ranking with Google. This trade is also known as the 'black market for links'.

Other manipulations of search results with political overtones are also exercised. For many years, a Google search for the queries 'miserable failure' and 'failure' returned the personal webpage of George W. Bush. [19] Similarly, a Google search for the query 'liar' returned the personal webpage of Tony Blair. This manipulation is possible because Google counts how often a site is linked to, and with which words (also known as 'anchor text'). Hence, information-skilled users and those who produce online content through weblogs and forums can group together to manipulate search results, a phenomenon that is also known as 'Google bomb' (BBC News, 2003). Empirical tests indicate that a Google bomb effect does not need a large number of websites, but rather a small number of dedicated online users (Battelle, 2005; Bar-Ilan, 2007).

The technique of Google bombing, i.e. manipulating search results by deliberately cross-linking certain words to certain websites, was widely used in the run-up to the 2006 US election. Many Republican candidates became targets for a Google bombing campaign, so that seeking their names through Google yielded negative campaigning and criticism in the top search results (Zeller, 2006). Still, politicians and political parties also exploit search engines, associating their websites with certain keywords and investing in search engine optimisation. Using Google AdWords, politicians can either promote their party or fight against their competitors, so that a search for their competitors will lead to negative advertising.

Vise and Malseed (2005) suggest that the decisions regarding inclusion or exclusion of certain issues in AdWords are not transparent and often reflect the personal views of Google's founders, Page and Brin. When it comes to political advertisements, the system often rejects advertisements that attack personally or slander political candidates, but can accept hostile advertisements that distort and denounce the political views of a candidate. Many decisions regarding the inclusion and exclusion of advertisements, which involve both automatic and manual mechanisms, are managed and controlled internally in Google and are not transparent to the public. Such practices expose users to certain information and products, while denying access to others. The growing popularity of AdWords as a dominant advertising online channel therefore has tremendous economic, political and cultural implications, which are worth examining in further studies.

While diverting search results is still not illegal in any country, Google is aware of such attempts to impede the 'integrity' of its own page-ranking system. Thus, once it discovers a link farm website, it permanently excludes it and its clients from the search results. In other words, there is no punishment for link 'prostitution' at the national level, yet there is an emerging online system of regulations with its own rules and punishment mechanisms. Thanks to our capitalist world system, these mechanisms can be developed and enforced entirely by search engines. Although Google has been sued in the past by various companies for being 'undemocratic' for removing or marginalising their websites, the US Court has consistently rejected such allegations, ruling in favour of Google's right to organise online information in its own services (BBC News, 2007c).

As well as attempting to divert search results, hackers and cyber-criminals have developed a method, known as the 'click fraud', to divert revenues from search engines. As discussed previously, based on the principle of cost-per-click (CPC), search engines get money whenever someone clicks on a sponsored link and, with the introduction of AdSense, Google provided website owners with the ability to distribute advertisements through their own websites as resellers. Consequently, a click fraud may occur if a person or an automated script imitates the legitimate action of clicking on advertisements in order to generate illegal revenues or harm competitors. Click fraud is considered a felony in some jurisdictions, and has therefore been prosecuted by the relevant national authorities.

The click fraud phenomenon poses a real problem for search engines and their business model. It is estimated that click fraud generates damages of $3.8 billion annually in advertising revenues (Hinman, 2005).

Google has established a special department to deal with specific cases as well as to limit click fraud in general. Yet Google makes enormous profits from click frauds, does not immediately compensate its affected clients, and often requires them to provide evidence for their claims (Vise and Malseed, 2005).

Conclusion

This chapter examined the operations of Google and the various information services it offers. Although 'organising the world's information and making it universally accessible and useful' is one of the most important challenges of the information society, Google has to innovate and add new products constantly in order to retain the loyalty of its audience and compete with other search engines. Its strategic position as the most popular information agent requires dealing with local authorities and governments, complying with local laws and fighting against new cyber-crimes. As a mass communication channel, it also has to comply with individual needs for privacy and national needs for security, while minimising its damage and maximising its profits.

Behind the 'automatic' organisation of online information there are various commercial considerations (e.g. page-ranking mechanisms, promotion deals, locking mechanisms) as well as international politics. The fact that there are various interests also means that the information in Google is not and cannot be unbiased. Apart from the basic organisation of information and the obvious preference for popular, bigger and commercial websites, Google also frequently excludes certain information and actors based on local laws and corporate considerations. The following chapters will examine more specifically the implications of those practices on the perpetuation of information inequalities through Google's search channels for news and maps, as well as through the analysis of popular search queries in various countries.

Together with the growing market share of the big search engines and their continuous acquisitions and mergers, such inequalities can be further intensified. This would never have been possible without the users themselves, who increasingly need tools to obtain immediate and relevant information and to control and organise the massive and growing flow of information and disinformation. They are empowered by search engines but, increasingly, they depend on them and thus contribute to their popularity and strength.

Notes

1. Some members of Google's board of directors also serve in companies such as Intel, Sun Microsystems, Yahoo! and Amazon (Google, 2007b).
2. The quotes for keyword promotion were obtained directly from Google AdWords in July 2005.
3. See, for example, Google (2008), Nunberg (2003) and Introna and Nissenbaum (2000).
4. Some search engines, such as Google, analyse mostly the visible content of webpages, while others also include the metatags in their index, i.e. the code lines that webmasters use to specify information about their webpages (e.g. authors, keywords and short descriptions).
5. A Google search for the term 'apple' was conducted by the author on 23 July 2006 and repeated on 2 April 2008.
6. Google is currently developing an open source platform known as Google Co-op, in which online users can voluntarily add related topics for each query. Thus, for example, when a person types a city name such as 'New York', Google automatically suggests refining its search results to dining guides, lodging guides, shopping destinations and other attractions.
7. Overture, which developed and patented the CPC technique and used to power the search and marketing solutions for Yahoo! and MSN, used to display the higher bidder first in its sponsored links (Battelle, 2005).
8. In 2007, Google moved some of these features to its homepage to make them more accessible.
9. Norris (2001) referred to this gap between the politically engaged and the disengaged created by customised media channels as the 'democratic divide'. See also Chapter 1.
10. The competition between Google and Microsoft over equity stakes in Facebook (McCarthy, 2007) exemplifies the great interest of search engine companies in SNS.
11. Agarwal (2008) used data provided by Compete, a web analytics company, indicating that Google Scholar attracts around 2 million unique users a month.
12. For example, AltaVista (Babel Fish), AOL, Yahoo and MSN, which use the dictionary translation of Systran (Senellart and Senellart, 2005).
13. See, for example, the study on Google Earth and Google Maps in Chapter 5.
14. This, in fact, happened to the author after searching for the search query 'Tiananmen massacre' in Yahoo China on 16 June, 2006.
15. The article was accessed in June 2006 and translated from Chinese to English using Google Translate: *http://translate.google.com/translate? sourceid=navclient-menuext&hl=en&u=http://www.people.com.cn/GB/ shizheng/252/2139/index.html*.
16. During the same period, Google attempted to recruit a network of lobbyists in Europe that would examine various aspects of privacy, copyrights and regulation of online information, enhancing its ability to shape information policies in Europe (Bounds, 2007).
17. A recent report by Privacy International claimed that Google's privacy practices are the worst among the internet's top destinations (BBC News, 2007b).

18. In 2005, Google introduced the Founders' Award to recognise the extraordinary innovative achievements of its employees. Similarly, it constantly searches to acquire small yet promising start-up companies in order to retain its competitive position (Battelle, 2005).

19. The lifecycle of Google bomb is varied. The search queries 'failure' and 'miserable failure' linking to the personal page of George W. Bush appeared in December 2003 (BBC News, 2003) and still appeared in October 2006. By the end of 2006, Google made massive changes in its index to tackle this problem.

Users and uses of Google's information

The previous two chapters looked at the significance of search engines in shaping the information society and deepening its digital divide. This chapter explores the various information uses in Google more specifically, identifying the opportunities and limitations of online search. The assumption lying behind this examination is that the increasing use of search engines inevitably creates more hierarchies and inequalities as a result of different information skills and abilities in manipulating online information. While UNESCO (2005a) and other international organisations have tried to measure and assess the different information skills in different countries, they have often applied more traditional top-down definitions to describe information inequality, such as technical divide (number of users in different countries), formal economic divide and education divide; as well as age, culture and language divide. To this end, little has been done to examine the actual information uses in the context of the digital divide,[1] and particularly the utilisation of online search engines such as Google.

In this chapter a new methodology to analyse popular search queries in different countries is developed and assessed. It suggests several indicators such as content, variety and accuracy of search in order to reflect the different information skills and uses. Subsequently, the main questions addressed in this chapter are:

- To what extent do popular search queries differ in different countries?

- What are the implications of such differences for the digital divide?

The findings suggest that some countries, in particular Germany, Russia and Ireland, demonstrate greater information skills, greater diversity of information uses and greater searches of economic and political value. However, they also indicate that in many countries (particularly the USA), search queries are poor in diversity and focus mainly on entertainments. This can imply a certain gap within the USA and similar countries between those users who are more politically informed and those who are less so. Hence, the relationship between information skills and economic and political powers is not always straightforward, as presented by previous measurements, and requires further assessment and academic attention.

The study of popular search queries in various countries not only reflects different trends, concepts and traditions, but also indicates the abilities of people in different countries to translate information into specific advantages. Together with top-down studies that observe national economic, educational and technological differences, it is important to continue and encourage more bottom-up studies that look at the actual content that users retrieve and produce. Of course, there is an ongoing interaction between the two, and global trends, particularly in media and communications, have been constantly shaping public preferences and their information usage patterns.

The digital divide can follow two different paths, driven by two different perspectives. From the top-down approach, some capitalist countries display better information and communication technologies, as well as stronger economies, and therefore lead the information society and deepen the global divide (Sciadas, 2003; UNESCO, 2005a). From the bottom-up approach, commercialisation and privatisation of communication channels may have strengthened economic and financial capital, but they have also polarised contemporary society, and weakened its political engagement and social capital (Putnam, 2000; Holtz-Bacha and Norris, 2001; Scheufele, 2002; Bagdikian, 2004; R. Rogers, 2004; Turow, 2005; see also Chapter 1). The digital divide therefore has different implications in different contexts. Understanding its diverse applications and implications in the context of information search is exactly what is at stake.

Methodology

The object of analysis in this chapter is the most frequent search queries initiated by users in different countries, mainly in Google, but also in Yahoo! (for information uses in the USA, see below). The analysis of search queries can provide an important insight into popular information trends in different countries. Several studies have explored how people search the web (Silverstein et al., 1999; Wolfram et al., 2001). Bar-Ilan (2004) and Jansen and Spink (2004) suggest that web-searching studies fall into three categories: (1) those that examine search queries; (2) those that incorporate user surveys and observations; and (3) those that examine issues related to or influencing web searching (e.g. web structure, interface design, social and environmental conditions, and so on).

A study by Hargittai (2002) attempted to assess the digital divide of information uses by providing a random sample of users with a list of information search tasks. Individuals were asked to find information about local cultural events, political candidates, tax forms, and so on. Information skills were defined as the ability to find the desired information in the allocated time. The findings indicated that young and experienced users were more likely to succeed in completing the tasks quickly, while old users and newcomers were much slower, and sometimes could not complete all tasks.

Other studies (e.g. Silverstein et al., 1999; Jansen et al., 2000; Jansen and Spink, 2003) have focused on the search queries people use, but not from a digital divide perspective. Jansen and Spink (2004) conducted longitudinal research from 1997 to 2003, looking at search queries in Excite, AltaVista, Ask Jeeves, and alltheweb.com in order to explore how and what people search on the web in Europe and the USA. Their studies included pornography, health and business-related search queries, but did not look at the political, social or cultural implications of the searches.

In terms of query length and search session length, the study of Jansen and Spink (2003) indicated very little change over the years, with most users entering two or three terms per query, and viewing about five web documents per query, without query reformulation or modification. In the distribution of search queries, Jansen et al. (2000) assumed the existence of the power law; that is, a few terms were used repeatedly and many terms were used only once. This further strengthens the importance of studying popular search queries in Google Zeitgeist (see below), which can shed light on the information-searching habits of many users worldwide.

In another study, Spink et al. (2002a) attempted to classify search queries from the Excite search engine into 11 'non-mutually exclusive, general topic categories', such as 'Entertainment or recreation', 'Health or sciences', 'Commerce, travel, employment, or economy' and 'People, places, or things'. However, the reasoning behind their taxonomic system is unclear, and the categories themselves seem to overlap (e.g. entertainment and people).

A study by Chau et al. (2007) compared popular Chinese search queries in a Hong Kong-based search engine with those in English search engines for content variety, query length and the use of search operators. Their study indicated similarity with English search engines in search topics and the average query length. Apart from pornography-related queries among the top 100 search queries, there were many queries related to travel, e-commerce and music downloading.

Finally, a study by Ross and Wolfram (2000) analysed popular queries from the Excite search engine, identifying the various topics using cluster analysis. Similarly, Pu et al. (2001) classified popular search queries in three Taiwanese search engines. Both studies attempted to apply automatic systems to classify popular search queries into topical categories, resulting in several well-defined clusters of subjects. The main principle of their classification was to obtain highly ranked web documents based on each search query, and then to analyse the content of these documents, and to identify their main topics.

Previous studies of search queries have suggested methodologies for manual or automatic analysis and topical classification, but have not specifically looked at the problem of the digital divide. This chapter continues the investigation of online search, attempting to shed light on the digital divide of information uses by analysing the content, diversity and accuracy of search queries. Another contribution is in developing a cross-national comparison of popular searches in a relatively large number of countries, a comparison that has not been done by previous analyses of search queries.[2]

Three indices are developed in order to examine three different aspects of the digital divide of information uses: the economic and political value (EPV) of search queries, the variety of uses (VoU),[3] and the specificity of search (SoS). Observations were performed during 24 months from January 2004 to December 2005. The relationships between those indices are examined, and countries are subsequently clustered based on the different attributes of the searches. The implications of those differences are discussed, calling for further development and implementation of search query databases and new analytical tools to study the digital divide in information uses.

Data sources

Most data have been automatically gathered and published on the Google Zeitgeist website (Google, 2005). The term 'zeitgeist' is commonly attributed to J. G. Herder's German translation of the Latin expression 'genius seculi', referring to the spirit of the century (Barnard, 2004). For Google it is now technically possible to explore what information is being sought by almost a billion users worldwide each month, map their interests and trace patterns and trends over time.

The drawback of Google Zeitgeist is that it does not regularly provide popular searches in the USA.[4] By way of contrast, Yahoo!, another leading search engine, provides a weekly summary of the most popular search queries in general (a service known as Yahoo! Buzz). Yahoo! does not divide information uses by countries, and therefore may provide a more global notion of information uses. That said, a number of sources have suggested that in terms of nationality, the highest share of Yahoo.com users are, by far, American.[5] As such, the data published by Yahoo! provide an indication of information trends in the USA.[6]

Jansen and Spink (2004) have made a similar attempt to compare the use of information in various countries by looking at popular search queries in several search engines (namely, Fireball, a predominantly German web search engine; BWIE, a Spanish web search service; and Excite, a US-based web search engine). In another study, Spink et al. (2002b) examined search queries to FAST (also known as alltheweb.com) during 2001, which was largely used by Europeans at that time. Popular queries to FAST were compared with those to Excite (used mainly by US users), suggesting that FAST's users searched more for people and places, while Excite's users focused on e-commerce. Regarding methodology, these studies suggest that there are some functions, such as the content of search queries and time of search sessions, which are comparable between different search engines in different countries. However, the comparison of some interface-dependent functions, such as the use of search operators, is less straightforward.

As for this study, the comparison between Google's and Yahoo!'s popular search queries is in terms of content, variety and accuracy, which are not interface-dependent functions, and can therefore be compared. In this sense, a possible methodological risk in such a comparison is that some people may use both Google and Yahoo!, but for different purposes (e.g. Google for information-seeking, and Yahoo! for entertainment purposes). This is most unlikely, however, as both Google and Yahoo! are *general* rather than niche search engines, consisting of very similar functions.[7] Moreover, the data used for the analysis consist of the most popular search queries, which are almost always general rather than specific queries. In any case, Google Zeitgeist displayed popular search queries in Google.com for some months. These data were used in order to validate the Yahoo! results, and clearly confirmed and supported the results, which showed that the most popular search queries to the parent-sites were about entertainment.[8]

In January 2004, Google Zeitgeist displayed the most popular search queries from nine countries: the UK, Canada, Germany, Spain, France, Italy, the Netherlands, Australia and Japan. Another seven countries – Brazil, China, Denmark, Finland, South Korea (hereafter: Korea), Norway and

Sweden – were added to the report in July 2004. Four more countries – Ireland, India, New Zealand and Russia – were included in January 2005. Finally, another seven countries – Chile, Greece, Israel, Poland, South Africa, Turkey and Vietnam – were added in September 2005 (see Appendix B for the complete list of countries and the months of inclusion in Google Zeitgeist). In sum, this study exploits data from Google's archive on 27 countries,[9] and from Yahoo!'s archive on general information searches, which mainly refers to the USA.

It is possible for users in one country to connect to search engines in other countries. For example, users in Germany can search in Google.de, but also in the parent US-site, Google.com, or the French version, Google.fr. The monthly report of Google Zeitgeist shows the most popular search queries used to search in Google's national interfaces. Thus, for example, search queries that were counted for Google Germany are those which were used to search in Google.de. This does not necessarily imply that all the users who searched Google.de reside in Germany. They could theoretically be in China, in the USA, or anywhere else. However, it does mean that users who searched in Google.de, and made up the monthly statistics of popular search queries, were most likely to be familiar with the German language, as the interface of Google.de is in German. This means that language is an important factor in the analysis.

Nonetheless, customisation mechanisms in Google also promote and reinforce local and national factors. Google automatically recognises the IP address of its users, and therefore also the location from which they search. Subsequently, it automatically loads the interface that is appropriate to their country by default. This 'user-friendly' process considerably increases the probability of local users employing the national interface of the country from which they search. It is therefore reasonable to assume that Google Zeitgeist broadly presents popular information searches of people in different countries speaking different languages.

On average, this study analyses between 150 and 200 popular search queries from each of the national interfaces of Google during the 24 months of 2004 and 2005.[10] All together 4,474 different search queries are analysed. Following enquiries,[11] Google has indicated that data in Google Zeitgeist were compiled using the in-house versions of their recent tools (i.e. Google Trends and Insights for Search). This list reflects the most popular searches in Google Search, excluding porn-related queries, duplicate entries (including misspellings) and spam results.[12] Obviously, many search engine companies hesitate to share a large volume of search queries or reveal the processes behind the data collection and reporting in their different services.[13] Nevertheless, the longitudinal investigation has enabled the collection of a relatively large volume of data for a cross-national comparison, and has been instrumental in the utilisation and demonstration of new methodologies to study the digital divide of information uses.

A cross-national comparison

There are two main reasons for using a cross-national comparison in this study. First, as mentioned earlier, the literature on the digital divide often describes the technology and information differences between states, as well as within states (Norris, 2001). Initially there is a technical divide, which refers to the internet infrastructure, and the physical differences in access to the network in terms of equipment, internet service providers, costs, and so on. Furthermore, different countries have different economic power, which is strongly related to the different percentages of online population (see also Appendix B, Table 12). Then there are also political differences between countries. Democratic regimes allow access to most websites in the world, while undemocratic regimes impose censorship and restrict access to certain websites for political, cultural and social reasons. These restrictions and limitations are mostly exercised at the national level. Finally, the digital divide of information is also a result of the different knowledge of languages. Most websites provide information in English. Official national languages and learned second languages are a direct result of national policies, and thus it is more likely that national division also affects language division, and both have crucial implications on the digital divide of information uses. Subsequently, the following analysis uses countries as a unit of comparison in the study of the digital divide.

The second reason for applying a cross-national comparison is the nature of the data in Google Zeitgeist, which also divides search queries by country. It is therefore a straightforward process to exploit these data, analyse the different popular information searches in different countries, and discuss their implications for the digital divide. The methodology developed here could be also applied in further studies to explore the digital divide within states, looking at popular search queries of users of different age, ethnicity, region and the like.

Main classification system

To compare information uses in different countries, this study employed a classification system of content integrated in Google Search, called the Open Directory Project (ODP), which is a very comprehensive human-edited directory developed and constantly updated by the online community. Each chosen editor qualified to add and maintain the open directory has to prove a good knowledge of the language, the culture and the field of the category to be edited. New information appearing on the web is constantly classified by the network community itself, and categories and subcategories are added and edited through a system of checks and balances and quality assurance. The Open Directory powers the core directory services in Google, AOL/Netscape Search and many other large and popular search engines and portals (DMOZ, 2005).

One of the main principles that ODP editors are required to follow is to organise websites by topics (e.g. news, business and games), rather than simply by region. This principle works well with the concept of functionality and usability of information, and refers directly to the research problem of this study. Furthermore, there are two main advantages in exploiting the ODP classification system in this study. First, content has already been classified, which means consistency and accuracy in the classification process – different coders using the ODP classification system will always attain similar results. The second advantage is that the ODP enterprise is international and its editors are local. It therefore already contains wide knowledge and experience, and provides an expert-specific classification of content by culture and language. As ODP editors are required to have the cultural, language and even topical background of the category they manage, it is reasonable to assume that they classify and sort information more accurately than people who do not know the field, the language or the cultural context of the classified content. The ODP's central management, hierarchical structure of editors and its developed system of checks and balances ensure consistency and accuracy of classification, even when done by different editors.

Google Web Directory is based on the ODP and provides 14 different topical categories. For each category there are 1–17 subcategories, which are divided again into 1–20 third-level subcategories, and so on. The main categories of Google Web Directory are: Arts (with 12 subcategories, such as Movies, Music and Television), Business (with eight subcategories, such as Employment, Financial Services and Investing), Computers (with seven subcategories, such as Hardware, Internet and Programming), Games (with six subcategories, such as Gambling, Role-playing and

Video Games), Health (with four subcategories, such as Alternative, Beauty and Nutrition), Home (with four subcategories, such as Do-It-Yourself, Cooking and Family), News (with four subcategories such as Breaking News, Online Archives and Weather), Recreation (with 13 subcategories such as Humor, Outdoors, and Travel), Reference (with five subcategories, such as Education, Dictionaries and Maps), Science (with three subcategories: Astronomy, Technology and Earth Sciences), Shopping (with eight subcategories, such as Auctions, Clothing and Flowers), Society (with nine subcategories, such as Chats and Forums, Government and Religion and Spirituality) and Sports (with 17 subcategories, such as Basketball, Football and Soccer). Appendix B displays the full list of categories and subcategories.

A search query submitted to the ODP or to Google Web Directory provides in return not only a list of results with their specific classifications, but also the main and most frequent classification of most results.[14] Because of this, it was possible for the study to automatically ascribe the most frequent and common ODP classification for each popular search query. Even though the process of classifying search queries into categories and subcategories was mostly automatic, there was careful human control involved for each query, checking the integrity, and filtering the regional effect of the classification process. Hence, for example, the query 'herr der ringe' (in English: 'The lord of the rings') appeared in Google Germany in January 2004, and was automatically classified as World > Deutsch > Arts > Films > Titles > H, as the query was written in German. In this case, the first regional categories were manually filtered and the classification started with Arts > Films > Titles, as the three categories to be checked and compared. When a query was automatically classified as regional, the subcategories were used as the main classification in order to maintain integrity with results from other national interfaces. Another example is the query 'eastenders' in Google UK. This query was classified automatically as: Regional > Europe > United Kingdom > Arts > Television > Programs, and was counted only as: Arts > Television > Programs, for research purposes. The only case in this research when a query was classified as regional was when the query itself was a region, such as the query 'france' in Google France in July 2004. Apart from exceptional and very rare regional queries, all search queries were classified first by their topic and usability, using the automatic subcategories suggested.

To reiterate, although the main method of classifying search queries was Google Web Directory, the automatic classification process for each query was also manually monitored in order to maintain the integrity of the results and to filter the regional effect, resulting in a better comparative exercise.

Reliability of coding: the hidden intention

Even knowing the search query, it is impossible to be completely sure what kind of information each individual user intended to acquire. However, it is possible to follow the main theme of each query and assign its relevant topic with a high degree of confidence. The classification process is based on the *majority* of search results and the subsequent Open Directory classification. Additionally, as mentioned above, the automatic classification was manually controlled by the researchers to keep its coherence with other results.

In most cases the classification was straightforward, as most queries were very simple and popular. For example, the query 'Britney Spears' was classified as: Arts > Music > Bands and Artists. However, in some particular cases the classification process was not as straightforward. For example, the query 'heart' is very general, and could be classified in different ways by the ODP. By searching for the query 'hjärtan' (which was actually one of the popular search queries in Google Sweden in February 2005 and translates into 'heart' in English), not everyone intends to find the same kind of information. Some may refer to Society and Relationships and others to Health. It is therefore the duty of the coder to analyse the relevant results, to refer to data from other months in order to develop a comprehensive picture, and finally to decide what is the *most common* information retrieved, or reasonably intended to be retrieved, by using this query.[15] Similar to the query 'hjärtan', less than 1 per cent of the search queries were too general or vague, leading to a more complicated process of classification. As those cases were very rare, it is unlikely that a mistake in an intelligent guess would have adversely affected the results.

Economic and political value index

The construction of the first index was inspired by the argument that certain information skills and uses can empower individuals with political and economic advantages (Webber, 2000; Bawden, 2001; Norris, 2001; Ciolek, 2003; Castells, 2004; R. Rogers, 2004). A study of television audiences by Robert Putnam (2000) revealed that the more time people spend watching news, the greater their civic and social engagement. In contrast, the more time people spend watching soap operas and game shows, the lower their civic and social engagement. This does not necessarily suggest a causal relationship, i.e. retrieving information related to politics leads to greater civic engagement, but it clearly implies a link between the two. When it comes to the internet, retrieving information about news, tax, law, government, society or business provides users with economic and political knowledge. This information also includes, for example, newly available positions, price comparison, education opportunities, political websites, fund-raising, and so on.

Looking at the digital divide among users, DiMaggio et al. (2004) compared the information skills, effectiveness and productivity of information uses for economic and political purposes. They analysed data from the 2000 and 2002 General Social Surveys, and subsequently distinguished between uses that are primarily recreational and uses that increase economic welfare (e.g. job-seeking, consumer information, education), as well as political and social capital (e.g. following the news, searching for information on public and civic issues).

DiMaggio and Hargittai (2002) have linked higher education and economic status with greater use of 'capital-enhancing' information, which is financial, political or governmental information. Similarly, a study by Bonfadelli (2002) found that higher education is positively associated with information and service retrieval, and negatively associated with using the web for entertainment purposes. The framework developed by DiMaggio and Hargittai (2002) was implemented a year later in a study by Robinson et al. (2003) that linked the digital divide with the use of online information for various purposes. Their study indicated, for example, that higher education and the income of users were associated with greater search for jobs, health, education, news and other economic and politically-related information. In contrast, lower education and income of users were associated more with searches for entertainment, music, games, sports and leisure activities. Subsequently, they concluded that the digital divide is deepened by different uses of online information, and particularly by political and economic uses.

Following this distinction between the various information uses (see also Howard et al., 2001; WSIS, 2003; Warschauer, 2004), and in line with distinction of the political divide made by Norris (2001), the economic and political value (EPV) index was articulated to examine the extent of search queries of high political and economic value (i.e. related to governmental information, news, jobs, business, and so on). It is impossible to infer how users will employ information from search queries. However, as indicated above, there is a strong correlation between searching for political and economic information and greater information literacy and skills.[16] This does not suggest that entertainment-related information cannot empower users and provide them with certain advantages. This distinction was primarily meant to examine the inequality of economic and political opportunities between users worldwide. Thus, there is room for further studies to examine the link between acquiring entertainment-related information and gaining social and emotional advantages.

Google Web Directory categorises search queries on movies, music bands and celebrities as Arts. Similarly, it categorises search queries on political, economic and social affairs as News, Business and Society, respectively. This division between entertainment and political, economic and social affairs is crucial for this study, as it provides an insight into the different national uses of information, and is directly linked with the distinctions made by the abovementioned studies on the digital divide. Subsequently, three levels of political and economic value are defined. *High-level* categories refer to the search queries of high economic and political value (i.e. business, news, shopping[17] and society – only the subcategories of issues, politics, government, organisations and law). *Medium-level* categories refer to search queries of middle economic and political value (i.e. recreation, home, regional, reference, science, computers, health and society – apart from the subcategories of issues, politics, government, organisations and law). These categories are not directly related to economic and political uses, but are also not entirely related to entertainments. However, they have been mentioned by previous studies as more 'capital-enhancing' information with a certain political or economic value.[18] And finally, *low-level* categories refer to entertainment-related search queries (i.e. arts, games and sports), which have relatively lower economic and political value.

The EPV index was constructed by providing a weight to each of the suggested categories and subcategories of the search queries, depending on the category's political and economic value. Table 4.1 shows the relative weights ascribed to each of the categories in this study. Ordinal weights were chosen to enable a simple comparison between countries and rank them according to the political and economic value of their searches.[19] A high weight (e.g. = 3) reflects a higher extent of political and economic value, while a low weight (e.g. = 1) reflects a lower extent of political and economic value.

The EPV index of a certain country in a certain month is the number of queries from each EPV group multiplied by its weight and standardised to 1. Definition 1 provides a simple formula for calculating the EPV index in a country each month:

$$EPV_i = \frac{(\text{no. high-level queries} \times 3) + (\text{no. medium-level queries} \times 2) + (\text{no. low-level queries})}{3 \times \text{total no. queries}} \quad (1)$$

Table 4.1 Weight of economic and political value

Level	Categories	Weight
High-level categories	Business, news, shopping and society (only the subcategories of issues, politics, government, organisations and law)	3
Medium-level categories	Society (apart from the subcategories of issues, politics, government, organisations and law), reference, science, computers, regional, home, health and recreation	2
Low-level categories	Arts, games and sports	1

The EPV index can range from 0.33, which is the lowest extent of economics and politics-related searches in a certain month, to 1, which is the highest extent of economics and politics-related searches. When it is close to 1, it indicates that there are many queries of economic and political value among the popular queries in a certain month. For example, in November 2004, the EPV index in Google France reached a record of 0.93, entailing mainly business, news and shopping-related queries.[20]

Variety of uses

Apart from the content aspect, it was previously suggested that skilled and creative users are empowered by the variety of information uses and their ability to control information. It is therefore suggested that countries with a greater variety of online information uses may also experience a wider range of opportunities to benefit from the internet. Stated differently, they demonstrate a greater understanding of the internet's potential, and are empowered by online information in various fields, such as economics, politics, education, society, business and entertainment.

This view has been supported by recent studies. Bonfadelli (2002) noted that a variety of online information can empower skilled users, and thus increase information inequalities. Similarly, the study of Robinson et al. (2003) revealed that a variety of information uses, particularly the search for jobs, health, education and other economics and politics-related information, correlated highly with better education, and indicated better information skills.

The aspect of information variety could therefore be applied in the study of search queries. For example, in the Netherlands in January 2004, seven of the ten most popular search queries were about arts and entertainment, while two concerned sports and one concerned society. It is clear that popular searches in the Netherlands in January 2004 were relatively homogeneous, and concentrated mainly on entertainment. In contrast, in the same month in Italy there were only four search queries about arts and entertainment, two about games, one about health, one about society, one about science, one about reference and one about business. This implies that popular search queries in Italy in January 2004 were more diverse than those in the Netherlands. Again, it is impossible to infer from the search queries how users employ the information. However, as indicated above, a variety of search topics suggests a better understanding of the various applications of online information, and was found to be correlated with greater information literacy and skills.

The variety of uses (VoU) index was constructed to study this variety of search topics. It is based on the coefficient of variation (standard deviation/average), which is a dimensionless number reflecting the spread of search queries among the categories.[21] The reciprocal of the coefficient of variation (average/standard deviation) was calculated separately for each country in each month. The reciprocal was used because a smaller variation indicates an even spread of queries in each category, and therefore a greater variety of uses. Hence, for example, the reciprocal of the coefficient of variation in the Netherlands in January 2004 was 0.38, while in Italy it was 0.78, meaning that in January 2004 there was a greater variety of uses in Italy than in the Netherlands. Definition 2 provides a simple formula for calculating the VoU index for each country each month:

$$\text{VoU}_i = \frac{\mu_i}{\sigma_i} \qquad\qquad (2)$$

where μ = average queries in a category; σ = standard deviation of queries; and i = for each country each month.

The VoU index can range from 0.27 to 1.52,[22] as 0.27 indicates that all search queries are related to one category in a country (e.g. Arts), and 1.52 means that information uses are very heterogeneous in a country in a particular month.

Specificity of search index

Specific search also means specific results, which can further provide users with more relevant and immediate information. A focused and detailed search indicates better search skills. If the VoU index indicates how heterogeneous and rich information uses are in different countries, the specificity of search (SoS) index indicates how skilled and controlled information uses are in various countries. The SoS index is therefore another way of assessing the digital divide of information uses.

Each search query can be classified into up to three categories and subcategories. For example, the search query 'lord of the rings', which is a very specific one, was classified based on Google Web Directory into three categories and subcategories: Arts > Movies > Titles. The search query 'games', which is a very general one, was classified into only one category: Games. Hence, the number of categories and subcategories can help assess whether a search query is more general or more specific. Definition 3 provides a simple formula for calculating the SoS index in each country each month:

$$SoS_i = \frac{No.\ subcategories}{3 \times no.\ queries} \tag{3}$$

The value of the SoS index can range from 0.33 to 1, where the former indicates relatively general search queries and the latter indicates relatively specific search queries.

Extent of locality

The principle of locality is relevant to this study, as it reveals another aspect of the digital divide of information uses. A majority of local search queries may indicate less interest in the outside world, and therefore less awareness of the international potential of the internet. However, as will be argued later, some search queries may also indicate greater interest in local political and social affairs. Thus, depending on their categories, local search queries have different meanings in the context of the digital divide discourse.

A local search query was defined as one that refers to local events, places or people. Local queries can deal with local news, the economy, sports or entertainment, and are mostly written in the language of the national interface. For example, the query 'Карта Москвы' in Google Russia, which in English means 'map of Moscow', or the query 'firemen's strike' in Google UK, which refers to local news in England, were both considered as local queries. In contrast, the query 'BMW' in

Google Germany was not considered as a local query. In this case, it is difficult to assess whether a particular product, service or technology is purely related to a certain country. Only queries that specifically refer to local events, places or people can be considered as local for the purpose of this study. Abstract ideas, technologies, brand items and information products tend to spread easily and quickly across the global network and are therefore much more difficult to localise.

Initial predictions

It was previously suggested that online information uses derive from socio-economic, political and cultural differences between countries. Thus, it was expected that economically and technologically strong countries, such as the USA (in which online networks are well established and the majority of the population has used the internet for a relatively long time) would also display greater versatility and accuracy in their use of search queries. Similarly, as most online content is in English (Lazarus and Mora, 2000; Pastore, 2000; O'Neill et al., 2003; UNESCO, 2006), it was expected that users from English-speaking countries would demonstrate a relatively high variety of uses. At the international level, greater information skills might also imply greater potential in competing, and in leading the global information society in politics, economics, culture and many other fields.

Results and analysis

Economic and political value index

Figure 4.1 summarises the average of the EPV indices over 2004 and 2005 for each country. As Google Zeitgeist displays only 10–15 popular search queries for each country each month, the average of EPV indices over two years provides a more comprehensive estimation of the information trends in different countries.

The EPV index indicates that Russia, Germany, Sweden, France and Ireland have relatively more search queries of high economic and political value (score 0.62 and above). The data used to compute the EPV index for the 'general' search were taken from Yahoo!, and refer to

Figure 4.1 EPV index by country

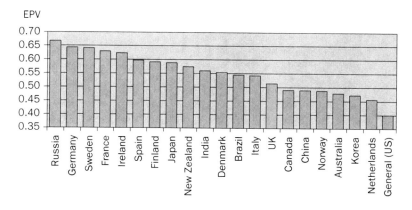

the top search queries in Yahoo.com over 2004 and 2005. These data mostly reflect information trends in the USA, and display very few search queries of economic and political value. This is also true for the popular information uses in the Netherlands, Korea and Australia, all of which have a low EPV index value (0.48 or lower). The findings suggest that Russia, Germany, Sweden, France and Ireland demonstrate a relatively high level of political and economic information uses, while the USA, Australia, the Netherlands and Korea demonstrate a low level of political and economic information uses. In the latter, most popular search queries concern entertainment.

Variety of uses

Figure 4.2 summarises the average of the VoU indices for 2004 and 2005, showing that Spain was the leading country during 2004 and 2005, with a relatively high variety of uses, followed by Denmark, Sweden and Ireland. Not surprisingly, countries like Korea, the USA, Canada and Australia, which scored low on the EPV index because of the dominance of entertainment-related uses, also have the lowest VoU value, which means that their uses of online information are more homogeneous. European countries, such as Spain, Denmark, Sweden, Ireland and Germany, which reported medium and high EPV index values, also have a high VoU value, as they demonstrate a relatively even distribution of information uses.

Figure 4.2 VoU index by country

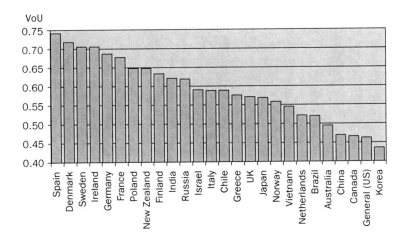

Specificity of search Index

Figure 4.3 summarises the average of the SoS indices over 2004 and 2005 for each country. As with the other indices, the average of the SoS indices over two years provides a more comprehensive estimation of the information trends in different countries.

Figure 4.3 indicates that in Korea, the USA, China, India and Australia, search queries are relatively more specific. The average SoS index value of 0.97–0.99 reveals that more than 90 per cent of search queries in these

Figure 4.3 SoS index by country

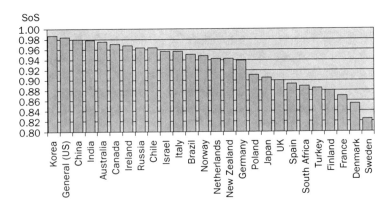

countries are very specific and detailed. In contrast, in Sweden, Denmark, France and Finland, search queries are relatively less specific. The average SoS index value of 0.82–0.88 indicates that more than 40 per cent of search queries in these countries are relatively general. These findings are especially interesting if compared with the VoU index, in which the results were almost the reverse. Sweden, Denmark and France were among the leading countries in terms of variety of information uses, while in terms of information specificity they lag behind. In contrast, countries such as Korea, the USA and China had relatively homogeneous information uses, while in terms of specificity they lead. This is probably because in all of these countries the use of information for entertainment purposes is dominant, and people tend to search for more specific information, such as particular performers, music bands, television programmes, and so on.

The fact that users employ the internet mainly for entertainment purposes does not necessarily mean that they possess less information skill. The ability to use specific search terms to retrieve information more accurately and promptly is another important factor. It indicates that most users know exactly what to look for, and may further imply that online information is highly customised in these countries. Hence, the SoS index reveals another aspect of the politics of online information: the ability to control and retrieve relevant information. The findings suggest that countries such as Korea, Australia and the USA, which display a low level of economic and political searches and variety of information uses, have relatively more specific information uses. Although they do not exhibit a high variety of information uses, their searches are more focused, and therefore can yield more relevant and immediate results.

Relationships between indices

Table 4.2 summarises the rankings of the EPV, VoU and SoS indices, indicating possible relationships.

In theory, very high scores EPV index mean that most search queries are concentrated in economic and political-related categories. Similarly, very low EPV index scores mean that most search queries are concentrated in entertainment-related categories. In both extreme cases (of very high and low EPV scores) the VoU index is supposed to be low, as the spread of search queries is not even among the different categories. However, in practice, Table 4.2 implies a possible positive correlation between the EPV and the VoU indices. It indicates that countries with low EPV scores (e.g. the USA, Canada, Australia, Korea and China) also have low VoU scores,

Table 4.2 A summary of index rankings

EPV	VoU	SoS
Russia (0.67)	Spain (0.74)	Korea (0.99)
Germany (0.64)	Denmark (0.72)	India (0.98)
Sweden (0.64)	Sweden (0.71)	Australia (0.98)
France (0.63)	Ireland (0.71)	China (0.98)
Ireland (0.62)	Germany (0.69)	USA (0.98)
Spain (0.60)	France (0.68)	Ireland (0.97)
Finland (0.59)	New Zealand (0.65)	Canada (0.97)
Japan (0.59)	Finland (0.63)	Russia (0.96)
New Zealand (0.57)	Russia (0.62)	Italy (0.96)
India (0.56)	India (0.62)	Norway (0.95)
Denmark (0.55)	Italy (0.59)	Brazil (0.95)
Brazil (0.55)	Japan (0.57)	Germany (0.94)
Italy (0.54)	UK (0.57)	New Zealand (0.94)
UK (0.51)	Norway (0.56)	Netherlands (0.94)
Canada (0.49)	Brazil (0.52)	Japan (0.91)
China (0.49)	Netherlands (0.52)	UK (0.9)
Norway (0.49)	Australia (0.5)	Spain (0.89)
Australia (0.48)	China (0.47)	Finland (0.88)
Korea (0.47)	Canada (0.47)	France (0.87)
Netherlands (0.45)	USA (0.46)	Denmark (0.85)
USA (0.40)	Korea (0.44)	Sweden (0.83)

while countries with high EPV scores (e.g. Sweden, Ireland and Germany) usually also have high VoU scores. Yet, there are no countries in Table 4.2 with high EPV scores and low VoU scores. This is primarily due to the fact that there are no countries with a very high concentration of economic and political-related searches. The countries with the highest EPV scores (e.g. Russia, Germany, Sweden, France and Ireland) still have 20–40 per cent of entertainment-related searches, and thus display a greater variety of searches than other countries (i.e. greater VoU scores).

As a positive correlation between the two indices is expected, and there are no assumptions regarding their distribution, a Spearman[23] single-tailed correlation test confirms that the EPV index and the VoU index have a strong positive correlation with a p-value of less than 0.01 (Table 4.3).

Table 4.3   Correlation between the EPV and the VoU indices

			VoU_IND
Spearman's rho	EPV_IND	Correlation coefficient	0.807**
		Sig. (1-tailed)	0.000
		N	21

**Correlation is significant at the 0.01 level (1-tailed).

A combination of the two correlated indices in one graph provides a vivid presentation of the differences between countries in terms of the content and the variety of searches (Figure 4.4).

While the EPV index reflects the content aspect, the VoU and SoS indices reflect another two aspects of the digital divide in information uses: volume and control. Table 4.2 implies that many countries that scored highly on the VoU index (e.g. Sweden, Denmark, Spain and France) tend to have low SoS index scores. Similarly, countries with low VoU scores (e.g. USA, Canada, Korea and China) tend to have high SoS scores. Thus, a negative correlation between the two indices is expected. As there are no assumptions about their distribution, a Spearman[24] single-tailed correlation test confirms that the VoU index and the SoS index have a strong negative correlation with a p-value of less than 0.01 (Table 4.4).

Figure 4.4   Content vs. variety of searches

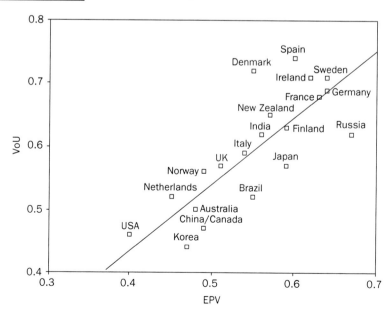

Table 4.4   Correlation between the VoU and the SoS indices

			VoU_IND
Spearman's rho	SoS_IND	Correlation coefficient	−0.696**
		Sig. (1-tailed)	0.000
		N	21

**Correlation is significant at the 0.01 level (1-tailed).

This significant negative correlation suggests that countries with more specific search queries (i.e. high SoS index) will usually also display a lower variety of search topics (low VoU index) and vice versa. In other words, there is a certain trade-off between the variety and the specificity of searches. One possible reason for this is that entertainment-related search queries (e.g. 'hilary duff' or 'green day' which were popular in Canada in February 2005) tend to be more specific and focus on certain people or television programmes, while politics and economics-related search queries (e.g. 'aftonbladet' or 'expressen' which were popular in Sweden during 2004 and 2005) tend to refer to general news or shopping portals (in which users are often required to continue and search for more specific information). This assumption gets further support in a Spearman[25] single-tailed correlation test that indicates a strong positive correlation between the SoS values and the percentage of entertainment-related searches in each country. Similarly, a strong negative correlation was indicated between the SoS values and the percentage of shopping-related searches, indicating that many shopping-related searches are more general (e.g. referring to general shopping portals rather than specific products and services).

While most countries with high SoS values tend to have a greater concentration of entertainment-related searches and thus less variety, findings also indicate that it is possible to maximise the two. A combination of the VoU and the SoS indices in one graph reveals the differences between countries in terms of the specificity and the variety of searches.

Figure 4.5 shows the negative relation between the indices. It suggests that countries with more specific search queries exercise a greater control and manipulation of online information, while countries with a greater variety of searches are exposed to a wider range of information, which means that they display a better understanding of the various applications of online information. Those who can maximise the opportunities of the search engine as an instrument for providing and retrieving information in a wider range of fields and with greater accuracy and depth display better information skills (see also Bonfadelli, 2002; Florida, 2002). Looking at the international

Figure 4.5   The trade-off between variety and specificity

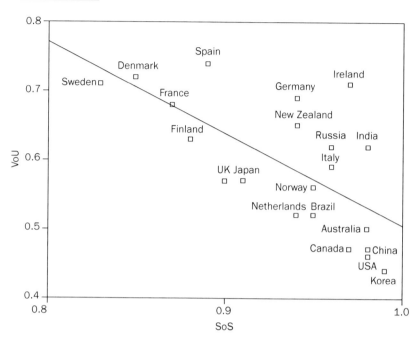

level, the model indicates that countries above the best-fit line exercise a better politics of online information in terms of search accuracy and variety of information uses. In particular, search queries from Ireland and Germany exhibit a higher balance of variety and accuracy than searches from other countries. Although they are as varied as searches from Sweden, Denmark or France, they are also more accurate and specific. Thus, while news-related searches in Sweden and Denmark were for general portal-sites, in Germany and Ireland popular searches were more specific, for example, 'george bush', 'pope' (or 'papst' in German) or 'vatican' (or 'vatikan' in German).[26]

Cluster analysis

A useful integration of the three indices in a comprehensive cross-national comparison can be achieved by employing hierarchical cluster analysis (S. C. Johnson, 1967; Lance and Williams, 1967; Aldenderfer and Blashfield, 1984). The idea of cluster analysis is to measure the distance between each pair of objects (e.g. countries) in terms of the variables suggested in the study (e.g. indices), and then to group objects which are close together. In this case, the cluster analysis is not used as a separate methodological approach, but rather as a complementary method for validating and supporting previous results, as well as for providing a better insight into the differences in information uses in different countries. While the various indices indicate the *ranking* of countries in terms of different information uses, cluster analysis allows a more specific look at the *similarities* and *differences* between countries, thus identifying groups of countries with similar information searches.[27]

The clustering was performed based on the method of Ward (1963), which was found to be most suitable as it creates a small number of clusters with relatively more countries. Additionally, the Ward method was proved to outperform other hierarchical methods (Punj and Stewart, 1983; Harrigan, 1985) in producing homogeneous and interpretable clusters.

Figure 4.6 shows the results of a hierarchical cluster analysis of countries based on the three indices.[28] The horizontal axis shows the distance between each cluster using the Ward method, in which six clusters were identified with an optimal number of 2–5 countries in each.

Figure 4.6 Hierarchical cluster analysis

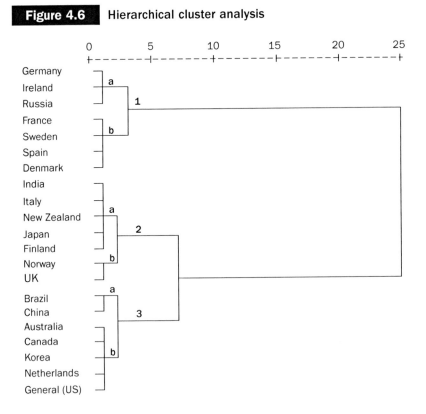

Figure 4.6 shows that Germany, Ireland and Russia are included in cluster 1a. The previous analyses (see Figures 4.4 and 4.5) help to trace the factors behind this classification, indicating that cluster 1a contains the leading countries in terms of all three aspects of the digital divide of uses. They all have a relatively heterogeneous use of online information of high political and economic value. They exercise a strong politics of online information by using accurate and specific search queries. Cluster 1b comprises four countries: France, Sweden, Spain and Denmark. The common factors for these countries are a variety of political and economic information uses, combined with a low specificity of information use.

Cluster 2a consists of India, Italy, New Zealand, Japan and Finland, which have a medium variety of searches, and medium economic and political value. Cluster 2b comprises Norway and the UK, also having a medium variety and specificity of searches. However, those countries demonstrate fewer economic and political information uses, and a greater use of online information for entertainment purposes.

Cluster 3a comprises China and Brazil, which demonstrate a low variety and a high accuracy of information uses. They both exercise an extensive use of socially related information, and therefore their EPV index is medium. Cluster 3b comprises Korea, the Netherlands, Australia, Canada and the USA. The common factors of these countries are their low variety of information uses, their extensive use of entertainment-related information and their high specificity of search queries.

Table 4.5 summarises the cluster analysis of countries and the different compositions of information uses and skills in each group.

Table 4.5 Summary of cluster analysis

Cluster 1: High scores		Cluster 2: Medium scores		Cluster 3: Low scores	
Cluster 1a:	Cluster 1b:	Cluster 2a:	Cluster 2b:	Cluster 3a:	Cluster 3b:
high variety high accuracy high EPV	high variety low accuracy high EPV	medium variety high-med accuracy high-med EPV	medium variety medium accuracy med-low EPV	low variety high-med accuracy medium EPV	low variety high accuracy low EPV
Germany Ireland Russia	France Spain Sweden Denmark	India Italy New Zealand Japan Finland	Norway UK	China Brazil	Canada Australia Netherlands Korea USA

This information divide has important political and social implications. Countries that can maximise the variety and accuracy of information search, especially Germany, Ireland and Russia, also display greater information skills. Other countries, notably the USA, fail to exercise a competitive politics of online information, at least in the context of the suggested framework, based on certain parameters of search queries.

Locality of information uses and their politics

Figure 4.7 summarises the percentage of local queries each month, and portrays the general trends of locality in 2004 and 2005.

In general, Figure 4.7 indicates that 10–30 per cent of search queries are local. It also illustrates a consistent increase in the percentage of local queries over time, which may suggest that users worldwide increasingly utilise information for local and customised purposes.

Figure 4.8 summarises the percentage of local queries and local political or economic queries in each country in 2004 and 2005. It shows that the USA, Korea and China make very extensive use of local information, with 60–70 per cent of popular search queries being local. In contrast, there are very few local search queries in Denmark, Sweden, Norway, Germany, Ireland and Canada.

The fact that most search queries are local in the USA, Korea and China indicates that many users in these countries are more concerned with local issues. However, the high extent of locality does not necessarily mean narrower opportunities. The search query 'receita federal', for example,

Figure 4.7 Trends of locality (percentage of local queries)

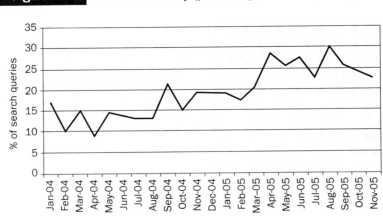

Figure 4.8 Locality by countries (percentage of local queries)

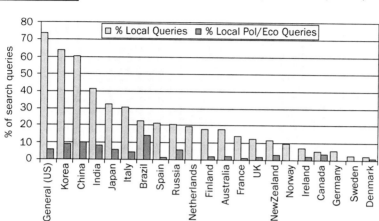

which was popular in Google Brazil during 2004 and 2005, and refers to the Federal Revenue and Customs Administration, was categorised as Business > Financial Services, and therefore as a local search query of high economic and political value. This query indicates that one of the most popular searches in Brazil was related to obtaining citizenship information about taxation. In contrast, the query 'Lee Eun-joo', which appeared frequently among the most popular search queries in Google Korea during 2004 and 2005, and refers to a popular Korean actress, was categorised as Arts > Television > Programs, and also as a local search query of low economic and political value (i.e. entertainment-related).

Hence, it is important to analyse the *content* of local information, while assessing the digital divide implications. Figure 4.8 also shows the percentage of local search queries of high economic and political value. This includes mainly local news, local political and economic issues, local law and governmental information, and any other citizenship information. Findings suggest that among popular search queries worldwide, the interest in local information of economic and political value is very low. Most local information acquired is about entertainment and sports. Less than 5 per cent of the search queries in most countries are related to local economics and politics. The only exceptions are Brazil, China and Korea, in which about 10 per cent of the popular search queries are related to local economics and politics. Further analysis of the content of local search queries leads to an interesting observation. While economic and political search queries in Brazil and most other countries refer to governmental websites or taxation, in both China and Korea there are also unusual search queries such as '16th Communist Party Committee Meeting', 'Lei Feng' (a soldier of the People's Liberation Army who became an idol to many), 'Roh Moo-Hyun' (Korean President) and Kang Hyun-Wook (Korean Governor).

The great popularity of these search queries implies that there could be a relationship between locality of search queries and national politics. It could be, for example, that countries with more local economic and political searches experience greater governmental or media influence and control.[29] Hence, an interesting question is the extent to which the locality of search queries reflects a free and democratic regime. Although assessing the level of freedom can be a problematic and highly political process in itself, various studies have suggested measurements and indices to compare the level of democracy and freedom in different countries (Kaplan, 1994; Vanhanen, 1997; Hill and Hughes, 1998). Freedom House (2005) publishes an annual assessment of freedom in all countries. Based on the Universal Declaration of Human Rights, each country is evaluated each year in terms of its political rights and civil liberties. Table 4.6 summarises the rating of relevant countries on a scale of 0 to 6, with 0 representing the lowest degree of freedom, and 6 the highest degree of freedom, as published by the Freedom House.

As it is to be expected that countries with a low Freedom Index will usually indicate a high level of locality, and as there are no assumptions about the distribution of the Freedom Index or the locality level, a Spearman[30] single-tailed correlation test confirms the significant negative correlation between the Freedom Index and the extent of information locality. There are significant negative correlations between the Freedom Index, the extent of locality in general ($= 0.565, p < 0.01$) and the extent of local search queries of high economic and political value ($= 0.581, p < 0.01$). The meaning of these consistent high correlations is that countries in which most information uses are local are usually also regarded as less free by other measurements. It is therefore suggested that social practices, education, culture and governmental involvement are all important factors in shaping public interests. There are exceptions, such as the USA, which scores highly on the Freedom Index, while also displaying a very high level of locality. Hence, the high locality of search queries in the USA may not be associated with its level of freedom, but probably, as a result of most US search engine users' general disinterest in international affairs.[31]

To conclude, the locality of search queries should be examined in conjunction with the content. High locality can be associated with certain political regimes (such as in China), but can also indicate a greater interest

Table 4.6 Freedom level in 2005

Country	Freedom Index
Australia	6.0
Brazil	4.0
Canada	6.0
Chile	5.0
China	0.5
Denmark	6.0
Finland	6.0
France	5.5
US	6.0
Germany	5.5
Greece	5.0
India	4.5
Ireland	6.0
Israel	5.0
Italy	5.5
Japan	5.5
Korea	5.0
Netherlands	6.0
New Zealand	6.0
Norway	6.0
Poland	5.5
Russia	2.0
South Africa	5.5
Spain	5.5
Sweden	6.0
Turkey	2.5
UK	5.5
Vietnam	0.5

in national and local affairs (such as in Brazil). While users in most European countries seem less interested in local information, most popular search queries in the USA, China, Korea and Brazil are local. Countries such as Japan, Russia, India and Italy are located in the middle, which means that users in these countries maintain a balance between the domestic and the international politics of online information.

Summary and discussion

One of the early attempts (Sciadas, 2003) to monitor the digital divide and construct a digital divide index took into account not only ICT resources, but also information skills (which were measured by education indicators). Subsequently, a report for the WSIS ranked countries by their 'info-density', which is the extent of ICT resources in each country, and 'info-use', which is the uptake and intensity of their uses. Similar to various other recent attempts by UNESCO (2005) to measure the digital divide, it indicated the very high scores of Western European countries, the USA, Canada, Hong Kong, Singapore, South Korea, Japan, Australia and New Zealand, compared with the very low scores of developing countries. Moreover, ranking was highly correlated with GDP per capita.

The methodology of this study was designed to provide a view from a different angle on the digital divide, by looking at the most popular search queries in Google and Yahoo! in various countries. In line with WSIS reports, it was expected that the leading countries in terms of economics and technology would display a greater versatility and accuracy in their information search. Additionally, as most content is in English, it was expected that users from English-speaking countries would demonstrate a greater variety of searches, and therefore a better politics of online information.

In terms of economics and technology, however, the findings indicate that many leading countries display a relatively narrow variety and extent of political and economic searches. Countries with higher EPV and VoU scores such as Russia do not lead in terms of GDP per capita or percentage of users. Together with Germany, Ireland, Spain, France and Sweden, they display the greatest variety of searches, as well as the highest extent of political and economic searches. In contrast, countries such as the USA, Canada, Australia and the UK, which are all native English-speaking countries, exhibit the lowest EPV and VoU scores, in spite of the fact that, together with Korea and the Netherlands, they are also the leading countries in terms of percentage of users. Popular search queries in these countries were relatively homogeneous, although more accurate, and concentrated mainly on entertainment.

The narrow range of information uses in some developed countries, such as the USA, Canada and Australia, matches the increasing internet commercialisation and the dominance of popular channels, which have reinforced highly concentrated internet traffic. Empirical studies indicate that the vast majority of visits are aimed at only a small percentage of websites (Waxman, 2000; Webster and Shu-Fang, 2002; Simmons, 2007; comScore, 2009a). Dominant and popular websites continuously customise information and advertisements for the specific interests of their users, reinforcing a narrow range of information uses in favour of commercial and popular content (Holtz-Bacha and Norris, 2001; R. Rogers, 2004; Turow, 2005; Barzilai-Nahon, 2006a). The high degree of entertainment-related search queries, the narrow range of popular searches and the very specific queries in the USA, Canada and Australia reflect this trend, suggesting that information in these countries is highly customised, popularised and commercialised.

One of the implications of relatively low economic and political searches is the increasing digital divide among users within each of these countries. While many users focus on entertainment, there are comparatively few information-skilled users making a greater variety of searches. This empowers those few, politically and economically, and therefore can result in social and information inequalities. Norris (2000) argues that the ability to customise information propagates a 'virtuous circle' between media and political users, where those who are interested in politics acquire their political content, which in return further empowers them to act politically. Those who are interested in entertainment acquire their preferred content, which in return further reduces their ability and interest to act politically. Hence, the growing ability of users to customise their information through search engines encourages social polarisation (Sunstein, 2001), and deepens the digital divide between users in these countries.

In contrast, countries with higher scores in all indices, such as Germany, Ireland and Russia, display greater search skills based on the suggested indicators, which may have several possible reasons. First, it is important to note that there is a significant digital divide of *access* among the countries observed in this study (see also Table B2 in Appendix B for the percentage of users in each country). The high EPV score in Russia, for example, can be attributed to its comparatively recent exposure to commercialisation and privatisation processes. Likewise, as less than 17 per cent of the population in Russia subscribe to the internet, it could be also argued that there is a higher percentage of information-skilled users among the Russian online community, and among Russian Google users in particular.[32] The implications of the digital divide of access may be observed when looking at the popular search queries in India and China, where the percentage of online users is significantly low (4.6 per cent and 8.5 per cent respectively). Both countries displayed a relatively high number of searches from the category 'reference', focusing on subjects such as educational tests and higher education. This may indicate that a higher percentage of Google users in China and India are students.

Second, when disregarding countries with a very low percentage of online users and comparing only countries with more than 40 per cent of online users, a negative correlation was found between the percentage of online users and the percentage of business-related searches ($p < 0.05$). In particular, countries with relatively higher percentages of online users, such as the USA, Canada, the Netherlands, Sweden, Denmark and Norway, had fewer business-related searches, while countries with relatively lower percentages of online users, such as Germany, Ireland, France and Spain, had more business-related searches. A possible explanation for this difference may be the higher percentages of youngsters among the online users in the former group of countries, who usually search more for entertainment-related information (rather than business-related information), and thus further contribute to the low EPV values.

However, as no significant correlation was found between the percentage of online users or the GDP per capita and the EPV scores, it is believed that apart from commercialisation and internet usage, there might be some other demographic, social, political and cultural reasons why certain countries, such as Germany, France, Ireland and Russia, displayed higher scores in all measurements, while other countries, notably the USA, lag behind. It could be, for example, the results of the intense national political or economic changes that some countries have undergone, engendering greater political and economic concerns in these countries. Looking at their popular search queries revealed an ongoing trend of relatively more accurate searches from a wider range of topics (e.g. business, news and society).

As was previously suggested, the study in this chapter only opens a route to investigate search queries in the context of the digital divide, suggesting new methods of studying, measuring and conceptualising the digital divide of information uses. Obviously, a study that focuses on search query analysis is limited to the users and uses of a specific search engine. It does not and cannot predict, for example, the ability to reach websites directly without the help of search engines while acquiring political and economic information. Similarly, it cannot indicate what happens after people search and how they actually use the information available to them. Complementary studies should be designed to observe the demographic profile of search engine users, and examine in depth the processes of information retrieval in various countries, and their economic, political, social and cultural implications. These kinds of observations may be more limited in scope, but may also help to better understand the reasons behind the current findings.

In terms of locality, the findings indicate that the USA, Korea and China displayed an exceptionally high use of local information, with more than

60 per cent of the popular search queries being local. The reasons for this are different in each country. While China displayed a relatively high interest in local politics, in the USA there were very few society and politics-related search queries. Similarly, the Freedom Index scored highest in the USA and lowest in China. Hence, it may be argued that while the high locality in China is related to political and media control, the high locality in the USA is probably a result of Americanisation processes in information production and consumption. As will be demonstrated in the next chapters, the oligopoly of a very few US communication conglomerates and their global reach have constantly reinforced a US-centric view worldwide. Consequently, there is a greater tendency for US and non-US users to consume US information products (e.g. Hollywood and television idols, US music bands and in some cases also US news). This is probably why various European countries, which increasingly consume these products, displayed very low locality.

The relatively high level of local political searches in Brazil is particularly interesting in the light of the rise of the Brazilian Workers' Party, and its successful utilisation of a local alternative means of communication that operates outside the mainstream capitalist media (Wilkin and Beswick, 2005). As was previously argued, it can also be related to a higher percentage of information-skilled users among the online community in Brazil. In both cases, the findings shed new light on the digital divide of information uses in the growing gap of information searches in some capitalist states on one hand, and on the other, the ability of certain states to resist this paradigm to some extent, and employ a stronger politics of online information. Together with economic inequalities (Dahl, 1985), the technological and information divide within many capitalist states threatens the practice of meaningful democracy. Those who can access, control and manipulate resources, communications and information are eventually also those who can influence and shape political outcomes.

Finally, it is important to mention that the internet develops very quickly. While this chapter covers only two years of study of internet institutionalisation and penetration, findings may vary and change in predictable, but also unpredictable, ways in the near future. Nevertheless, there is a reasonable basis to expect that both information skills and commercialisation processes will continue to shape the information society. Together with the increasing ability to customise online information through search engines, and the growing understanding of its various applications, it is expected that internet corporations and information-skilled individuals will strengthen their positions and deepen the digital divide of information uses.

Notes

1. See also the study of Hargittai (2002) and more recent studies as described in the methodology section.
2. See also the section on cross-national comparison and its limitations.
3. The variety of search analysis is based on a method developed in a previous longitudinal study (Segev et al., 2007) which examined the diversity of content and form of the national homepages of MSN and Yahoo!
4. Between 2004 and 2005, Google Zeitgeist regularly displayed the most popular search queries in general only for its local interfaces (e.g. Google.co.uk, Google.co.jp, and so on). For its main interface, Google.com, which has a majority of US users, it displayed the most popular search queries in specific topics (e.g. news, sports, television and so on). During the study, it was not possible to obtain further data on popular searches directly from Google apart from the publicly available data.
5. See also Table A.10 in Appendix A as well as more recent data from Alexa (2009).
6. Following the information provided in Yahoo! Buzz (*http://buzz.yahoo.com*), it is estimated that around 0.5 per cent of the online users in Yahoo! searched for one of the most popular search queries. Thus, each popular query that appeared in Yahoo! Buzz was searched by more than a million unique users. Consequently, it could be estimated that for the national interfaces in Google, each query was searched by between 50,000 and 500,000 unique users.
7. See also Appendix A for data on the most popular search engines.
8. In Google.com, 70 per cent of search queries in 2004 and 2005 were about entertainment, which is identical to the results in Yahoo.com.
9. The latter group of countries was not used in most analyses due to the relatively small number of search queries available and the short duration of sampling.
10. During the sampling period, Yahoo!'s archives displayed 20 and Google's archives 10–15 popular search queries for each country each month. For the complete list see Appendix B, Table B.2.
11. These data were obtained following an e-mail to Google representatives in December 2008.
12. Similar filters are used in Google SafeSearch, Google Hot Trends and Google Suggest. See also the explanation on the construction of Google Hot Trends data (*http://google.com/intl/en/trends/about.html*) and the filtering of porn-related queries in Google Suggest (*http://labs.google.com/suggestfaq.html#q12*).
13. Google maintains very tight policy regarding the exposure or sharing of corporate data, and was even invited to court after refusing to hand in a list of search queries to the US government (Hafner and Ritchel, 2006).
14. The features and data of the ODP and Google Web Directory were observed and analysed in 2005 and 2006, and may change in the future.
15. In the same month and the same country, the other query was 'alla hjärtans dag' (which in English means 'the day of the hearts' and refers to Valentine's Day). In this way, the query 'alla hjärtans dag' could provide new information about the query 'hjärtan', which was subsequently classified as Society > Holidays > Valentine's Day. It is still possible that there were some users who

used the word 'hjärtan' in Valentine's Day to find information about anatomy, health or recreation; however, the initial goal was to identify intelligently the major purpose and the main interest that most users have in a particular month and a particular country.

16. The term 'information uses' in this context refers to the use of information in Google and Yahoo!, and particularly to popular search queries, and not to what people actually do with the information they acquire.

17. Shopping-related search queries, which mostly referred to e-commerce, consumer information and price comparison portals, were considered as economic-related searches. See also DiMaggio et al. (2004).

18. DiMaggio et al. (2004) stressed the importance of socially-related information, which is associated with higher education, higher income and the digital divide, particularly by enhancing the social networks and opportunities of online users. Similarly, Robinson et al. (2003) stressed the importance of education and health-related information, which is also associated with greater information literacy and skills. Subsequently, these categories were considered as medium-level categories for the purpose of this investigation.

19. Based on the abovementioned previous studies on the digital divide of information uses (e.g. Howard et al., 2001; Robinson et al., 2003; DiMaggio et al., 2004; Warschauer, 2004).

20. Interestingly, despite the local elections in France, many popular search queries in this month were related to shopping and did not refer to this specific event. To this end, the most popular search queries tend to be more constant and similar from one month to another, and therefore reflect more general trends. In contrast, the 'top-gaining' search queries (which were not included in this study) tend to be more sensitive to local social and political changes, and therefore reflect more specific trends. On some rare occasions, such as the US presidential election in 2004, the death of Pope John Paul II or the South-East Asian tsunami, popular search queries reflected these regional and global events in many countries. Yet, the longitudinal investigation over 24 months helped to minimise the possible impact of specific events on the findings.

21. It is important to mention that not all categories in Google Web Directory are associated with a similar variety of information. For example, health or games may be associated with less information than arts and entertainments. Nonetheless, Google Web Directory covers a wide range of topics and the VoU index is designed to provide a more general distinction between countries that display mostly entertainment-related search queries and countries that display also politics, economics and society-related searches. See also Segev et al. (2007) for the methods of diversity analysis of information.

22. The lower limit of the VoU (= 0.27) is a theoretical case where all ten queries are from one of the 14 categories (e.g. all ten search queries are entertainment-related). The upper value of the VoU (= 1.52) is a theoretical case where all ten queries are divided equally along the 14 categories (ten categories have one query and four categories have no queries). From August 2005, Google Zeitgeist started reporting 15 search queries per country, and therefore the upper value of the VoU could theoretically reach 4.01 (i.e. 13 categories have one query and one category has two queries), with the lower limit staying at 0.27. For the USA, Yahoo! Buzz reported 20 search queries, and therefore the

upper value of the VoU could theoretically reach 2.78 (i.e. six categories have two queries and eight categories have one query), with the lower limit staying at 0.27. In practice, the highest value of the VoU was found to be 1.17 both in Google France in August 2004 and in Google Spain in October 2004. The lowest value of the VoU was 0.3 in Google Korea in September 2004 and in January 2005, where nine out of ten search queries were entertainment-related.

23. A Pearson correlation test yielded similar results, supporting the positive correlation between the two indices.

24. A Pearson correlation test yielded similar results, supporting the negative correlation between the two indices.

25. A Pearson correlation test yielded similar results with a p-value of less than 0.01.

26. It is very possible that Google is used in Sweden, Denmark or France relatively more as a general gateway to local news and shopping portals, where more specific second-level searches are made. To this end, the study is limited to the examination of the search differences in Google only.

27. Cluster analysis was also applied as a complementary method in a previous study (Segev et al., 2007), which examined the similarities and differences between the homepages of MSN and Yahoo! in terms of content and form.

28. Standardised values of the indices were used for this analysis. As Punj and Stewart (1983) suggest, using standardised variables in a cluster analysis reduces the effect of the outliers, and thus enables the examination of all the countries in the dataset.

29. The high locality of search queries in the USA might be an exception for this assumption, and should be related to different factors (such as corporate rather than government control on media channels and the expansion of US media worldwide), to be analysed further.

30. A Pearson correlation test yielded similar results, suggesting a negative correlation between the Freedom Index and the extent of locality of information uses in different countries.

31. This trend has been also observed by Bagdikian (2004), who argued that Americans increasingly prefer local rather than international news as a result of the high commercialisation and customisation of content and the dominance of advertising mechanisms. Similarly, it has been argued that the US audience has generally shown little interest in international news that does not directly affect US 'interests' (McLeary, 2006). This claim will be supported further in Chapter 5, which explores the bias of mainstream online news, most of which originates in the USA.

32. This assumption requires further investigation. The data indicate that in Russia there are more than 20 million users; thus, even if the majority of users are relatively highly information-skilled, they still represent a significant number of users. Moreover, there was no significant correlation between the percentage of online users in different countries and their index values.

5

Mass media channels and the world of Google News

It is not just the queries used in search engines that can reveal something about the digital divide of information, but also the information that is organised and disseminated by the search engines themselves. This is particularly true if search engines are perceived as the gatekeepers for the growing volume of political, economic and social information online. While many scholars have described the role of previous mass media channels in shaping the way people envision and understand the world (McLuhan, 1964; B. Anderson, 1983; Foster, 1991; Robertson, 1992), the increasing connectivity of online networks and their global diffusion, entails the possibility of challenging this imagining in the longer term. As people from different countries can read the same popular news through common international multilingual interfaces such as Google News, BBC or CNN, contemporary mass media channels now have the ability to shape multiple perceptions and understandings of the world. These perceptions may still be under the domination of specific powerful states. It has been argued, for example, that following the Gulf War, the US-based and owned CNN 'dominated television screens around the world. One definition and one account of this momentous geopolitical event was given to global audiences' (Schiller, 1996: 113).

A report by the Pew Project for Excellence in Journalism (2009) based on data from comScore indicates that Yahoo! News is the most visited news site in the USA, with more than 40 million unique visitors each month. In other words, some search engines have a growing role in the organisation, dissemination and provision of news based on specific considerations and priorities. This chapter investigates Google News, an increasingly popular news channel that pulls together thousands of news websites and ranks them according to their popularity. As it combines news sources from different countries, it should display different local points of view, irrespective of the user's origin. That is to say, users in

Japan can read world news written by US sources, and vice versa. However, Google News may also reinforce certain views provided by particularly popular news websites. For example, Google's PageRank mechanism may score the website of the *Washington Post* higher than many other news websites, and therefore the *Washington Post* would appear as a dominant and 'authoritative' source in many of the world news links. In this case, it will be primarily US mainstream views that shape the notion of the world as perceived by a growing number of users.

Findings indicated that indeed the USA and Iraq were by far the most frequently occurring countries in English and non-English world news over the period of observation. This conforms to the argument that US news sources dominate the English-language media and provide news to non-English news sources (Thompson, 2000), but it also suggests that this trend is very significant, and particularly within automatic news aggregator tools such as Google News. One of the possible implications of this dominance is the continuous dissemination of official and mainstream US views worldwide,[1] even through more customised information agents such as search engines. The analysis of news content further supported this trend, where Russia and China were often criticised for their policies regarding democracy and freedom. Additionally, findings suggested that the UN and the EU play an increasingly important role in world news as organisations that work to maintain international peace and security and the balance of power respectively.

Apart from conventional statistics, this chapter applies network theory to examine not only the popularity, but also the position and relations between countries as represented by popular news sources (referred to as 'news-links'). This analysis revealed that the USA, together with the UN, the UK, Iraq, Russia, the EU and India, are main hubs, located at the centre of the international network, with news-links to many other countries. Asian and South American countries are located in the middle and have more regional links. African countries tend to be located at the margin of the international network as perceived by popular online news.[2]

Online transformation of media and news

The growing popularity of the internet has had significant implications for the operation and communication abilities of other media (e.g. press, radio and television), which have been driven to widen their online activities in order to reach more users, become more interactive, and survive in a mercilessly competitive market. Most popular newspapers already have internet editions, enabling users all over the world to read news mostly free of charge. Radio channels increasingly broadcast online and are listened to all over the world, bypassing national borders and regional frequencies. Television channels release special features on the internet, constructing online communities and interacting with global audiences. Together with the growing success of online video services, News Corporation and NBC Universal have announced plans to team up with Yahoo!, MSN and AOL to distribute popular television programmes sponsored by advertisers (La Monica, 2007; Wray, 2007). Being online in the information age is increasingly the sine qua non of media existence.

Media channels, which produce and channel the flow of information, seek therefore to embrace the online network in all possible forms. Rather than a unidirectional flow of information, new technologies enable interactivity; thus the television of today is increasingly structured as a computer. It enables storage of digital data, customisation of desired programmes, retrieval of video on demand (VOD), communication with other users, game-playing, and so on. Castells (1996) predicts that due to high decentralisation, diversification and customisation, television and the internet will be eventually combined into a single domestic system that can broadcast interactive entertainment, news and customised internet content. Media channels, such as television, radio and newspapers, are therefore transformed into hybrid communication corporations that join forces and expand their control over the global network of information.

This fusion makes it more difficult to distinguish the qualities and characteristics of each media form independently. Previously, McLuhan (1964) separated the different media by their resolution and density of information. The hot or the high-definition media, such as radio, photography and film, provide a relatively higher volume of information than the cool ones, such as speech, cartoons and television. In contrast, cool media forms leave, according to McLuhan, more space for additional participation or completion by the audience. Both hot and cool media have different impacts on different social groups and public opinion.

By translating reality into words, the press has enabled the storage, documentation and dissemination of ideas and events. However, its main power derives from its repeatability, the dimensions of diffusion and its extension in space. Thus, it has reinforced a homogeneous language and a common way of thinking among large communities (McLuhan, 1964; B. Anderson, 1983). Similarly, radio and television initially reinforced homogeneous and local trends by providing similar content to a mass local audience. However, nowadays, together with the growing diversity of channels, the ability to customise content, and the emergence of satellite television and internet radio, both homogeneity and locality are challenged. Moreover, the emergence of high-definition television and home cinema systems further challenges the simplistic distinction between cool and hot media. As it has been suggested that contemporary media channels, i.e. television, radio and the internet, will gradually merge into a single domestic system, it is impossible to indicate whether they are cool or hot à la McLuhan, or whether they are local, national or global. Contemporary media channels tend to combine homogeneous and heterogeneous, global and local trends, and can perhaps be better understood as 'glocal' and 'tepid' media.

The variety of media forms (e.g. text, images, video), the new abilities to customise news (e.g. focused search, homepage design, e-mail alerts, news source comparison) and the advanced features of interaction (i.e. talkbacks, sending news articles to friends, e-mails to the editors, and so on) make studying the internet in general, and news websites in particular, more complex. The advanced ability to customise news channels is particularly what makes them local or global, deeper or shallower, and heterogeneous or homogeneous for different users. There is no doubt that this variety brings about more opportunities and empowers skilled users to obtain more relevant information. While media channels used to prioritise news articles based on decisions by editors, news aggregators today increasingly rely on automatic algorithms which require specific academic attention. The main purpose of this chapter is therefore to analyse the news provided by Google News in order to shed light on this automatic organisation and its implications.

Commercial motives and their implications

It appears that both manual and automatic organisations of news reflect the specific commercial motives of media and advertisement companies. In both cases, preferring more popular, entertaining or commercial news reflects the need of media companies to increase the size of their audience, and thus to enhance their control over the production and dissemination of information. Bagdikian (2004) believes that narrow controlled information also means narrow controlled politics. He demonstrates the growing concentration of media ownership in the hands of a few dominant corporations, and warns that while dominant media channels cannot tell the public what to think, they definitely tell their audience what to think about.

In contrast, Compaine and Gomery (2000) challenge this view, indicating that when looking at the single industry level, there are trends toward both consolidation and greater competition. They believe that these trends became even more prominent after the emergence of the internet, which lowered the entrance barriers for smaller media companies (see also Shapiro and Varian, 1999; Caves, 2000). In this sense, news channels, and particularly Google News, theoretically offer more opportunities for smaller news sources. However, as argued previously, there is also constant competition for the limited attention of users, who often rely on the information presented on the homepage of popular portals, or the first page of search engine results (Jansen and Spink, 2003; Van Couvering, 2004; Barzilai-Nahon, 2006a). Thus, the commercialisation of news means that, together with more opportunities, there is also an increasingly asymmetrical flow in favour of larger and richer websites.

The ongoing debate regarding media consolidation or diversification can also be seen in the light of the broader discussion of media homogeneity and heterogeneity (see also the Preface and Chapter 1). Both Bagdikian and Compaine have recognised the significance of the commercial motives behind the operation of media companies and information production; however, each emphasises a different aspect. This debate directly links to the two commercial principles: popularisation and customisation, which oppose, but also complement each other, and are so essential in this book.

While search engines and portals channel users' attention to more popular websites and content, they are also required to provide advanced means of customisation. Indeed, a study by Segev et al. (2007) revealed that customisation in popular portals and search engines often increases the heterogeneity of information production in terms of content and form. However, in each of these specific channels, the principle of popularisation still operates in the background. For example, a search for the term 'Iraq' in Google News will return specific news on Iraq, yet within this list of results the automatic ranking will still favour larger and more popular news sources. This tendency corresponds to marketing logic, i.e. providing specific advertisements to maximum users. It is often also a useful principle for many users, who usually search for the more popular news sources, and are less or hardly interested in smaller news sources. Hence, advanced customisation of news creates more opportunities to obtain specific information, but this does not necessarily mean that smaller and less popular news sources can reach more audiences. Even when users search for more specific news, there is increasing competition over the position of results within the page, and it would be much more difficult for smaller sources to gain the attention of users who do not specifically search for them.

In the beginning of 2005, Google filed patents in the USA and around the world (WO 2005/029368) that revealed the ranking mechanism behind its news results. In order to evaluate the 'authority' and 'quality' of a news source, Google monitors its popularity and worldwide traffic, the number of stories it provides, the average story length, the number of authors and staff employed, the number of bureaux cited and the duration it has been in business (Fox, 2005). Thus, the practice of Google News and its ranking mechanisms support the growth and strengthening of the larger and more popular news sources.

Although Google News complies perfectly with the commercial principles of popularisation and customisation, its business model is much more complex and subtle. While pulling text and images from other news sources, Google is constantly subject to lawsuits for copyright infringement (D. Riley, 2007; Auchard, 2007b). In fact, Google pays large news groups in the USA and Europe to license content for its news channel (Vass, 2008). This probably explains why it was only in February 2009, after six years of operation, that Google started experimenting with advertisements in its US news channel (Helft and Stelter, 2009). Nevertheless, even without advertisements, the popularity of this service[3] helps Google to maintain its position as an important hub and gatekeeper among news readers, and thus increases the affiliation and dependency between its users and the company.

Obviously, the ability to obtain, organise, search and customise news from many online sources is very useful for users. It may be even more beneficial for search engines that can follow and store the information consumption habits of their users. In a way, this service is also beneficial for news companies, as it channels more traffic to their websites. Hence, lawsuits, content licensing and a subtle business model do not prevent Google from developing new features in Google News and translating the service to more new languages, clearly indicating its commercial interests.

The question is, what are the implications of news aggregators with popularisation and customisation mechanisms with respect to the digital divide? On one hand, they bring together various news sources and enable comparison and plurality of expressions. On the other, they exhibit another form of concentration, drawing the attention of international audiences to the more popular and 'authoritative' news sources based on their page-ranking mechanism. The following analysis of online news examines this trend. Through the study of Google News, it attempts to identify the dominant political voices produced online and their biases.

While addressing this question, it is important to keep in mind that many US media companies have a significant international impact. An early study by Nordenstreng and Varis (1974) indicated the asymmetry in the international flow of television programmes. It demonstrated the one-way traffic of news and entertainment from some countries, such as the USA, the UK and France, to the rest of the world. Similar trends were observed in the film and music industry of the USA and other capitalist states, which dominate the production, distribution and exchange of entertainment and cultural goods (Schiller, 1992; 1996; Herman and McChesney, 2000). Looking at the news industry worldwide, Thompson (2000) believes that there is an increasing globalisation of international news agencies. Early technological developments, such as the telegraph, and later the radio, supported the emergence of international news agencies, and contributed to the formation of global communication networks. The four major international news agencies that survived after the Second World War were Reuters from the UK, Agence France-Presse (AFP) from France, and Associated Press (AP) and United Press International (UPI) from the USA. Today they are still the dominant international news sources, and efforts by international organisations (e.g. UNESCO) to create a more equal and democratic information and communication order have had a very limited effect (Boyd-Barrett and Tantanen, 1998; Mattelart and Mattelart, 1998; Thompson, 2000). Thus, it is expected that Google News, which aggregates popular news sources rather than producing original content, will reflect and further disseminate this trend globally.

Google World News

A study by the Pew Internet and American Life Project in December 2005 indicated that 35 per cent of internet users in the USA, or about 50 million people, check news online every day. Additionally, news portals such as Yahoo! News and Google News are among the most popular online news sources, with more than 40 per cent of visits (Horrigan, 2006; Pew Project for Excellence in Journalism, 2009). In order to examine the main issues and actors involved in news reporting, researchers suggest looking at their frequency of appearance. Dearing and Rogers (1996) measured the number of news stories that appeared in newspapers as an indication of media attention and the popularity of certain issues (see also Benton and Frazier, 1976; Pritchard, 1986; Wu, 2000; Golan and Wanta, 2001; Kiousis, 2004). Another way to assess popularity is by examining the position of news articles within the text (Williams, 1985; Ghanem, 1997; Kiousis, 2004). Some scholars have further combined the principles of volume and position of news articles under the category of 'visibility' (Manheim, 1986) in order to explore media attention, priorities and agendas.

Subsequently, the 'visibility' of certain issues and states in Google News was examined and assessed. On each day, Google News displays the 20 most popular world news articles, integrating more than 4,000 news sites (Google, 2007a). For each of the news articles, it also displays the number of online-related sources available, thus indicating the global coverage level of the issue. The top 20 news articles of Google World News were documented daily over a period of six months between August 2005 and January 2006. The following aspects of each news article were documented: date, relative position (out of 20 news articles), the main countries to which it referred, the news source, the number of other sources dealing with the same issue or event and a précis of the article. The main purpose of this experiment was to determine the dominant countries and issues appearing in popular world news, and thus to picture the global political map as perceived by popular news sites.

Apart from news in English, Google News provided world news in 11 other languages during the period of observation. The popular world news in each language was slightly different, as news sources were usually different (not all news sources have an English edition, and certainly not multilingual content). As there are only a few dominant international news agencies that provide world news to all other local news sources, one would expect to find similar world news in different languages. Nonetheless, popular news in different languages can also promote different issues and agendas, which are crucial to the study of the digital divide of information. Thus, each of the 11 non-English interfaces of Google World News was analysed on a weekly basis for a period of three months.

A study by Ulken (2005), which explored political biases[4] in Google News during the US elections of 2004, indicated that although news articles are based on an automatic algorithm and are claimed to be apolitical, they tend to represent also 'non-traditional news sources' that skew its content toward political extremes. Ulken defined traditional or mainstream news sources as wire services, newspapers, magazines, television stations, radio stations, broadcast networks or cable networks. Thus, his analysis revealed that 40 per cent of Google News results came from non-traditional news sources, while only 24 per cent of Yahoo! News results came from non-traditional sources. This is to suggest that smaller and internet-based news sources (such as weblogs and opinion sites) have more chance of appearing in Google News (which is an automatic news aggregator) than in Yahoo! News (which employs editors). Subsequently, he found that Google News tends to be more politically biased in one direction or the other compared with Yahoo! News.

However, Ulken's study is different from this study in two important ways. First, it looked at the content of news articles returned in specific searches (for presidential candidates), while this study looks at the top stories automatically pulled into Google World News. While customised search on specific political candidates may yield more results from smaller websites, it is expected that in the front pages of Google News, the top stories will be taken from more popular and mainstream sources. Second, Ulken's study examined the 'political bias', i.e. if news articles favoured one candidate over the other, while this study examines the most popular issues and states in world news in different languages in order to explore the extent of US dominance in popular news sources. Hence, the term 'bias' in this work refers more to the dominance of US views rather than a predisposition to the political left or right wings.[5]

Interestingly, Ulken's study suggests a certain relation between the popularity and the content of a news source. His study indicates a tendency for smaller and 'non-traditional' sources to be less neutral and more politically biased in one way or another. This tendency is less obvious when looking at the 'bias' of news in the context of US dominance. Here it is reasonable to expect that many of the larger and more popular news sources (which often originate in the USA or the West) will also represent US-centric or Western-centric views. Sometimes, however, popular sources such as Al-Jazeera, offer alternatives to US-centric views, and thus news sources can be popular and still not US-centric. The aim of this experiment is therefore to identify the main issues and states appearing in Google World News in English and other languages in order to assess the extent of US dominance among popular news sites worldwide.

Dominant online states

Figure 5.1 summarises for each country[6] and international organisation (such as the UN and the EU) the number of news articles in English referring to it, and therefore indicates the countries and organisations which appeared most frequently in online news sources over the period of six months between August 2005 and January 2006.

The figure shows that Iraq was the country that occurred most frequently in online world news in English. Some 235,928 news articles in

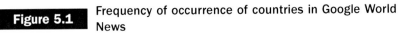

Figure 5.1 Frequency of occurrence of countries in Google World News

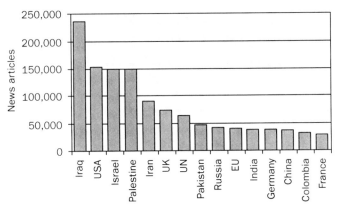

Google World News mentioned Iraq over this period – an average of more than 1,600 articles per day. The next most frequently cited countries were the USA, Israel and Palestine, each being mentioned in about 150,000 news articles – an average of more than 1,000 news articles per day. An analysis that took the position of the news articles in the page into account yielded very similar results, where all four countries led in frequency.

Another way to determine the order of interest in countries in news sources is to conduct a search for each country name in Google News. This makes it possible to determine the number of news articles mentioning each country in all news sources. Figure 5.2 displays the search result count[7] for country names in Google News in a search conducted on 7 February 2006.[8]

Figure 5.2 shows that the USA has by far the most news items, being mentioned in more than one million news articles per month.[9] The other most frequently occurring countries, such as the UK, Iraq, China and Canada, were mentioned in fewer than 180,000 news articles per month. The USA, and not Iraq, is the most frequently occurring country, as the analysis includes *all* news, while in Figure 5.1 it included only world news. This difference implies that most news in English is produced by US sources, is mostly focused on the USA, and views Iraq as the most widespread international concern, given the USA's involvement there. Other English-speaking countries, notably the UK, Canada and Australia, become more prominent because they also produce news in English. Findings provide strong evidence for the Western-centric point of view that dominates news in English. There is a very minor presence of South American countries among popular news sources, and hardly any presence of African countries.

Figure 5.2 Frequency of occurrence of countries in Google News

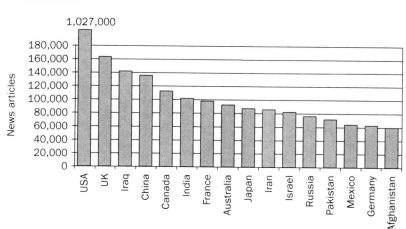

This is not to suggest that there were fewer events to cover in these countries. For example, during the same period of observation, the IRIN news service, which is part of the UN Office for the Coordination of Humanitarian Affairs, established to 'bridge the information gap', reported civil wars in both Uganda and Somalia (see also McLeary, 2006). Although the IRIN reports revealed that the number of casualties of violence and displacements in these countries exceeded those in the war in Iraq (IRIN, 2006a), this information was marginalised from a Google World News perspective. Somalia, for example, was ranked in 116th place, with only 282 news articles over a six-month period (compared with 235,928 news articles mentioning Iraq). While it is possible to obtain news on Somalia in Google News by making a specific search, African countries are unlikely to appear in the top stories as they seldom make headlines in the key news sources upon which Google News depends. As such, most users, who are not aware of significant world conflicts apart from the war in Iraq, have very little opportunity to learn about them from the top stories in Google News.

A further analysis examines which countries dominate the *production* of news in English. Figure 5.3 portrays the share of each country in producing Google World News over a period of six months.

Figure 5.3 shows that US news sources are the most productive, generating 37 per cent of the total English-language news articles. British news sources are in second place, producing 24 per cent of the English-language news articles. Each of the other countries produces less than 5 per cent of the English-language news articles in Google World News.

Figure 5.3 Online news sources by country

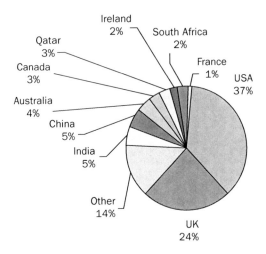

As Google News integrates thousands of news sources, it could reflect a certain estimate of the market share, where the USA and the UK together provide around 60 per cent of the popular world news in English. Other native English-speaking countries such as Australia, Canada and Ireland, provide together around 20 per cent of the popular world news in English. Only 20 per cent of the popular world news in English is provided by non-English speaking countries, usually as the English version of their local news online.

The dominance of the USA and the UK in popular news in English can explain why Iraq was the country that occurred most frequently in world news. Both the USA and the UK were engaged in military operations in Iraq during the period of observation. Consequently, users from other countries who read world news in English were channelled to view the military operations in Iraq as the dominant international event. The bias of news thus supports the formation of a global image in which the USA, its allies and their foreign politics and priorities, are the main international concern.

International concern

Apart from the frequency of appearance in Google World News, it is worth looking at the main issues with which each country is concerned. Figure 5.4 summarises the number of news articles and the main political issues

Figure 5.4 Online news articles about Iraq

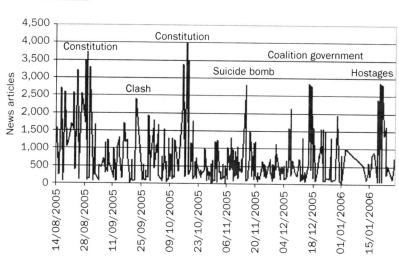

concerning Iraq over the period of six months between August 2005 and January 2006.

Figure 5.4 shows that the most frequently occurring issues related to Iraq were the process of establishing a democratic regime, and the constant insurgency and terror attacks that interfered with and threatened this process. Figure 5.5 shows the main issues discussed in relation to the USA, the country which occurs second in frequency in world news in English.

Figure 5.5 Online news articles about the USA

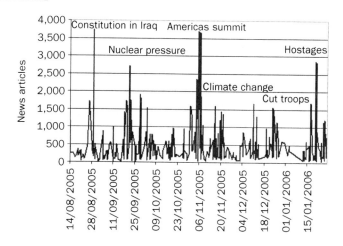

Figure 5.5 shows that the involvement of the USA in Iraq was one of the issues appearing most frequently in world news during the period of observation, from the political pressure to establish a democratic constitution, to the military operations and counter-attacks. Apart from its role in Iraq, the USA is also mentioned in the context of the Americas Summit, anti-nuclear pressure on Iran and North Korea, and climate change. In terms of numbers, although the population of Iraq and the USA together comprise only 4.8 per cent of the entire world population, more than 21 per cent of world news in the observation period was about these countries.

Figures 5.6 and 5.7 portray the main issues discussed in relation to the other prominent region in world news, which includes Israel and Palestine.

Similarly to the previous example, Figures 5.6 and 5.7 show that the politics of Israel and Palestine are interrelated. In August 2005 they were both mentioned in the context of the Israeli withdrawal operation from Gaza. Both then maintained a constant level of occurrence, where each was engaged in internal political processes and elections. In terms of interest, although the populations in Israel and Palestine together represent only 0.15 per cent of the entire world population, more than 16 per cent of the world news in the observation period was about these countries.

Finally, findings also indicate the increasing popularity of international organisations such as the UN and the EU, which were ranked within the ten most popular political entities in world news. Interestingly, the EU was

Figure 5.6   Online news articles about Israel

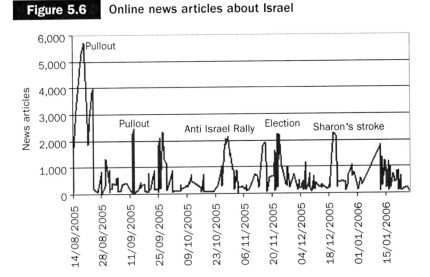

Figure 5.7 Online news articles about Palestine

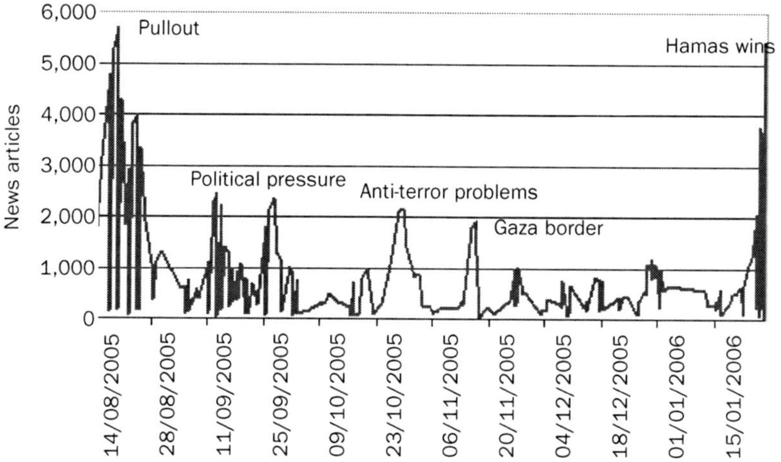

mentioned more than most European countries. Figures 5.8 and 5.9 reveal the main issues discussed in relation to these two international organisations.

These figures suggest that both the UN and the EU play crucial roles in maintaining international security and the balance of power. While the EU was mentioned more in the context of the Iranian nuclear plan, which is of primary concern to the USA, the UN was also mentioned in the context of Asian earthquake relief, the intrigues surrounding Hariri's death in the Middle East and environmental issues.

Figure 5.8 Online news articles about the UN

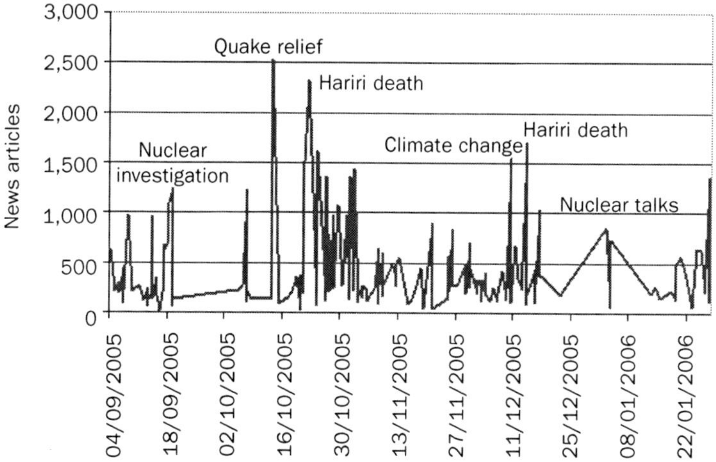

Figure 5.9 Online news articles about the EU

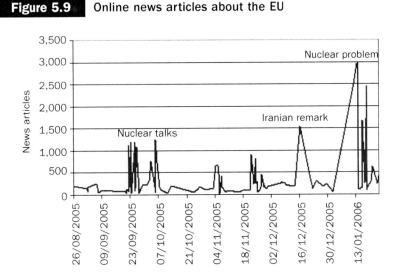

International network

Network theory provides a useful framework for understanding and envisioning the relationships between states as reflected through news. In many cases, news articles indicate formal or informal relationships between two or more countries. An international network emerges when countries are considered as nodes, and news articles provide a descriptive map of the links between them (hereafter: news-links). Hence, the analysis of the relations between countries as an international network may reveal which countries are more connected and serve as central and dominant hubs in the network, and which countries are less connected and play a more marginal role. It should be noted that the following analysis is not necessarily a presentation of the actual political relations between states, but rather a *representation* of the international network as perceived by popular news sources.

While the previous statistical analysis looked at the frequency of occurrence of countries in news, the network analysis focuses on the news-links, i.e. the relations between countries and their structures (Wasserman and Faust, 1994). It can indicate not only which countries appear more frequently in mainstream news, but also with which other countries they are frequently engaged, and what their overall position is in relation to other countries. Thus, the network analysis provides a much more detailed and visual conceptual map of the world's politics as represented by news sources worldwide.

Some studies (Snyder and Kick, 1979; Nemeth and Smith, 1985) have realised the benefit of network analysis in understanding the complex political and economic world systems, the position of countries and transnational interactions as indicators of economic growth. Recent studies have also employed network theory to examine the structure of international telecommunications (Barnett, 2001), indicating the dominance of North America and Western Europe in the production and dissemination of information. Similarly, Barnett and Kim (1996) utilised network analysis in order to examine the flow of international news, indicating a clear asymmetry where the Western industrialised countries dominated the production and dissemination of international news. Their study also suggested that the growing exchange of news among these countries further marginalised the position of other countries. Finally, they revealed that the structure of international news flow is influenced mainly by the economic development, and also by the language, geographic location, political freedom, and population of each country. Thus, network analysis has become an increasingly useful method for studying the complexity of the global communication flow, and particularly the flow of news. The main contribution of this section is also to apply these methods in the study of Google News, not in terms of news flow, but rather in terms of content, i.e. the analysis of the relations between states as represented by news articles, and thus shed more light on the evolving imagined communities online.

The following network analysis is based on the same data that were sampled between August 2005 and January 2006 from Google News. It uses Borgatti's (2002) software, NetDraw Version 2, to produce visual networks of news-links between countries as represented in Google News, and thus also in popular news sources in English. Figure 5.10 delineates the centre of the news-link network. The size of a node indicates its degree, i.e. the number of news-links that each country has with other countries. The width of the links indicates the strength of the tie, i.e. the number of news articles mentioning each pair of countries.

Figure 5.10 shows that the USA is at the centre of the network, with ties to 54 other countries, i.e. it is the main and largest hub of the international network, linked to more than 45 per cent of countries. Interestingly, the UN is the second most linked node, with links to 32 countries. The UK has 25 links, Iraq 24 links, Russia 21 links and the EU and India 20 news-links to other countries.

The strength of ties indicates the number of news articles mentioning each pair of countries. It may therefore signify which countries are more frequently engaged with each other. Figure 5.10 reveals that the USA and

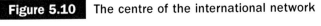

Figure 5.10 The centre of the international network

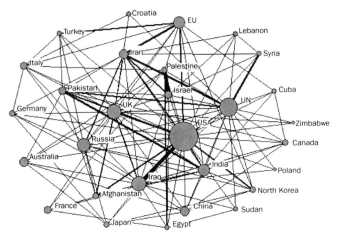

Iraq are deeply engaged with one another, as are Israel and Palestine. Further, there are frequent engagements between the UN and both Iran and Syria. The EU has frequent engagements with Iran, Pakistan with India, and the UK with the USA. As the previous discussion on international concerns revealed, these strong ties often indicate tensions between the two states/organisations, and less often cooperation (which can be explained in that tensions and conflicts tend to be better reported by the mass media than cooperation and peace).

Apart from international organisations, the centre of the international network also includes most English-speaking countries (the USA, the UK, Canada and Australia) and some European and Middle Eastern countries. Asian and South American countries are located in the middle. African countries tend to be located in the margin of the international network as perceived by English news sources. As such, this network is obviously biased and represents a very partial picture of the world. Between August 2005 and January 2006, civil wars, health problems, food shortages and massive displacements of communities were taking place in the Congo, Uganda, Somalia, Liberia, Burundi, Senegal, Nepal and Yemen (IRIN, 2006a; UN News, 2006). Most of these events were marginalised in the news. Similarly, in the same period, IRIN news services reported on the growing tensions between Chad and Sudan and between Gambia and Senegal. News in English did not mention Gambia and Senegal at all, while Sudan was mentioned only in relation to the USA and the UN. Thus, news-links between African countries did not get much representation in the international network of Google News. African international relations seemed of interest only when their relations mattered to countries and organisations outside Africa, and particularly the main hubs (i.e. the USA, the UN and the UK).

Furthermore, it is possible to separate each country and analyse its international environment (i.e. ego-centred network) as represented by popular news sources in English. The ego-centred network (Wasserman and Faust, 1994) allows one to focus on one specific actor, in this case a country, and its relations or news-links with other countries. The UN is the second most important hub, and it is also the hub that connects most African countries to the international network. It could be argued that it is primarily because of UN concern that African countries get some news coverage.

Figure 5.11 shows that, in addition to links with many African countries, the UN has strong ties with Iran, Syria and Pakistan. With Iran there is the issue of the nuclear problem, with Syria the investigation of Hariri's death, and with Pakistan the earthquake relief. Popular news articles do not mention the UN so much in relation to Asian, South American and European countries, but there are certainly news-links with

Figure 5.11 The international network of the UN

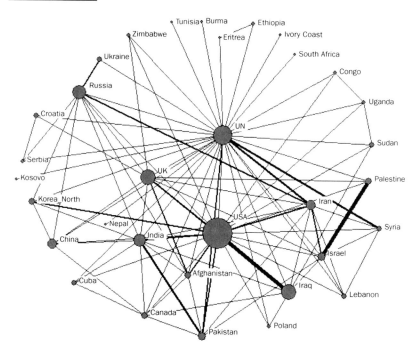

the main hubs, the USA, the UK, Russia and China. Here, the international network of the UN can provide a visual illustration of its main activities and concerns as perceived by popular news sources.

Figure 5.12 illustrates the international network of the EU. As a regional organisation it has obviously more links to European countries, but it also acts as a hub, linking to many other countries, such as Iran and North Korea, as well as to other hubs such as the USA, the UK, Russia and India. Through this particular structural framework, the EU is viewed as an international hub – in a way, a smaller version of the UN. It has fewer links and its ties are weaker than those of the UN. The heterogeneity of links to a few African, Asian and Middle Eastern countries may imply that its international political function and concern are still not entirely shaped (or recognised by popular news sources).

Similarly, the international network of the UK (Figure 5.13) is relatively large and scattered. It has links to some other European countries and to main hubs, such as the USA, the UN, the EU, Russia and China. Additionally, it has relatively strong ties with Iraq and Afghanistan, where

Figure 5.12   The international network of the EU

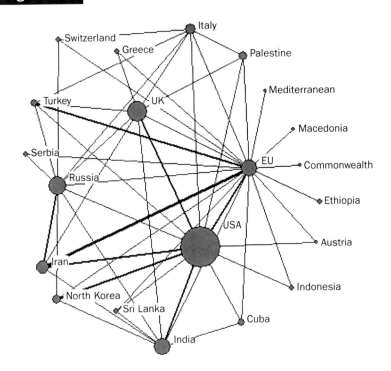

Figure 5.13 The international network of the UK

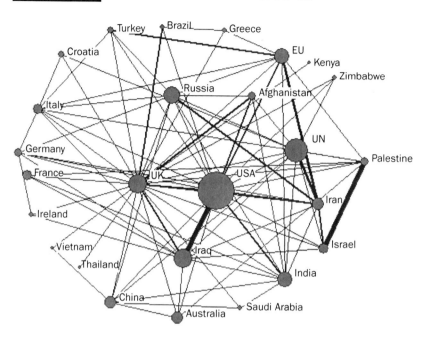

it is engaged in military operations, and with Brazil, with which it had diplomatic tensions following the police shooting an innocent Brazilian man in July 2005. Finally, there are some weak links to Asian, Middle Eastern and African countries.

The international network of Iraq reveals a very different picture. Here there is almost full representation of many English-speaking as well as European countries and some Middle Eastern countries. Apart from Japan, there are no Asian countries linked to Iraq.

Figure 5.14 shows that Iraq's strongest ties are with the USA and then with the UK. As Iraq is mentioned mainly in the context of the USA's military operation and its 'nation-building' efforts, the international network represented by news sources is highly biased toward Western interests. In this case, Figure 5.14 particularly shows which countries were the key players in these operations. Interestingly, there were no news-links between Iraq and Syria, Lebanon or Turkey. This is despite the major effects of the war in Iraq on these countries. For example, in December 2005, IRIN News (2006b) reported on almost a million Iraqi refugees who had fled to Syria to escape US-led offensives, their plight as well as their role in the Iraqi elections.

Figure 5.14 The international network of Iraq

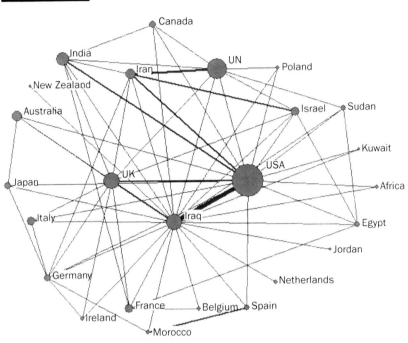

The international networks of Russia and China reveal (Figures 5.15 and 5.16) that they have relatively more news-links to Asian countries in their region. Similar to the role of the UN as an international hub to African countries, the network analysis indicates that both Russia and China serve as crucial hubs to some Asian countries.

Both China and Russia have news-links to the main hubs (i.e. the USA, the UK and the UN) and to some countries in their region. However, they have almost no news-links with Middle Eastern, African or South American countries. Interestingly, there were no news-links between Russia and many of its central Asian neighbours, such as Uzbekistan, Kyrgyzstan, Kazakhstan and Tajikistan. In November 2005, for example, IRIN News (2006c) reported on a treaty signed by Russia and Uzbekistan, offering mutual assistance and providing each with the right to use military facilities in either country. This event did not, however, make headlines in Google News. Similarly, the strategic ties between China and West African countries, as well as China's economic investments (IRIN, 2006d) were not mentioned in popular English-language news in January 2006.

Figure 5.15 The international network of China

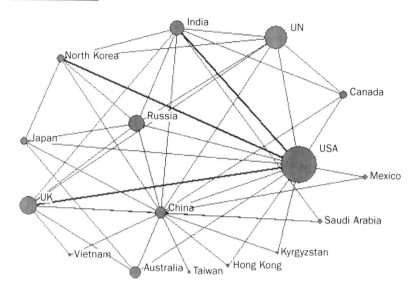

Figure 5.16 The international network of Russia

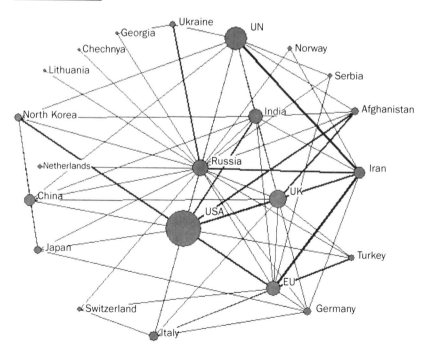

Again, the news-link networks indicate that Russia and China are mentioned mostly when the issues are also related to the USA. The content of news-links provides clear support to this claim. To begin with, Russia and China are both mentioned in the context of military cooperation. Further, China has news-links with the UK, Australia, Canada, Mexico, Vietnam, Saudi Arabia and North Korea, all of which deal with enhancing political and economic ties with these countries. In contrast, China's news-links with the USA are mostly about growing tensions: US and UN criticism of human rights abuse in China, US concern about the militarisation of China, and US pressure on Chinese political reforms. Similarly, in relation to Hong Kong and Taiwan, China is mentioned as a regime that exercises tight control and limits democracy and freedom initiatives. Obviously, China is pictured by popular news in English as a growing international actor that may threaten US security. Moreover, China is often mentioned in the context of human rights abuses, such as the killing of protesters over property rights or the journalists' protest against censorship in December 2005. All examples suggest that in popular news in English, China is viewed as a problem or an increasing economic and political challenge for the West.

Similar to the representation of China, the representation of Russia in English-language news is mostly one-sided. Russia has news-links with North Korea and Iran dealing with its support of their nuclear plans and its involvement in international arms deals. Further, Russia has news-links with India, Germany, the Netherlands, Italy and Turkey, all of which deal with enhancing political and economic ties with these countries. In contrast, within Asia, among its neighbours, Chechnya, Lithuania, Georgia and Ukraine, news-links deal with political and economic tensions. The USA is only mentioned as expressing criticism and concern over Russian support of Iranian nuclear plans. Additionally, Russia is mentioned in the context of Khodorovsky's hunger strike and the governmental control of NGOs. Hence, the content of popular news-links in English clearly underlies a dominant US concern over the 'unresolved' international identity of Russia. Has Perestroika really changed the face of Russia from an 'enemy' to a 'friend'? Will it succeed in fighting internal corruption (Khodorovsky) and governmental control (NGOs) on its way to become a more 'democratic' and 'free' state?

Finally, the international network of Israel (Figure 5.17) indicates its importance as a regional hub in the Middle East, although many other countries have news-links with each other and with the USA. The Middle Eastern network is therefore a particularly tied cluster, in which each country has either positive or negative relations with other countries in the region.

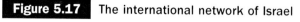

Figure 5.17 The international network of Israel

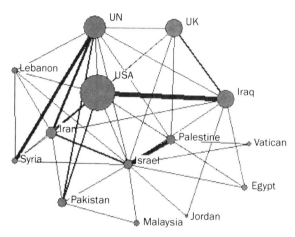

The analysis of international networks as represented by English news sources could not reveal a regional hub in South America. To this end, the USA serves not only as a global hub, but also as a regional hub for the American continent, probably as most international news in English provides a biased and narrow view of the region through a US lens. Of course, an analysis of international news in Spanish and Portuguese might reveal different networks with different hubs, though see below for some general trends.

The language dimension

While US dominance in English news may be anticipated, it is less obvious whether online news in other languages follows a similar trend. Google News allows this investigation as it displays world news pulled from popular news sites in various languages. Table 5.1 displays the 20 countries most frequently mentioned in news sites in 12 different languages during a period of three months between March and May 2006. In order to emphasise the differences between English and non-English sources, countries frequently appearing in *both* English and non-English news are shown in italics.

The dominance of italicised countries in Table 5.1 indicates that there is not a great difference in the focus of world news in different languages. In all sources, English and non-English, the USA is one of most frequently

Table 5.1 Frequency of occurrence of countries in Google World News by language

Rank	English	Spanish	Dutch	French	Portuguese	German	Italian	Chinese (Mandarin)	Chinese (Cantonese)	Japanese	Korean	Hebrew
1	USA	USA	USA	Italy	USA	USA	USA	USA	USA	USA	USA	Iran
2	Iraq	France	Iran	Iran	France	Iraq	Palestine	Iran	China	China	Canada	USA
3	Iran	Iran	Belgium	USA	Italy	UK	Iran	Japan	Japan	Iraq	S. Korea	Italy
4	Russia	Italy	Netherlands	Russia	Iraq	Italy	Iraq	China	Iran	Japan	China	France
5	Palestine	Peru	Iraq	France	Iran	UN	Israel	Iraq	Iraq	Iran	Japan	Germany
6	Italy	Mexico	Poland	Israel	Israel	Afghanistan	France	S. Korea	Russia	S. Korea	N. Korea	Israel
7	Israel	Iraq	EU	Iraq	Russia	Iran	Italy	Serbia	S. Korea	EU	UN	Russia
8	Afghanistan	UN	Italy	Palestine	Palestine	Russia	Russia	Russia	Taiwan	Palestine	Vietnam	EU
9	Australia	Spain	Russia	EU	Serbia	Palestine	India	Italy	Serbia	UN	Australia	Iraq
10	Nepal	Serbia	UK	Serbia	Peru	Switzerland	UK	Thailand	UN	Russia	UK	UK
11	France	Vatican	Israel	Egypt	UK	Bolivia	China	Ukraine	Palestine	N. Korea	EU	Jordan
12	UK	Colombia	Palestine	Serbia	Chile	France	Peru	Palestine	Egypt	Taiwan	Africa	Palestine
13	Sudan	Cuba	Afghanistan	Spain	EU	S. Leone	Afghanistan	Pakistan	Ukraine	UK	Iraq	Syria
14	EU	Israel	Serbia	Ukraine	Liberia	World	Canada	India	France	India	Nigeria	Australia
15	India	EU	Germany	Belarus	Nepal	Germany	Germany	UN	Thailand	Syria	France	Sudan
16	Sri Lanka	Brazil	India	Ivory Coast	Egypt	Ukraine	EU	France	India	World	Iran	Egypt
17	Canada	Uruguay	Vatican	Chad	Venezuela	Israel	Brazil	UK	UK	Sudan	Syria	Pakistan
18	UN	Russia	Spain	China	India	Austria	Israel	Germany	Egypt	Nigeria	India	Lebanon
19	Ukraine	Serbia	France	Switzerland	Ukraine	Amenia	Somalia	Taiwan	Indonesia	Somalia	Taiwan	Serbia
20	Pakistan	Nepal	UN	Canada	China	Australia	Egypt	Belarus	N. Korea	Cameron	Israel	Ireland

mentioned countries in world news. Interestingly, Italy is mentioned more than the USA in French news, and Iran more than the USA in Hebrew news. However, in both French and Hebrew news, the USA is ranked second or third. Generally, news in European languages (including Spanish and Portuguese, which are also popular in Latin America) has a very similar focus to that of English news. World news in Spanish, French, Dutch, Portuguese, German and Italian focuses mainly on the USA, Iraq, Iran, Russia and the Middle East, all of which also occur frequently in English news. African and Asian countries have very little presence in world news in most European languages. Obviously, in world news in Asian languages, notably Chinese, Japanese and Korean, there is a dominant presence of Asian countries, in addition to the high presence of the USA and the Middle East.

Apart from the USA's dominance in non-English news, there are also some significant regional trends. News in Spanish and Portuguese often mentions countries in Latin America, such as Peru, Mexico, Colombia, Cuba, Brazil, Uruguay, Chile and Venezuela, which occur far less frequently in English news. Similarly, news in Hebrew often mentions countries in the Middle East, such as Jordan, Syria, Egypt and Lebanon, which occur far less frequently in English news.

Figure 5.18 portrays the international network as reflected by world news in different languages. Each of the 12 languages was linked with the 20 countries most frequently mentioned in it. The large nodes represent languages and the small nodes represent the most frequently mentioned countries. The size of a node indicates its degree of connection, i.e. in how many languages the country was mentioned. The width of the links indicates the strength of the tie, i.e. the number of news articles mentioning each country.

Figure 5.18 indicates that the USA, Iraq and Iran are the most frequently mentioned countries in world news in all languages. Immediately following, France, Russia, the UK, the UN, the EU, Palestine, Israel, Italy and India, play a central role in world news in different languages. Finally, similarly to previous indications, Asian and Latin American countries occur frequently only in news in Asian and Latin American languages respectively. Most African countries occur far less frequently in news sources in different languages, and therefore constitute only a minor part of the imaginary international communities as perceived by users worldwide.

Figure 5.18 clearly demonstrates regional trends, where South American countries dominate Spanish and Portuguese news; Asian countries dominate Japanese, Chinese and Korean news; and Middle Eastern

Figure 5.18 The international network by language

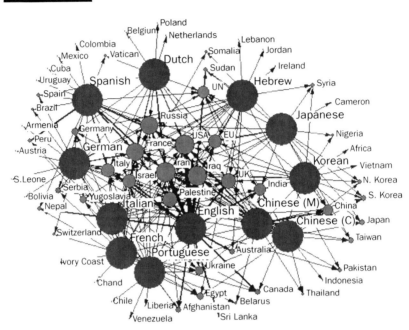

countries dominate Hebrew news. Apart from regional trends, there are also very obvious global trends. The centre of the international network reflected by non-English news is very similar to the centre of the international network reflected by English news. Considering the USA'S recent military involvement in Iraq, and its growing concern over the Iranian nuclear plan, these global trends suggest that, as with English news, non-English news in Google News is also biased toward US-centric priorities and agendas.

Summary and conclusion

The study of Google News suggests that, together with informing the public, it has also shaped a certain global image, in which the USA, its allies and their foreign politics were the main international concern in the second half of 2005. One of the reasons for this partial representation of the world is that the USA and the UK together provide around 60 per cent of popular world news in English.[10] Other native English-speaking countries, such as Australia, Canada and Ireland, together provide around

20 per cent of popular world news in English. Only 20 per cent of the popular world news in English is provided by non-English speaking countries, usually as the English version of their local news websites. Thus, a US-centric view is reinforced, mainly as US news sources also dominate the English media. Google News, which gathers and organises thousands of these news sources, reflects this trend.

A network analysis also revealed the relations between countries, and mapped their relative positions in the news-link network as perceived through Google News and popular news sources. It indicated that, in addition to the USA, the centre of the international network also includes the UN, the UK, Iraq, Russia, the EU and India as main hubs that link to many other countries. Asian and South American countries are located in the middle and have more regional links. African countries tend to be located at the margin of the international network as perceived by news in English. Thus, the network analysis indicated that many countries appear in news only because of their relations with the main hubs. In this context, the UN plays a crucial role as a central hub that connects many African countries with the rest of the international network, bringing them into public consciousness. This shows the importance and potential of certain international organisations in the global political map, or at least in the imaginary world as represented by popular news sites.

Strikingly, the centre of the international network reflected by non-English news was very similar to the centre of the international network reflected by English news. This suggests that popular news in different languages is still very biased toward US-centric priorities and agendas. A possible reason for this is the dominance of few international news agencies, which originate in English-speaking countries and provide world news to all other local news sources. Thus, most international news is translated from English sources and distributed through local media channels.

The study of Google News reveals the same overarching narrative that lies behind the operation of commercial search engines, involving popularisation and customisation mechanisms with their advantages, disadvantages and inevitable implications. As previously suggested, popularity is often an indication of relevancy, and thus the reasons behind implementing page-ranking mechanisms and prioritising 'authority' sites are both practical and commercial. While Google News automatically pushes more popular news sources to its front pages, it also appeals to larger audiences and generates more traffic. This is true, not only for its news channel, but also for its e-commerce channel (i.e. product search), its academic channel (i.e. Google Scholar), and so on. The idea is that if most users find an information source relevant and appealing, there is more chance that a random user will also find it appealing. As has happened with other media (see Bennett, 1990; Herman and Chomsky, 2002; Entman, 2004), the implementation of advertisements in Google News can further strengthen the dominance of mainstream news channels and contribute to the commodification of news, with all the previously discussed political implications.

Indeed, advanced customisation, which is another important commercial motive, often works in the opposite direction, and when it comes to news it increases the variety and possibilities of means for skilled users to find smaller and less popular news sources. However, users who search for these sources usually also know what they are looking for, and are able to search skilfully for more specific information. The internet and the increasing customisation power of search engines may certainly provide easier and quicker access to that information, but people who search for alternative views, and knowing unique ways to get alternative information, were around well before the advent of the internet. Many users, however, are not aware of specific non-mainstream news sources, and do not search for them frequently. They are part of a vicious circle, defining the popular and retrieving it in return. The page-ranking mechanism in Google News is not and cannot be the cause; it is merely an essential agent that contributes to this process.

Similar to the other experimental chapters, the main value of this study, which looks at the production of information in Google, is that it can be used and applied in various ways. It is therefore important to continue and investigate the different uses of Google News, i.e. what search queries are used and what top stories are read. However, the current analysis of main issues and states in Google News in its English and non-English versions suggests that, together with local and regional trends (based on the different news languages), there are also very significant global trends of US-centric views. These trends portray another angle of the digital divide of information, and in a way correspond to observations of other scholars regarding the dominant role of US views in online media and international news production (Barnett and Kim, 1996; Thompson, 2000; Wu, 2000; Kroes, 2003). The world as reflected by Google News, and therefore also by popular news sources, is one in which the USA's relations with Iraq or Iran are, or should be, everyone's business. It is a world in which Asian and South American countries have limited importance primarily within their own region and vernacular news. Finally, it is a world in which African countries that produce a very small fraction of online news sources are completely marginalised and neglected from the imagined international communities.

Notes

1. See also the section on US dominance in the Preface, particularly its dominance of communication means, and its various implications.
2. The terms 'centre', 'middle' and 'margin' are used in a general sense to specify the location of countries in the news-link network and not in the more specific sense as found in the WSA literature (i.e. centre, semi-periphery and periphery).
3. In July 2007, Google News attracted 9.6 million visitors (Liedtke, 2007).
4. The term 'political biases' in Ulken's (2005) study refers to the overall conservative or liberal slant.
5. See also the Preface for the concept of US dominance and the use of the term 'bias' in this book.
6. Palestine refers to the Palestinian territories and particularly to world news mentioning the West Bank or the Gaza Strip.
7. Also known as 'search engine count estimates', see the study by Janetzko (2008) that examined the objectivity, reliability, and validity of the search result count.
8. The investigation focused on the website *http://news.google.com*. However, similar results can be obtained when looking at other English versions of Google News such as *http://news.google.co.uk* or *http://news.google.ca*. Additionally, the analysis is sensitive to the various names and spellings that certain countries may have (e.g. 'United Kingdom', 'the UK', 'England' or 'Britain').
9. During the observation period, Google News displayed news articles for the recent month only. A search for a country in Google News would have therefore returned all the news articles mentioning this country over the last 30 days.
10. As was measured in Google News during the sampling period, but as Google gathers thousands of news sources, these figures can provide a good estimation of the more general trend.

6

Google's global mapping

The study of Google News indicates the dominant US presence in popular online news sources in different languages, and thus sheds light on the digital divide of information which is evident in this channel. This chapter continues the investigation of Google and its contribution to the bias of knowledge by observing Google Earth and Google Maps. Although many users may regard maps and images as 'neutral', it was found that some of Google's depictions are political and biased, providing for a start much deeper and wider information about the USA than other countries. It is important to note that the biases found in Google Earth and Google Maps (as in other Google services) are not always intentional. They will often be the result of political and economic considerations, agreements with other companies and the available market of users.

An interesting example in this context is the high-resolution imagery of military installations, which many governments perceive as a threat to their national security. Strikingly, there is a structural bias here as well: while Google Earth provides clear images of military installations in South and North Korea, Iran and China, various military installations in the USA and allied countries have been censored. Similar to many other global information and communication corporations, Google is a US-based company, and thus it appears that the US government has a considerable ability to control and censor sensitive information in its channels.

Google Earth and Google Maps

Google Earth and Google Maps are very similar products, providing directions, interactive maps and aerial images of the world. Google Earth provides a more detailed three-dimensional view in a user-friendly interface installed and run on the personal computer, while Google Maps is a web-based interface. In some regions, users are able to zoom in and view high-resolution satellite images of streets and buildings. In some cities, it is possible to search further for businesses, public transportation, driving directions, hotels and restaurants. The maps in Google were purchased mainly from Tele Atlas and NAVTEQ, while most patches of aerial images were purchased from DigitalGlobe and its QuickBird satellite, as well as from other US government sources (Google, 2009b). The imagery in Google Earth and Google Maps is taken from a variety of sources, and pieced together in a mosaic to make up a pseudo-continuous image of the globe (Ullmann and Gorokhovich, 2006).

It is believed that, even if maps and images are produced automatically, they are socially constructed, subject to direct manipulation, and have further social and political implications. Zook and Graham (2007) develop the concept 'DigiPlace', i.e. the use of code and data located and ranked in cyberspace to represent physical spaces. They suggest that digital mapping, like other forms of cartography, incorporates certain distortions and structural biases, which promote the interests of those who create it (see also Harley, 1988; Pickles, 2004). However, unlike previous mapping systems, DigiPlace is automatically generated by the code, constantly updated, and enables advanced customisation of maps and images. These innovative features empower skilled users and provide new opportunities for the production and consumption of mapping-related information. For example, Google Earth and Google Maps enable users to generate their own annotations, graphics and photos within the maps and images, and share them with others in a community layer. In this way, skilled users can easily impart their perception of places to others.

Many mapping services existed before Google introduced its own version. However, one of its important contributions was to popularise online mapping services, making them easily and freely available, and applicable to various fields. Subsequently, more websites (e.g. hotels, restaurants and property agencies) have integrated these maps, allowing people to navigate and easily find their businesses and services. For example, the maps and images in Google have been used by militants to plan attacks and escape routes. Another growing use is the integration of Google Earth and Google Maps with GPS systems. Users can locate other people in real time by tracking signals from their GPS systems or mobile phones.[1] The Brazilian police force has also used Google Earth in order to track down a notorious criminal (Estadao, 2007).

Apart from the obvious benefits, the increasing openness and wide availability of high-resolution images pose threats to the privacy of individuals and groups, and also to the national security of states. Without international policies, there is currently no way to protect and regulate these various interests at a global level, and it often happens that US and commercial interests provide the dominant framework.[2]

Biases in scope

There is no doubt that online mapping services can present many opportunities for producing personal and customised maps, as well as for searching for more specific information. However, a study by Zook and Graham (2007) indicates that even specific search results in Google Earth and Google Maps incorporate certain structural biases based on the code and the automatic ranking mechanisms. Their study suggests, for example, that Google Maps ranks larger and more popular businesses (with a larger number of links) higher, and thus local businesses with no, or very limited, web presence risk being invisible, even if they provide relevant products or services. While there is an obvious difference between the visibility of popular and less popular businesses, the main focus of this chapter is on the different representations of *countries* in Google and their implications for the digital divide.

Although many users may perceive automatic mapping services such as Google Maps as relatively 'neutral', it has been found that depictions in Google Earth and Google Maps are often political and partial.[3] First, the naming in Google Earth and Google Maps is highly political. It has been reported, for example, that Google Earth is regularly criticised by Korean users for what they claim is the 'wrong' use of Korea's geographical names. Among the issues in dispute are the Dokdo Islets and Mount Baekdu, which are also given Japanese and Chinese names respectively. In response to these claims, Google Korea's spokesperson announced plans to launch a Korean version of Google Earth, adding that 'much attention from Korean netizens will help us [Google] prepare for better service, and their advice will be reflected in the launching preparations' (Yoon-Mi, 2007). This suggests that local customisation and exclusion of 'sensitive' information will help Google to deal with controversies, and enhance its penetration into national markets. In return, it might be that users in different countries will be exposed to different information. Similarly, the Chilean government asked Google to correct an 'error' in its maps, relocating a Chilean village in Argentina (ABC News, 2007). Finally, until October 2005, a search for the island 'Taiwan' in Google Maps would have returned the result 'Taiwan, a province of China'. This highly political assertion prompted the Foreign Ministry of Taiwan to put pressure on Google to change its results. This incident also provoked intense pressure from legislators of the pro-independence Taiwan Solidarity Union to modify this entry. A month later, after Google had deleted the entry from its Google Maps interface, it was heavily criticised by Chinese officials, and many users in China demanded a boycott of its services (Gluck, 2005).

Second, as a result of Google's agreements with aerial imaging companies and the commercially available data, there is a bias in the regional coverage of high-resolution images. The USA has a very large coverage of high-resolution images in Google Earth and Google Maps. West Europe has less coverage, while the lesser developed world has relatively little coverage of high-resolution images (Google, 2007c). Figure 6.1 and Figure 6.2 show that, while for New York and most other US cities, Google Maps provides a very detailed and high-resolution view of buildings, cars and people, including a street view (on the right),[4] for Benin City in Nigeria, which has a population of more than 1 million people, it provides a relatively low-resolution view. This projects the notion that the USA is more developed than other countries, and even that it is an 'open information society'. Not only is it difficult for many people in the 'periphery' to acquire information about their own location, but it also remains difficult for Americans to acquire information about them. This is probably a dynamic and changeable situation, as Google Earth is continuously widening its coverage, and more cities worldwide are gradually becoming available as high-resolution images. In June 2006, Google noted that it was working in conjunction with DigitalGlobe in order to increase its coverage of high-resolution images (Google, 2006d). In the same period, it claimed to

Figure 6.1   Google Maps in New York

Google Maps, accessed in January 2008
(*http://maps.google.com/maps?hl=en&lr=&q=Empire%20State%20Building*)

Figure 6.2 Google Maps in Benin City, Nigeria

Google Maps, accessed in January 2008
(*http://maps.google.com/maps?hl=en&lr=&q=benin,nigeria*)

already have high-resolution image coverage of over 20 per cent of the planet's land surface (Claburn, 2006). This suggests that high-resolution images of the 'peripheries' are technically available from various sources, however, their integration requires Google to invest both money and time.

The current level of image resolution in Google Earth reflects the commercial interests of Google and the available market of users in various cities. An ongoing survey indicates that more than 80 per cent of Google Earth users are from the USA, Western Europe and Australia (Zook and Graham, 2007). Hence, from an economic perspective it is clear why Google provides more detailed images and advanced features for these states, while overlooking others. This unequal representation through maps and images (similar to the unequal representation through online news) reveals another aspect of the digital divide, and certainly affects the way users perceive their world.

Finally, the additional features provided with Google Maps (e.g. route planner and business locator) are only available in particular countries, such as the USA, Canada, Australia, New Zealand and Japan. RideFinder, for example, is another feature of Google Maps that integrates GPS systems in taxi and limousine services, and thus enables users in the USA to search for available taxis in their neighbourhood (Figure 6.3). This suggests that, together with the expanding coverage of the world, there is

Figure 6.3 Google RideFinder in New York

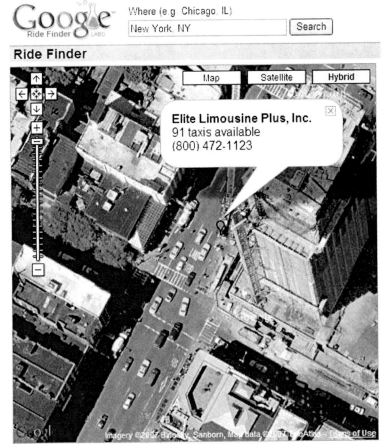

Google Maps, accessed in June 2006
(*http://labs.google.com/ridefinder?z=8&near=New%20York%2C%20NY&src=1*)

also an increase in the depth of information available in the USA and in some other capitalist countries. While Google works at increasing its high-resolution coverage, it also introduces new mapping tools and services for its US users.

Google continuously comes up with new ideas to integrate its search engine into daily life. As often happens, instead of answering peoples' needs, new technologies create new needs. Market forces lie behind the increasing dependence on ICTs, and therefore also the increasing gap between the information-rich and information-poor. In April 2007,

Google launched a new project together with the US Holocaust Memorial Museum, integrating high-resolution images and up-to-date information on the atrocities committed in Sudan (Butler, 2007). Although this move seemingly indicates a positive step towards a more equal representation of the world, it is important to note that US officials and media often criticise the Sudanese government, and consider the crisis in Darfur as genocide. Google only reinforces this official view by focusing on those particular political events that draw the attention of the Western audience. This suggests that Google Earth is gradually becoming a political tool par excellence. The more economic, political and social uses it introduces, the more popular and essential an information agency it becomes.

The national security dimension

The increasing availability and popularity of information is sometimes at odds with 'national interests'. The excitement that Google Earth brought to users worldwide has been matched by the anxiety of national governments over the open online exposure of military and security installations. An interesting example in this context is the Mintongseon, or the Civilian Control Zone of the Demilitarised Zone (DMZ) between North and South Korea, which is one of the world's most heavily fortified borders. For security reasons, the borders of the DMZ were left unmarked on maps produced in South Korea. Similarly, for many years the North Korean government omitted military bases and defence facilities from official maps (Card, 2006). Google Earth, which provides a free satellite view of the area, is perceived as a threat to national security by both North and South Korea, as it clearly displays military installations. Although South Korean officials tried to put pressure on US authorities, they could not change the situation, as Google is a private entity (Haines, 2005b). In a way, as new alternatives to the official maps became easily available and popular, the South Korean government has for the first time lost control over the representation of Korean terrain to the public.

Similarly, the President of India expressed his concern over the security threat posed by Google Earth, revealing high-resolution images of army headquarters and Parliament House (Techtree, 2006). Since 1967, Indian law has explicitly forbidden satellite and aerial images of bridges, ports, refineries and military establishments (Hafner and Rai, 2005). In the USA, defence experts contended that aerial images of Google Maps in Iraq helped terrorists to locate and attack British and US military bases

(Copping, 2005). An army intelligence source argued that many attacks on British bases in Basra were based on aerial images in Google, claiming that documents seized during raids on the homes of insurgents yielded print-outs from Google Earth (Harding, 2007a).

In July 2007, a researcher from the Federation of American Scientists noticed that a commercial satellite image of one of China's nuclear submarines was available on Google Earth (Shankland, 2007). A Pentagon official said that the very detailed aerial view in Google Earth revealed the entire nuclear zone and secret military facilities in China, which were previously highly classified and an exclusive domain of the US technical intelligence agencies. Obviously, this kind of imaging has been perceived as a threat to the national security of China.

While China is known for its strict and advanced censorship mechanisms in Google and elsewhere,[5] there is currently no evidence of censoring or manipulating images in most versions of Google Maps or Google Earth. However, Leung (2007) has demonstrated manipulation of maps in the Chinese version of Google Maps. For example, he noticed that the disputed region of Arunachal Pradesh (which is currently under Indian administration) was labelled in most versions of Google Maps as a separate region by dashed lines indicating a dispute, while in the Chinese version of Google Maps it was not labelled, and was included as part of China. In other words, similar to Google News and the general Google search, Google Maps has a local version in China, which is controlled and manipulated by the Chinese government. However, while Chinese users cannot access sensitive results through the Google search engine or Google News, they can currently access the non-Chinese versions of Google Maps and look for discrepancies. Hence, unregulated and uncensored mapping information is still available for Google's users in China.

In Thailand, officials have considered asking Google to censor images of vulnerable government buildings (Haines, 2005a). Meanwhile, as Figure 6.4 demonstrates, Google Maps provides even more sensitive high-resolution images of the Thai air-force base in Korat and its top quality US-built aircraft.

In April 2006, the US Institute for Science and International Security (ISIS) published an analysis of the uranium enrichment progress in Iran, based on aerial images from DigitalGlobe, which are also available in Google Earth (Figure 6.5). Their report not only carefully estimates the current and future nuclear capacity of Iran, but also provides users with tools to further 'interpret' publicly available satellite images (Brannan and Albright, 2006). Thus, even if Iran prevents an official inspection from the UN or the USA, there are plenty of professional and amateur 'spies', who can follow the

Figure 6.4   Thai air-force base in Korat

Google Maps, accessed in January 2008
(*http://maps.google.com/maps?hl=en&tab=wl*)

Figure 6.5   Iran's nuclear plant in Natanz

Google Earth, accessed in July 2006 (*http://earth.google.com*)

development of the Iranian nuclear plants using free tools such as Google Earth. Information that was previously classified has become even more available and interpretable through dedicated online communities that constantly research the images in Google Earth and exchange place-marks. In the same way, there are many popular weblogs that specialise in locating biases and providing critical reviews on Google Earth and its threats to privacy and security (e.g. Google Earth Community and Ogle Earth).

While many governments view Google Maps and Google Earth as a potential threat to national security, some governments have more control over the production and distribution of online information than others. This is why, for example, certain Dutch buildings in Google Maps are obscured. Figure 6.6 shows a screenshot of the Dutch Ministry of Defence in The Hague.

Figure 6.6 shows that an area of the high-resolution image of streets and buildings is obscured by mosaic. In the case of the Netherlands, Google

Figure 6.6   **The Dutch Ministry of Defence**

Google Maps, accessed in July 2009
(*http://maps.google.com/maps?f=q&hl=en&q=netherlands&ll=52.078603,4.315926&spn=0.002466,0.010729&t=k&om=1*)

purchased aerial images from the Dutch company, Aerodata. Aerodata is subject to Dutch law, and was therefore obliged by the Dutch government to censor certain images, which were later used by Google (Wolfstad, 2006). Here the Dutch government could exercise greater control over online information than the South Korean or the Iranian governments, at least for the time being, as long as Google has a contract with the Dutch aerial imaging company. Similar image distortions appear when looking at some other sensitive government and military installations in Europe, such as airfields in France and various military installations in the UK, Germany and Spain, as has been reported by Google Earth Community members (PriceCollins, 2006; see also Kopytoff, 2007b). Figure 6.7 displays another example of censorship when looking at Google Maps images of NATO headquarters in Brunssun, the Netherlands.

Not surprisingly, however, most examples of censorship come from the USA. Figure 6.8 reveals that the US Naval Observatory is censored in Google Maps for national security reasons. As in Europe, images in the USA are usually not blurred directly by Google, but rather by its image suppliers, i.e. the aerial imaging companies, which comply with local security requirements (Zook and Graham, 2007).

As most high-resolution images of the world in Google Earth are purchased from DigitalGlobe, which is a US-based company, and so subject to US law, it seems that the US government has the greatest control over the exclusion and censorship of online information, while many other governments have less control. Some 'good' US allies may

Figure 6.7 AFCENT NATO HQ, Brunssum, the Netherlands

Google Maps, accessed in April 2008
(*http://maps.google.com/maps?f=q&ll=50.938514,5.977185&spn=0.006409,0.021544&z=16*)

Figure 6.8 The US Naval Observatory

Google Maps, accessed in June 2006
(*http://www.google.com/maphp?hl=en&tab=wl&q=United%20States%20Naval%20Observatory*)

occasionally benefit from its dominance over the distribution of online information. Thus, US law requires, for example, that certain images of Israel shot by US-licensed commercial satellites be made available at a limited resolution (Hafner and Rai, 2005; Kalman, 2007).

While the previous examples display self-censorship by aerial imaging companies as a result of national laws, the free availability and growing popularity of these images in Google Earth and Google Maps has persuaded governments to contact Google directly and to work together to censor certain 'sensitive' images. Although these commercial images have been available for purchase from aerial imaging companies for many years, with the introduction of Google Earth and Google Maps they have become more freely and easily accessible, and have thus attracted much more attention and uses. An interesting example in this context is of the aerial images of British military installations in Iraq. Until January 2007, Google Earth displayed relatively recent imagery of the British headquarters in Basra. However, after an alarming report from the *Daily Telegraph* (Harding, 2007a) about terrorists using Google Earth, there was an imagery 'update'. The 'current' image from Google Earth of the same place in Basra actually precedes the Iraq invasion and shows no military installations. Figure 6.9 displays this change as published in Ogle Earth (Geens, 2007).

The left-hand image, which was available in Google Earth until January 2007, and revealed the entire British headquarters in Basra, is more likely to have been taken in late 2004 or 2005, while the updated image on the right is from 2002. This discrepancy shows that Google replaced newer imagery with older imagery at the request of the coalition forces in Basra. Similarly, it has been reported that Google blotted out various sensitive installations, including the Trident nuclear submarine pens in Faslane, Scotland and the eavesdropping base at GCHQ, Cheltenham, at the request of the British government in order 'to hinder terrorist attacks' (Harding, 2007b).

While Google Earth technology is used by insurgents to plan attacks on military installations in Iraq, and by Western governments to censor those same targets, a report from the BBC News (North, 2007) indicated that Google Earth was also used to help people survive sectarian violence in Baghdad. Users established websites and integrated Google Earth's detailed imagery of Baghdad in order to plan escape routes from the violence of Shia vigilante police forces in local neighbourhoods. Thus, Google Earth can serve as a crucial means to gain political goals, or in this particular example, a means for immediate survival.

Figure 6.9 British headquarters in Basra before and after Google's update

Ogle Earth, accessed in January 2007
(*http://www.ogleearth.com/2007/01/did_google_cens.html*)

Following Google's cooperation with the US and British governments, the Indian government made a similar attempt to modify the information in Google Earth. In February 2007, during a meeting between officials from the Indian Ministry of Science and Technology and Google Earth representatives, it was decided to camouflage certain military and scientific installations identified by the Indian government (Deshpande, 2007). As it was felt that lower resolution or blurred images might attract further unwanted attention to sensitive locations, Google agreed to creatively distort buildings by adding structures and carefully masking certain aspects of the facilities without attracting the attention of users. It is therefore clear that Google Earth also engages in deliberate world misinformation if it is 'convinced' of the need to do so.

Nonetheless, the fact that Google cooperates with certain governments and obscures sensitive installations, cannot prevent the online community from searching for discrepancies and reconstructing high-resolution images of uncensored versions of the same places (which were previously available in Google, or are still available in other map services). Figure 6.10 displays, for example, the censored image of SAS headquarters in Credenhill (on the left), which is currently available from Google Earth, and the uncensored version of the same place (on the right), which can be downloaded from the Google Earth community website and integrated in Google Earth software.

Similarly, Google Earth community members have compared various sources and reproduced an uncensored overlay image of the US Naval Observatory (albeit at a relatively low resolution), which also includes the residence of the US vice president (Figure 6.11; PriceCollins, 2006).

Figure 6.10   SAS headquarters in Credenhil

Google Earth, accessed in January 2007
(http://earth.google.com)

Figure 6.11 Uncensored overlay of the US Naval Observatory

Google Maps, accessed in April 2008
(*http://maps.google.com/maps?q=http://bbs.keyhole.com/ubb/download.php?
Number=193866&t=k&om=1*)

This suggests that the power of the US government and its allies is not absolute, and information skills provide a significant advantage in this context. As well as Google Earth and Google Maps, there are various other mapping services that use different local and global sources.[6] Thus, governments may find it difficult to keep up with the increasing number of online mapping services and the various threats they pose. Consequently, some US officials have expressed their concern and announced that they may need to enhance their control over the dissemination of satellite images (Shrader, 2007).

Finally, an interesting example that demonstrates the dynamic politics of mapping is the headquarters of the Swedish National Defence Radio Establishment (FRA). Eniro, a popular Swedish search service much like Google Maps, provides the image of the FRA shown in Figure 6.12, which has been purchased from the Swedish aerial imaging company, Lantmäteriet.

Although the left-hand map indicates the existence of buildings, an aerial view on the right displays a forest. In contrast, Google Maps, which uses aerial images from a different source, provides a totally different image of the very same place (Figure 6.13).

Figure 6.12 The headquarters of the Swedish National Defence Radio Establishment in Eniro

Eniro.se, accessed in June 2007
(http://kartor.eniro.se/query?&what=map&mop=zi&mapstate=6%3B1616635%3B65809
71%3B0%3B1615633%3B6581776%3B1617637%3B6580165%3B)

Figure 6.13 The headquarters of the Swedish National Defence Radio Establishment in Google Maps

Google Maps, accessed in June 2007
(http://maps.google.com/maps?q=59.3332,17.8544)

This suggests that as with the cases in the Netherlands, the USA and the British bases in Iraq, the image produced by the Swedish aerial company, Lantmäteriet, for Eniro was intentionally obscured with a fake forest. These discrepancies indicate that different sources (and sometimes even different local versions of the same source, such as in Google Maps China) provide different maps and images, and thus behind the so-called 'transparent' services there are various political, economic and increasingly technological forces that continuously shape and reshape the representation of the world.

Summary and discussion

The analyses of Google Earth and Google Maps indicate another aspect of the digital divide of information. They reveal that even behind maps and images there are complex political and economic considerations. Google does not deliberately work to produce an unequal or partial picture of the world. It only tries to find a certain compromise between its commercial motives, its users' needs and the various interests of governments in protecting their national security, on the way to achieve its vision 'to organise the world's information and make it universally accessible and useful'.

This chapter looked at the maps and images that Google provides, revealing yet another structural bias, where information services in the USA are much more detailed and diverse. Moreover, as Google and most of its map and image suppliers are US companies, it was found that the USA and some of its allies have more control over the censorship of strategic military installations than many other countries (e.g. Iran, North Korea and South Korea), where Google Earth and Google Maps showed high-resolution images of 'sensitive' information. Although these images were previously available for purchase through aerial imaging companies such as DigitalGlobe, with the introduction of Google Earth and similar services, they have become much more popular and easily accessible free of charge to the online community, which can further share, compare, analyse, distribute and popularise sensitive information. In this way, Google Earth seems to contribute to the development of what Ahituv (2001) describes as the 'open information society', a society with no secrets, where everyone can easily obtain information about others. This trend has become even more prominent with the introduction of a community layer, which enables users to produce their own content (annotations, hyperlinks and photos) within Google Earth and Google Maps. An interesting example in this context is the use of the community layer to list 700 Palestinian villages that remained empty after the 1948 Arab-Israeli war (Darby, 2006). While Google Earth and Google Maps officially do not allow posting commercial, political, religious, racial or sexual material (Lrae, 2004), in practice many posts do have some of these overtones, and it is impossible for Google's administrators to enforce this regulation completely. Zook and Graham (2007) provide various examples of users' annotations and opinions in Google Earth on conflicts in Iraq, Sudan, Palestine, Cyprus, and so on. In contrast, they indicate also that Google Earth has in the past removed commercial postings that may breach copyrights or make it vulnerable to lawsuits. The problem is that in most cases there is no consistent pattern, and ultimately it is in the hidden hands of Google Earth administrators to decide what is too 'offensive', 'commercial' or 'political'.

Indeed, Google Maps and Google Earth provide very dynamic multi-layer maps and images, which open more opportunities for skilled users, companies and certain states to promote their economic and political interests, and shape their image and their perceptions of the world. However, the main concern of this chapter (which in many respects is similar to the concern raised in the previous chapter on online news) is that online mapping and the representation of the world are increasingly controlled by private corporations rather than by the public. There is no transparency in the way search engines organise, manipulate, detail or obscure certain maps and images. Moreover, many individuals, groups, and even states, find themselves unable to control the information produced about them, the extent of its accuracy and depth, and the means to protect their privacy.

As previously discussed, there is a growing number of conflicts of interest between governments, companies and individuals regarding privacy/security and freedom of information (production and consumption).[7] Together with the growing popularity of global mapping and imaging services, there is growing governmental concern regarding national security issues, and Google Earth keeps producing headlines, while cooperating with certain governments and deliberately obscuring its images (Kopytoff, 2007b).

Certainly, censorship of sensitive maps and images has been a common practice throughout history. Harley (1988) suggests that maps have always reflected certain ideologies which could be studied through the intentional and unintentional exclusion of information (or what he calls 'cartographic silence'). He differentiates between two types of cartographic silence: 'intentional censorship' (usually of military and governmental installations), and 'indeterminate silence', which often refers to the ideological presupposition that certain information is privileged. The latter also includes various manipulations by the state and its agents to acquire and maintain control over new and existing spaces, and reinforce official or hidden agendas.

While the examples of censorship in this chapter demonstrate the former type of cartographic silence, the differences in image resolution and services in Google Maps and Google Earth demonstrate the latter. Although there is no 'evil' intention to ignore certain states and provide more detailed images and advanced services in the USA and some other capitalist states, commercial motives indirectly contribute to the emergence of these inequalities. The US control over the process of 'cartographic silence' is supported by powerful US internet companies, is further disseminated worldwide and shapes our understandings of the world. While some other states with economic ties and market potential, such as India, can still negotiate for their control, other states, such as North Korea, Iran and some African countries, have, at least for the time being, less control over the representation of their spaces.[8]

An interesting example in this context is the street view feature in Google Maps. This service, which was first available only in the USA and was gradually introduced in some other capitalist states, enables users to navigate the streets of big cities based on photographs obtained by specialised Google vehicles. In this case, the privacy concern occurs at the individual's level, as the service allows one to view and sometimes to identify people and private property in the streets. In order to solve this, Google automatically detects and blurs faces and allows individuals to request for their photos to be removed. Additionally, it is required to negotiate with governments and adjust this service to the privacy standards of each country (Fleischer, 2007; Shankland, 2008; BBC News, 2009). However, even if some photos are removed as a result of specific requests or local laws, problematic photographs taken by Google may still appear in weblogs, online community bulletin boards and even mainstream online newspapers (see for example Helft, 2007; Weinberg, 2007).

This suggests that the 'open information society' is becoming a relative term, which is constantly shaped by a global network of political and economic powers. While certain countries get more detailed coverage, advance services and greater control over security issues, other countries lag behind. Apart from the obvious gap between the developed-secured centre and the undeveloped-vulnerable periphery, these imaging and mapping services further empower the skilled users and the info-rich with competitive opportunities, increasing the digital divide of information.[9] The use of Google Earth images by militant groups in order to target British bases in Iraq (Harding, 2007a) exemplifies some of the political opportunities that popular mapping and imaging services offer. The fact that the British government asked Google to censor those 'sensitive' images (Harding, 2007b) demonstrates another layer of political influence. This process becomes particularly problematic as it is not transparent, i.e. Google does not inform or disclose details regarding its cooperation with governments to censor sensitive images, and in some cases (as was indicated in Iraq or India) it deliberately manipulates and obscures sensitive images in a way that will not attract the attention of users.

The growing popularity of Google Earth and Google Maps and their various applications, including real-time navigation in mobile phones, increasingly influence our understandings of spaces. Consequently, it is important to recognise and raise the awareness of users to the manipulations and exclusion mechanisms that develop in those channels. Further studies should be designed to examine the various uses and understandings of mapping services and their social and political implications. Finally, there is certainly more room for policies and regulations that call for more accountability and transparency in the operation of search engines, which increasingly dominate our common pool of information.

Notes

1. The more advanced editions of Google Earth can read tracks and waypoints from GPS devices and integrate them in its high-resolution images (Google, 2009c).
2. See also the summary and discussion for more on the privacy implications.
3. The observations in Google Earth and Google Maps were made between June 2006 and January 2008. Due to the dynamic nature of the internet and the constant upgrades in Google, it could be that some of the examples for biases have become irrelevant. However, similar principles are expected to remain as long as commercial considerations rule.
4. See the summary and discussion for the privacy implications of the street view feature.
5. See also Chapter 3 for censorship examples in Google China.
6. Microsoft, for example, has launched Windows Live Local, an online local search and mapping service that combines maps, aerial images and bird's eye imagery (*http://local.live.com*).
7. See also the general discussion in Chapter 2 on privacy and conflicts of interests in the information society.
8. In some cases, instead of negotiation with Google, governments decide to entirely close down access to Google, as often happens in Iran, or specifically block access to Google Earth, as happened in Bahrain, Jordan and Morocco (Geens, 2006; Gharbia, 2007; Noman and Zarwan, 2008).
9. Clement and Shade (2000), DiMaggio and Hargittai (2002), Shade (2002) and T. B. Riley (2004) have addressed national censorship and the ability to manipulate online information as an important element of the digital divide; see also the discussion on the digital divide of information uses in Chapter 1.

7

Conclusion

The title of this book, *Google and the Digital Divide: The Bias of Online Knowledge*, suggested a new and less conventional approach to analysing and illuminating the growing inequality in the information society caused by the organisation and dissemination of online information. It was extensively argued that the digital divide is not only about access to online information and socio-economic differences, but also, and perhaps more importantly, about the different uses, misuses and abuses of information.

By focusing on online information and power, this book addressed the issue of information skills, as well as the direct and indirect manipulation of information exercised by individuals, corporations and governments. As each chapter demonstrated, this manipulation takes various forms and involves various actors, working to include, exclude and channel online information to promote their diverse interests and objectives. Search engines play a central role, as they provide tools for individuals, corporations and governments to acquire information and reach more audiences. Moreover, they serve as the main hubs, brokers, mediators and gatekeepers in the global information network, linking diverse actors. Hence, the politics of online information as practised by Google, the dominant search engine today, has been crucial to this book.

The importance of information and communication

Following from the work of Innis (1972) and Mattelart (1980), Chapter 1 looked at the historical significance of information and communication in producing 'monopolies of knowledge', and exercising control and order. Together with the growing integration of communication and transportation technologies into our daily routines, there is also a constant and accelerating flow of information, people and commodities.

This technological proliferation enhances the ability of people to interact and create tighter global networks.

In this debate, some scholars talk about the 'network society', emphasising the decentralised network form and the significance of communication between the nodes (Barney, 2004; Castells, 2004; Van Dijk, 2005), while others talk about the 'information society', emphasising the content and flow of information generated and distributed within the network (McLuhan, 1993; May, 2002; Mattelart, 2003). Both conceptualisations have merit, and although this book mainly examined the latter, it also occasionally referred to the former. It has been argued that the emerging information society also creates a growing need for relevant and immediate information. The network, with its hypertext technologies, can answer the need for relevant information by providing advanced *customisation* mechanisms. At the same time, the immediacy of information flow propagates a much more competitive environment, in which individuals and organisations are constantly required to be available/online/connected and follow current and relevant information in order to develop greater innovation (E. M. Rogers, 2003). This could, subsequently, bring about economic advantages (e.g. lower prices for services and products, better customer relationship management, more information about competitors) as well as social and political advantages (e.g. expanding social relationships, obtaining education and citizenship information, conducting political polls, recruiting members, and so on). However, one of the important implications of the accelerating speed of generating and consuming information is in some cases the lack of reflection, the commodification of information and the *popularisation* of mainstream content, leaving less opportunity for alternative views, debate and critical discourse.

This also means that the information society is increasingly concerned with social inequality and organisations, which are based not only on financial resources and capitalist markets, but also on information skills. Various examples in this book suggested that economic advantages and information skills often overlap and depend on each other, while information skills do not always comply with the market rules, and often introduce new practices and norms of their own.

The power of the search engine

Search engines have become the main instrument for people to acquire online information (Hopkins, 2007), and thus their position and significance within the information society have increased tremendously. In order to maintain their dominant role, search engines are constantly required to enhance their quality (relevancy and immediacy of providing information), and quantity of information. As search engines can technically cover only a small part of the entire world wide web, it has been argued that the deep web poses a major challenge for them. Database websites of the deep web offer a great variety of relevant economic, political and social information – much more than the surface web (Bergman, 2001). Moreover, the world wide web is only one dimension of the internet, which includes, among other things, e-mail, File Transfer Protocol (FTP) and peer-to-peer (P2P) communication. Retrieving information from the deep web and other online communication channels often requires extra financial resources and information skills. In particular, users have to be aware of the existence of particular websites so they can reach them directly, pay membership fees for password-restricted information (e.g. e-journals), use specific search engines that harvest the deep web, or have an extensive knowledge of the code and the internet infrastructure (e.g. hackers).

However, as argued in Chapter 2, making the deep web accessible and searchable does not necessarily mean bridging the digital gap. While database websites, such as library catalogues and e-journals, are increasingly included in Google Scholar, for example, articles are organised and prioritised by page-ranking mechanisms. In this way, popular articles become more popular and less popular articles are further marginalised. This is also true for Google News and other attempts by search engines to integrate database websites and 'bridge the information gap'. Eventually, in order to be more accessible, web owners have to comply with the search engine logic, i.e. page-ranking mechanisms, money promotion deals and greater dependence, giving up aspects of their privacy and independence. Paradoxically, unveiling the deep web can increase the digital divide, making online information even more economically and commercially dependent.

While the technical problem of accessing and indexing the deep web might eventually be solved, a new type of information inequality emerges as a result of the growing need to protect private information, property rights and national security. There is a continuous competition between states, organisations and individuals to protect their information interests, and search engines often play a central role as mediators between conflicting stakes, drawing the line between what is to be revealed and what should remain hidden or obscure.

'Googling' and the politics of online search

Two essential principles are involved in Google's organisation of online information: popularisation and customisation. While the former produces a certain information order for all users, the latter does so for each individual user separately. Together these principles play an increasingly central role in media production in general, and the operation of search engines in particular.

Popularisation lies behind the page-ranking mechanism of Google and other search engines. By analysing the number of back-links in order to estimate the popularity of websites and therefore also their 'authority', 'importance' and 'relevance', search engines further divide and polarise the information society: the rich get richer, the popular get more popular, and the less popular become further marginalised (Hindman et al., 2003; Cho and Roy, 2004). Moreover, studies have revealed that search results in popular search engines are biased in favour of commercial and US-based websites (Introna and Nissenbaum, 2000; Van Couvering, 2004; Vaughan and Thelwall, 2004). As with other mass media channels, the revenue of search engines is based on advertisements; thus, they end up promoting websites based on a bidding system. Those who can pay more for a certain search query have more chance of appearing first in the search results of that query. The fact that search engines can cover a great volume of information does not mean that online information is free and equally available. Specific information is often rather expensive or not available to all.

The increasing demand for customised information products benefits both users and search engine companies. For individuals, customisation means new possibilities for editing their own stories, and new instruments for including and excluding online information. In this way, Google and other information agencies empower information-skilled users to focus on desired content, reinforcing existing dispositions and dividing users into heterogeneous segments based on interests (Sunstein, 2001). For search engine companies, customisation also means the ability to gather more private information on their users' preferences and habits. Knowing the information needs of each individual, search engines can tailor personalised solutions and make it burdensome for users to change their information providers. Apart from direct search services, Google and other search engines provide community-related services, such as e-mail, weblogs and social network services, which increase the affiliation between the search engine and its users, and further propagate dependence.

Together with the growing influence of search engines and other global communication corporations, some national governments still have a significant influence on the information flow. Many democratic and non-democratic regimes exploit, for example, information exclusion mechanisms in the name of national security and law. Supported by global internet companies such as Google and Yahoo! that aim to increase their market share, they filter 'undesirable' information, or use their corporate databases to track down criminals or dissidents. While there are no global information policies, national laws still regulate the operation of transnational corporations and, to a certain extent, limit the diffusion of information. Interestingly, some information-skilled users take advantage of the automatic page-ranking mechanism of search engines to promote economic and political goals by using 'link-farms' and 'Google bombing' methods. While there are currently no laws against these kinds of 'cyber-crimes', search engines have the power to 'punish' web owners by excluding them from the network and permanently deleting their websites from search results.

The practice of Google, which claims to 'organise the world's information', illustrates the various economic and political uses of this information and the importance of search engines in the contemporary society, enabling information-skilled users and governments to develop various mechanisms and tactics to gain certain advantages and promote their interests and positions.

Information uses in Google and Yahoo!

Chapter 4 focused on popular search queries in Google and Yahoo!, revealing the information trends of users in different countries. Countries which demonstrated a relatively high degree of economic and political searches were Russia, Germany and Ireland. Popular search queries in these countries were also more varied and more specific, indicating higher information skills and greater potential to gain political and economic advantages. In contrast, the great interest of the USA, Canada and Australia in entertainment, and the more specific search queries, could reflect national processes of media commercialisation and customisation. This, of course, is only one possible reason, and there is a need for complementary studies to observe Google users' profiles in order to support and shed light on the findings. Nonetheless, the low extent of political search queries in the USA and other countries conforms to previous studies (Dordoy and Mellor, 2001; Norris, 2001), which similarly indicated that in the USA and some European countries, users make limited use of the internet for political activism or to be politically informed. These studies suggest a growing gap between the politically engaged and disengaged. Advanced customisation mechanisms in search engines, which utilise a narrow focused outlook, can further reinforce existing dispositions and contribute to this gap (Sunstein, 2001; Turow, 2005).

The digital divide of information uses is therefore the result of various factors. Chapter 4 suggested looking also at the use of search queries to assess the gap between those who utilise search engines as instruments to acquire local and global political and economic information and those who do not. While previous studies on popular search queries focused on the technical differences between searches (Silverstein et al., 1999; Wolfram et al., 2001; Bar-Ilan, 2004; Jansen and Spink, 2004), this chapter offered new techniques to examine the relationship between information search and the digital divide, calling for complementary studies to continue and explore the processes of information retrieval (Hargittai, 2002), and what people actually do with the information they retrieve.

The world of Google News

Better search results require understanding the context of search, and thus Google provides customised channels in different fields and contexts. Google News offers a fascinating opportunity to look at the bias of international news as it gathers news articles from thousands of news sources in many languages. The analysis of the main news articles in Google News during a nine-month period displayed how popular online news sources represent the world and construct certain 'issues' and 'realities'. While reading popular online news, worldwide users were channelled to view the US military operation in Iraq or the concern regarding the nuclear potential of Iran and North Korea as the most important international political events. Consequently, it is suggested that Google News and similar services, which integrate various news sources into one interface and become popular news channels in themselves, intensify US and Western perceptions of the world. This is mainly due to their page-ranking mechanisms which prioritise larger and more authoritative news sites that often originate in Western countries.

The content of popular online news supported this view, indicating that countries such as China and Russia were often criticised by mainstream media, and the focus of news articles was primarily on their negative political actions. A network analysis envisioned the relative position and the news-links between states and organisations. It clearly displayed the centrality of the USA in English and non-English news. It also revealed the important role of the UN as a central hub that connects many African countries with the rest of the international network. This suggests that international organisations, and particularly the UN and the EU, play an increasingly crucial role in the international network as perceived by popular online news sources, due to their central position and political influence as mediators and connectors between countries.

In short, the study of Google News revealed a structural bias based on Google's page-ranking mechanism, in which popular mainstream news sources are elevated, while alternative views are marginalised. Together with the growing competition of news agencies for public attention, they construct and shape political 'realities' that are dominated by US priorities and agendas. They picture a world in which Asian and South American countries have a limited representation, mainly through vernacular news, while African countries are completely marginalised from the imagined international community.

The bias of Google mapping

Google's organisation of online information and its structural biases were further observed in its other specific channels. A study of Google Earth and Google Maps found that, as most aerial imaging companies are American, the US government and its allies have the greatest ability to control and censor certain images, while many other governments are gradually losing such control. Thus, the open information society becomes a bogus term, which is in practice reshaped and redefined by dominant political and economic actors. The fact that many transnational information agencies are American provides the USA with major military, political and international advantages, as it plays a dominant role in framing what is to be cartographically known.

The impact of popularisation mechanisms

Looking at the different findings presented in this book leads to a certain paradoxicality concerning the power ramifications of online information.

On one hand, the analysis of popular search queries revealed that the perceived online power of the USA and many English-speaking countries may be implicitly undermined arguably due to extensive commercial processes of popularisation and customisation. On the other, the investigation of popular channels such as Google News and Google Earth, suggests a seemingly opposite trend, where the USA and other English-speaking countries dominate content, and consequently empower their global vision and priorities.

The key to understanding this apparent contradiction is perhaps the commercial motivations and principles that shape technologies and algorithms of information organisation. When looking at global mass media channels (i.e. popular news sites and maps), it is the popularity and dominance of US actors (e.g. companies and websites) and English content that often reflect US and Western views. However, when looking at local customised searches in the USA, it is already possible to identify the impact of media popularisation and customisation on users' behaviours and interests, where the majority sought commercial and entertainment content. The same mechanisms that maintain or even intensify the technological and information gap between the USA and some other countries, inevitably creates an inner gap within the USA between the few politically-engaged skilled users and the majority who are increasingly taking part in a commercial vicious circle. A similar trend has been observed by Schiller (1996), who argued that commercial global media channels that disseminate the US and Western cultures and views worldwide, are also responsible for the increasing polarisation and information inequality within the leading industrial states.

The studies presented in this book indicated that local and global trends, bottom-up and top-down views, do not necessarily always compete, but rather complete each other. From local and global, national and international perspectives, the digital divide is intensified as a result of popularisation and customisation mechanisms that polarise the information society. By extensively implementing these mechanisms, the USA and some of its allies indeed dominate global views and construct certain realities, but at the same time end up undermining the power of their own local domains.

The future of search engines

The study of Google and its various information channels has indicated that search engines are currently developing along two main paths. First, they are expanding their ability to index more parts of the deep web, and are constantly refining their search algorithms to provide more relevant and qualitative results. Second, they are deepening their knowledge about their users in order to increase their ability to customise online information. These trends have crucial implications for the development of the next generation of search engines.

While search engines continue to cover more of the deep web and are introducing new specific information channels (such as Google News, Shopping and Google Scholar), they are also aware of their users' difficulties in conducting searches in multiple channels. Google has therefore introduced a 'universal search', integrating websites, news, video and other results in one page (Hillis, 2007). This trend, which turns contemporary search engines into 'supermarkets' of information, makes it easier for users to 'shop' for information in one place. Yet, it also increases the competition between companies over their decreasing place on the 'shelf', where more popular and commercial companies always win.

As part of the race to cover more of the deep web, the next generation of search engines will focus on analysing and incorporating non-text based content in general, and multimedia content in particular, in their indices. As previously mentioned, the French government is currently engaged in developing a new search engine called 'Quaero', which aims to recognise and index audiovisual files (O'Brien, 2006). Users will be able to input sounds and images, and the search engine will return sound and image files that contain similar or identical patterns, enabling users to find songs, videos, lectures, shapes, colours and photographs. While contemporary search engines analyse the textual content of webpages, the search engines of the future will be required to use techniques that transcribe and automatically analyse and translate the content of image, sound and video files, maintaining a large multilingual index, and enabling efficient retrieval of relevant information.

One of the implications of multimedia search is that it will allow different pictures to be associated with search queries in different languages. Thus, for example, search queries such as 'beauty' or 'terror' will return images from various countries,[1] and not only images from English websites. To this end, the analysis and indexing of image and sound files may bring more information to more users regardless of their native language. This does not necessarily imply that multimedia search will challenge the dominance of English and Western culture. The principles of popularisation and commercialisation will still play a significant role, prioritising more popular information, most of which still originate from economic and cultural hubs such as the USA. However, multimedia search will open a new frontier for companies to compete for the attention of users. Together with the growing popularity of video and image-sharing services (e.g. YouTube[2] and Flickr), multimedia search is increasingly becoming indispensable for the information society. By analysing the actual content of multimedia files, search engines will enhance their influence and control over online information uses, and widen and deepen the ability of users to retrieve information.

Another interesting direction, in which Google as a search company is developing, is molecular biology and genetic engineering (Vise and Malseed, 2005). Having the greatest computing and processing power, it is involved in indexing the human genome in order to enhance its understanding. A different utilisation of Google's database in medical research is a study that looked at a large numbers of Google search queries to track influenza-like illnesses in a population (Ginsberg et al., 2009). This study assumed that a high volume of search queries related to influenza could indicate health-seeking behaviours of individuals. Hence, based on the frequency of search query, the researchers were able to predict more immediately and accurately the geographical centres and spread patterns of epidemics. Apart from medical research and development, it is reasonable to expect that the search engines of the future will play an important role in our health and medical practices, and will even enable users to 'Google' their own genes.

Apart from expanding the quantity of coverage, search engines are constantly concerned with increasing the quality of their search results. As a response to the struggle against link-farms and other manipulations of search results, it is expected that search engines will further elaborate their page-ranking mechanisms. They will enhance their ability to evaluate the popularity of webpages, which is currently based mostly on the number of back-links and the number of visits to websites from their search results.[3] At the same time, search engines are continuing to develop various other techniques for evaluating the actual popularity and traffic of a website. Google Toolbar and Google Chrome, for example, enable Google to analyse what websites are visited by its users, and thus to estimate their popularity on an individual basis.

Ultimately, the increasing popularity and significance of search engines as influential and 'authoritative' information agencies also means that more website owners are required to consider the search algorithm, and modify their website's content and design accordingly.[4] Gradually, search engines will set up global standards of content production, design and database structuring. Website owners who wish to increase their presence and reach more audiences will have to comply with these standards, which will in turn enhance their dependence on search engines.[5]

From personal advisers to global advertisers

Following from the study of Google, it is reasonable to expect that the search engines of the future will increase their abilities with respect to data-collection and learning more about individual searches and preferences, building an accurate profile of each user, and continuously refining their search results accordingly.[6] Search engines will elaborate their recovery (i.e. analysis of personal search history) and discovery techniques (i.e. integration of results of other people with similar interests) in order to enhance and perfect the relevancy and accuracy of search results (Battelle, 2005). Thus, if someone is interested in music and frequently searches for information about bands and songs, search engines will be able to prioritise and customise this user's search results so that music-related information appears first. Moreover, with greater access to e-mails and personal files, search engines will be able to integrate public information with personal desktop information or with organisations' intranet information. Additionally, it is expected that users will also be able to customise their own page-ranking to some extent, configuring the level of popularity, relevancy and currency of information.

It is therefore believed that the search engines of the future will serve more as personal advisers or information agencies. To provide their users with relevant and personalised information, they will be increasingly required to deepen their knowledge about them. This study examined various aspects of customised search and information provision, which are only the beginning of a long process, where search engines are bound to become more crucial instruments and dominant agents of the information society. Nevertheless, this process, which is increasingly followed by commercial interests and corporate mergers, will be constantly debated and resisted by private organisations and states with opposing interests.

Maybe the greatest power of search engines is their ability to store and analyse what kind of information users seek, and what webpages they view (i.e. their 'click-stream'). Currently, this knowledge is implemented only for enhancing the personalised search mechanism; yet its potential is much greater. This knowledge, which Bettelle (2005) calls the 'database of intentions', is a continuous and accurate measurement of cultural trends and the popular information, products and services required by users from different regions. Moreover, together with the growing need for immediate and relevant information, information search, intentions and interests are increasingly becoming a significant part of our identity, i.e. search queries can reveal a great deal about the searcher. In August 2006, AOL released a database of 20 million random search queries for research purposes. A couple of hours after discovering the controversy caused by this release, it decided to withdraw it, as it revealed the private names, addresses, health conditions, love life and leisure preferences of the firm's users (Barbaro and Zeller, 2006).

Using such data, search engines can gradually develop into media companies, catering content to demand. Google News is an example of a search engine that has already developed into a media company. The ability to provide news articles according to people's interests and preferences is probably the most desirable wish of any news company, thus placing Google News in a competitive position among news channels (albeit only as a news aggregator). Similarly, e-commerce portals, such as Amazon or eBay, have the ability to learn what kind of products and services people seek, helping them to customise and target their advertisements, sign contracts with appropriate suppliers, efficiently prepare inventory in advance, or even produce certain products in-house. Hence, being first to know about users' needs, search engines have a competitive advantage, which allows them to cooperate with other suppliers and significantly increase their span. Eventually, they will integrate the various information channels, i.e. internet, television, video on demand (VOD) and mobile phones, into one powerful search centre. Thus, search engines will continue to improve their ability to learn about the information consumption of their users, and will customise advertisements accordingly.

As previously argued, other media, and particularly television, radio and newspaper, should not be treated separately from the internet, as they gradually turn into hybrid communication corporations that facilitate the interactive and multi-directional production of information. Google foresaw this trend, and is working to integrate video and television content into its web services. It has recently been argued that in many places the current internet infrastructure cannot support the quality of services that customers expect. Instead, Google has offered to cooperate with cable companies, combining its video search technologies and customised advertising mechanisms with high-definition quality of information flow (*USA Today*, 2007). Similarly, Google has launched an automatic advertising system for radio stations in the USA,[7] suggesting that the media market is indeed turning into a hybrid communication oligopoly. Finally, in October 2006 Google acquired YouTube (BBC News, 2006c), applying its search mechanism and keyword advertising models, thus further increasing its coverage and control over the online media and advertising industries.[8] Even in the gaming industry, Google has drawn up plans to develop a program that compiles psychological profiles of gamers. The idea behind this program is to evaluate users' behaviour during the game (e.g. honest/dishonest, passive/aggressive, and so on) and customise advertisements accordingly (Adam and Johnson, 2007).

In its biggest acquisition so far, Google has purchased the internet advertising company DoubleClick Inc. for $3.1 billion, outbidding Microsoft, Yahoo! and AOL. While DoubleClick Inc. was one of the largest sellers of online advertising spaces; it is believed that this deal gives Google much more control over the web advertising market and access to a huge amount of information on consumer and supplier behaviour (Reuters, 2007a). Moreover, this acquisition clearly indicates that, apart from information agencies, search engines are increasingly becoming advertisement agencies, commodifying and monopolising more information space.

New abilities in narrowcast advertisements will further enhance the business model of search engines. While early advertisements in Yahoo! were based on cost-per-impression techniques, i.e. advertisers paid every time users were exposed to their advertisements, Google has popularised the cost-per-click (CPC) technique, i.e. advertisers pay only if users also click on their advertisements and visit their websites. However, even with the CPC, advertisers cannot guarantee that their visitors will actually purchase their products and services. This is why future search engines will be required to design even more efficient and attractive advertising packages. The cost-per-performance or the cost-per-action technique will enable advertisers to pay, not if users click and visit their websites, but rather if they actually purchase products and services, or register to obtain further information (Battelle, 2005). In this way, search engines will also be able to tackle click frauds and search spamming, which constantly threaten their reliability.

Google's vision 'to organise the world's information and make it universally accessible and useful' (Google, 2007d) has been demonstrated, not only through its global reach for online information, but also through its additional products such as Google Books and Google Earth, which have successfully expanded far beyond the web boundaries toward satellite images and libraries. Various practices have indicated that Google systematically documents and stores every piece of text, image, sound and video in its Google Grid, a powerful supercomputer, which contains more than 450,000 servers (Markoff and Hansell, 2006), and indeed organises the world's information. With the integration of mobile phones and GPS technologies, people increasingly rely on Google Mobile to navigate, find the exact location of their family and friends in real time, search for businesses and services nearby, and employ their portable personal adviser to make various decisions in life.

The digital divide of the future will be less about the technical difficulties of accessing the network, or the limited ability of search engines to cover the deep web, and more about the deliberate organisation of information and manipulation of dominant actors. Different users will have different information available, depending on their ability to configure search engines, defining what information to share and with whom, and customising their information preferences.

The future of the information society

The information society and its divides are constantly shaped by developments in technological standards and information policies. New technological standards increasingly allow people to share online information, and make it readily available through search engines. Information policies define the boundaries between individuals, organisations and governments, providing them with communication rights and certain abilities to customise the extent of information to be shared. As previously indicated, several international organisations are working to develop information policies and decrease the digital divide of access (ITU, 2006), protect local culture and heritage (UNESCO, 2005b) and support local authorities, cities and governments (UCLG, 2006; Mattelart, 2008). While the International Telecommunications Union and UNESCO tend to address the digital divide from the international level, United Cities and Local Governments focuses also on information inequality within the state, aiming to encourage knowledge and information rights for each and every citizen. Apart from the UN and the EU, there are various national and international, governmental and non-governmental organisations, such as Bridges.org, Digital Divide Network, The Digital Opportunity Initiative, and so on, all established to address certain aspects of the digital divide. 'One Laptop Per Child' (OLPC) is an example of a project designed to bridge the digital divide by producing Linux-based $100 laptops. Google and MIT Media Lab were among the organisations and sponsors involved in this project, which introduced a working prototype in November 2005 at the World Summit on the Information Society (Palmer, 2005).

The OLPC project was criticised by various scholars and politicians, including India's education secretary, who stressed the need for classrooms and teachers over tools. Other studies questioned the effectiveness of free access, a strategy embraced by the International Telecommunications Union and other organisations, as the digital divide is rooted in socio-economic stratifications that cannot be bridged by technology alone

(Norris, 2001; Williams et al., 2005). Even if some of the international initiatives for tackling the informational and technological inequalities succeed, they are still small-scale in comparison with the increasing global capitalist forces, which promote freedom of trade and extend their influence on politics, society and culture. Freedom of trade poses a serious challenge for information equality, and as this book has demonstrated in various examples, it supports the development and growth of global information agencies and their inevitable commercial biases.

Himanen (2004) argues that in order to bridge the increasing digital divide and information inequalities, governments and corporations should shift the focus from technological developments to social developments, including changing global economic structures and industrial practices. Based on different operations and social traditions, he identifies three different models: the Silicon Valley model, the Singapore model and the Finnish model. The Silicon Valley model focuses on a tight network of science, research and technology production based on capitalist principles, in which the rich get richer and the social divide deepens. The Singapore model (operating also in China and India) focuses on tax reductions and attracting transnational corporations and investments to the region. Finally, the Finnish model (as a representative of the European tradition) emphasises a combination of the information society (i.e. encouraging production of science, technology and innovation) and the welfare society (i.e. equal opportunities, freedom and inclusive policies).

In a way, the 'European' model is an attempt to find the balance between two extremes: the US market-controlled development and the Asian government-controlled development. Indeed, both the US and Asian models have led to economic and technological developments, but drawbacks have also been inevitable, most prominently the increase of social and information inequalities. In contrast, the European model, which aims at social and information equality, usually suffers from stagnation. People may be less motivated to compete and create in a welfare environment where they receive their social benefits anyway.

Probably one of the greatest current challenges for the information society is to organise the information flow in a more balanced way, resolving the various interest conflicts such as between freedom of information (production and consumption) and property rights, and between personal privacy and collective security (national and international). A good global information policy should be able to protect the privacy of users, and at the same time provide them with a certain degree of security. It should be capable of protecting the rights of those who produce original intellectual property, but at the same time prevent them from abusing their rights, enabling others to share this information in order to develop innovation. Despite the complexity of this challenge, it is not the first time that humanity has been called upon to introduce regulations and rules to respond to technical innovation. In short, the global dissemination of ICTs, and popular search engines in particular, calls for the adoption of global information policies that promote equality and transparency.

This does not mean that the problem of information asymmetries and inequalities could be entirely resolved in the future. Those who have a better strategic position in the network, as well as stronger attributes (financial resources, education, language and information skills), will continuously reconfigure the network and its role to promote their own interests. The growing ability of search engines to customise information and empower specific users only tightens their control and increases the digital divide within the information society.

Notes

1. A Google image search for the word 'beauty' in English, Spanish, Hebrew and Turkish was conducted in January 2007, revealing mostly images of white females. This trend can be explained as many search results are associated with popular and commercial websites of transnational cosmetic companies. The increasing role of search engines in framing our knowledge may therefore reinforce commercially biased understandings of the world.
2. It was estimated that in March 2009, YouTube had more than 100 million unique users in the USA alone (comScore, 2009c).
3. The more people click on a search result in Google, the more popular and 'important' a website is (Osinga, 2004).
4. The growing popularity of search engine optimisation companies supports this trend.
5. It is interesting to view in this context Google's official announcement that it is going into competition with Microsoft over the software application market with its 'Google Apps' (Reuters, 2007b).
6. Google Personalised Search, for example, is based on the history of searches. After opening an account with Google, one can configure Google to save one's searches. The more one searches with Google, the more refined and relevant one's search results are.
7. In December 2006, Google launched a radio advertising system called Google Audio Ads. This system connects advertisers directly to radio stations, enabling them to customise and track their radio campaigns in the USA (Rodgers, 2006).
8. In January 2007, Google and YouTube revealed their plan to introduce a revenue-sharing mechanism, where advertisements will be attached to the videos of their users and the revenues will be shared with them (Weber, 2007).

8

Epilogue

The age of the so-called information society is also that of the production of mental states. It will be necessary to rethink the question of freedom and democracy. Political freedom cannot be reduced to the right to exercise one's will. It also lies in the right to control the process whereby that will is formed. (Mattelart and Mattelart, 1998: 156)

This book attempted to disperse some of the clouds that cover 'the process' of our understanding of the world. It focused on the role of search engines in the growing production and consumption of information inequalities, and unveiled their particular politics of online information. It has been argued that, together with their increasing popularity, commercial considerations contribute to the construction of a certain information order, and subsequently intensify the digital divide between the information-rich and information-poor. The analysis of search queries in Google revealed that popular searches in many capitalist (and particularly English-speaking) states increasingly focus on entertainment rather than on politics and economics. While there are various explanations for these trends, they also correspond to the growing gap between the politically engaged and disengaged in these states and the social polarisation as a result of commercialisation and advanced customisation mechanisms.

The analysis of the increasingly complex and diverse search channels in Google (e.g. Google News and Google Earth) revealed a certain structural bias toward mainstream and often official US views, agendas and priorities. Serving as popular mass communication channels to retrieve political and economic information, these services have tremendous implications regarding the construction of social 'realities'. Moreover, it has been argued that even in the seemingly 'neutral' search mechanism of Google, which is often perceived as a highly customised channel designed to retrieve more specific and individualised information, search results are biased toward popular, commercial and English content. Hence, the digital divide is not only the result of different information skills and uses, but also of the growing dominance of global media and communication corporations, which originate mainly in the USA and some other capitalist states.

Far from being an exclusive question of access, the digital divide emerges within the internet, a most complex, diverse and elaborate medium, which provides a relatively stable infrastructure for the evolution of the information society, and new opportunities for various actors to generate and consume information and increase their presence and dominance. Its enormous potential for the capitalist market has been quickly discovered. As a result, one operating system (Windows), one browser (Internet Explorer) and one search engine (Google) have increasingly become the dominant standards in obtaining and maintaining a certain information order. The detailed study of Google and its various services has demonstrated that beyond its beneficial mission to 'organise the world's information and make it universally accessible and useful', Google also reproduces and intensifies the digital divide, and sustains the US-centric information order.

Appendix A:
Search engines statistics

Share of searches in the USA

Table A.1 displays the share of searches done in each of the search engines as published by two different search marketing companies: comScore (2009d) and Nielsen/NetRatings (2009). The table summarises searches done by US web surfers in June and July 2009.

Share of searches worldwide

Table A.2 displays the share of searches done by world wide web surfers in July 2009 in each of the main search engines. The data were extracted from statistics provided by comScore (2009e).

As the experiment in Chapter 4 is based on popular search queries in Google Zeitgeist from 2004 and 2005, Table A.3 displays the share of searches in different countries during this period. It shows that Yahoo! used to be a much more popular search engine in the USA, while Google kept its lead in Canada, France and the UK.

Table A.1   Share of searches in the USA

Search engine	Share of searches ComScore (%)	Nielsen/NetRatings (%)
Google	65.0	64.8
Yahoo!	19.6	17.0
Microsoft	8.4	9.0
Ask	3.9	3.1

Source: comScore qSearch (2009) and Nielsen/NetRatings (2009)

Table A.2   Share of searches worldwide

Search engine	Share of searches (%)
Google	67.5
Yahoo!	7.8
Baidu.com	8.7
Microsoft	2.9

Source: comScore qSearch (2009)

Table A.3   Share of searches worldwide, April 2004

	Canada (%)	France (%)	UK (%)	US (%)
Google Sites	70	80	77	44
Yahoo! Sites	17	10	14	37
MSN-Microsoft Sites	13	10	9	19

Source: comScore qSearch (2004)

Appendix B:
Data for statistic analysis

Countries in dataset

Table B.1 summarises the countries that appeared in Google Zeitgeist each month during 2004 and 2005, and were used in the analysis of popular search queries in Chapter 4 (excluding countries marked in italics which joined later and did not display enough searches).

Percentage of online users

Table B.2 summarises the percentage of online users in each of the observed countries, based on data from the CIA World Factbook.[1]

Categories and subcategories

Table B.3 summarises the first two category levels of search queries as classified by the Google Web Directory (see also Chapter 4). The numbers in brackets indicate how many search queries were classified under each category or subcategory.

Global uses of online information

Following the analysis in Chapter 4, Figure B.1 summarises the share of search queries in each topic during 2004 and 2005. Figure B.1 indicates that art and entertainment-related search queries comprise the majority of popular searches worldwide, accounting for more than 37 per cent of the total searches. The categories society, sports and recreation comprise about

Table B.1 Countries appearing in the Google Zeitgeist report

Country	2004	2005	Total queries
Australia	Jan-04 – Nov-04*	Jan-05 – Jul-05, Sep-05, Nov-05	220
Brazil	Jul-04 – Nov-04*	Jan-05 – Sep-05, Nov-05	175
Canada	Jan-04 – Nov-04*	Jan-05 – Jul-05	190
Chile	–	Aug-05, Sep-05, Nov-05	45
China	Jul-04 – Nov-04*	Jan-05 – Jun-05, Sep-05	135
Denmark	Jul-04 – Nov-04*	Jan-05 – Jul-05, Sep-05, Nov-05	160
Finland	Jul-04 – Nov-04*	Jan-05 – Sep-05	155
France	Jan-04 – Nov-04*	Jan-05 – Sep-05, Nov-05	235
General (US)	Jan-04, Apr-04* (in Google)	July-04 – Oct-05 (in Yahoo!)	820
Germany	Jan-04 – Nov-04*	Jan-05 – Jul-05, Nov-05	205
Greece	–	Aug-05	15
India	–	Jan-05 – Sep-05, Nov-05	110
Ireland	–	Jan-05 – Jul-05, Sep-05	85
Israel	–	Sep-05, Nov-05	30
Italy	Jan-04 – Aug-04, Oct-04 – Nov-04*	Jan-05 – Jul-05, Sep-05, Nov-05	220
Japan	Jan-04 – Nov-04*	Jan-05 – Jul-05, Sep-05, Nov-05	220
Korea	Jul-04 – Nov-04*	Jan-05 – Jul-05, Aug-05	145
The Netherlands	Jan-04 – Nov-04*	Jan-05 – Jul-05, Sep-05, Nov-05	220
New Zealand	–	Jan-05 – Jul-05, Sep-05, Nov-05	100
Norway	Jul-04 – Nov-04*	Jan-05 – Jul-05	130
Poland	–	Aug-05, Sep-05, Nov-05	45
Russia	Jul-04 – Oct-04*	Jan-05 – Jul-05, Sep-05, Nov-05	150
South Africa	–	Aug-05, Nov-05	30
Spain	Jan-04 – Nov-04*	Jan-05 – Jul-05, Sep-05, Nov-05	220
Sweden	Jul-04 – Nov-04	Jan-05 – Jul-05, Sep-05, Nov-05	150
Turkey	–	Aug-05, Sep-05, Nov-05	44
UK	Jan-04, May-04, Jul-04 – Nov-04*	Jan-05 – Jul-05, Sep-05, Nov-05	175
Vietnam	–	Aug-05, Sep-05, Nov-05	45

* Google Zeitgeist provided annual data on the popular search queries in general during 2004. These data were used to validate and support the results of the monthly data.

Table B.2 Percentage of online users in the observed countries

Country	Online populations (millions)		
	Population	Internet users	Percentages
New Zealand	4.08	3.20	78.4
Sweden	9.02	6.80	75.4
Australia	20.26	14.18	70.0
South Korea	48.85	33.90	69.4
Denmark	5.45	3.76	69.0
USA	298.44	203.82	68.3
Norway	4.61	3.14	68.1
Japan	127.46	86.30	67.7
The Netherlands	16.49	10.81	65.6
Canada	33.10	20.90	63.1
Finland	5.23	3.29	62.9
UK	60.61	37.80	62.4
Germany	82.42	48.72	59.1
Ireland	4.06	2.06	50.7
Israel	6.35	3.20	50.4
Italy	58.13	28.87	49.7
France	60.88	26.21	43.1
Spain	40.40	17.14	42.4
Greece	10.69	3.80	35.5
Chile	16.13	5.60	34.7
Poland	38.54	10.60	27.5
Russia	142.89	23.70	16.6
Brazil	188.10	25.90	13.8
China	1,310.00	111.00	8.5
South Africa	44.19	3.60	8.1
Turkey	70.41	5.50	7.8
Vietnam	84.40	5.87	7.0
India	1,100.00	50.60	4.6

10 per cent of the searches each. News comes in the fifth place with 8.7 per cent, and reference-related searches (e.g. online dictionaries, address books or maps) comprise only 5.1 per cent. Hence, it seems that the majority of information uses worldwide are of low EPV values (arts and sports rather than business, references and news).

Table B.3   Categories of search queries (first two levels)

Category	Subcategories
Art (1950)	Animation (165), Architecture (1), Body-art (8), Celebrities (187), Design (6), Entertainment (16), Events (4), Literature (17), Magazines and E-zines (2), Movies (174), Museums (2), Music (839), Performing Arts (265), Photography (4), Radio (5), Television (25), Visual Arts (1)
Games (167)	Board Games (1), Gambling (14), Hand-Eye Coordination (1), Online (34), Paper and Pencil (9), Trading Card Games (3), Video Games (83)
Sports (473)	Baseball (8), Basketball (14), Boxing (1), Cricket (13), Cycling (28), Darts (1), Equestrian (18), Events (33), Fencing (1), Football (32), Golf (2), Handball (1), Hockey (12), Martial Arts (1), Motor-sports (44), On the Web (12), Paintball (8), Skating (1), Soccer (185), Strength Sports (1), Tennis (28), Water Sports (4), Winter Sports (1), Wrestling (20)
Business (173)	Advertising (1), Agriculture and Forestry (1), Business Services (6), Conglomerates (1), Construction and Maintenance (1), Employment (46), Financial Services (53), Food and Related Products (1), Hospitality (2), Industrial Goods and Services (1), International Business (1), Investing (1), Marketing and Advertising (1), Real Estate (14), Shopping (6), Telecommunications (36)
Computers (86)	Data Communications (2), Hardware (11), Internet (20), Multimedia (1), Programming (3), Security (8), Software (41)
News (346)	Breaking News (110), Directories (5), Online Archives (107), Weather (124)
Shopping (180)	Auctions (35), Autos (3), Beauty (1), Classifieds (7), Clothing (15), Computers (2), Consumer Electronics (9), Entertainment (4), Flowers (15), Food (1), General Merchandise (52), Gifts (1), Home and Garden (28), Office Products (1), Price Comparisons (2), Sports (1), Vehicles (1)
Science (12)	Agriculture (1), Astronomy (8), Biology (1), Earth Sciences (2), Technology (10)
Recreation (418)	Autos (49), Boating (2), Collecting (12), Crafts (1), Drawing and Colouring (2), Food (5), Gardening (1), Humour (12), Motorcycles (5), Online (41), Outdoors (2), Parties (1), Pets (25), Sauna (4), Theme Parks (7), Travel (247)
Society (418)	Chats and Forums (69), Ethnicity (2), Folklore (8), Government (35), History (2), Holidays (181), Issues (9), Law (2), Organisations (2), People (13), Politics (15), Relationships (42), Religion and Spirituality (38)

Table B.3 Categories of search queries (first two levels) (*Cont'd*)

Category	Subcategories
Reference (197)	Dictionaries (48), Directories (36), Education (47), Encyclopaedias (12), Flag (1), Libraries (2), Maps (47), Units of Measurement (3)
Health (18)	Alternative (1), Beauty (1), Conditions and Diseases (1), Dentistry (3), Nutrition (9), Organisations (3)
Home (12)	Apartment Living (4), Consumer Information (1), Cooking (1), Do-It-Yourself (1), Family (1), Food (4), Home Improvement (1)
Regional (17)	Africa (2), America (1), Asia (2), Europe (12)

Figure B.1 Search topics worldwide

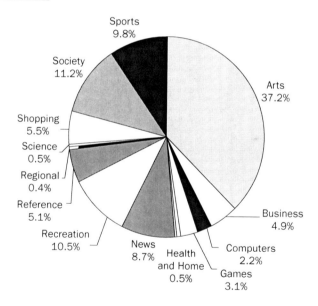

Information uses in different countries

Figure B.2 summarises the percentages of searches for arts and business in different countries. Interestingly, it shows that most countries with a relatively high use of arts-related online information also have a low use of business-related online information and vice versa. A Pearson correlation test[2] between searches in different countries reveals a significant negative correlation (~ −0.5, $p < 0.01$) between the low EPV categories (i.e. arts and

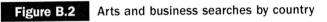

Figure B.2   Arts and business searches by country

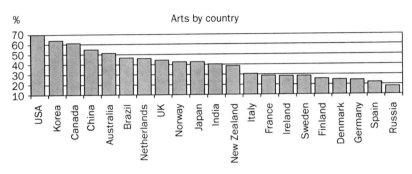

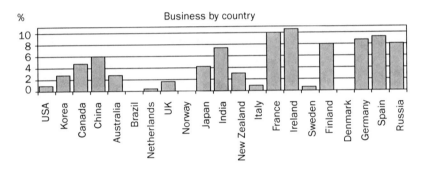

sports) and medium and high EPV categories (i.e. business, computers and references). These negative correlations suggest that online users in different countries understand the potential of the internet and its applications differently. While in some countries (e.g. the USA, Korea, the Netherlands and Australia) many online users tend to search mostly for entertainment, in other countries (e.g. France, Germany and Russia) there are more popular searches related to political and economic information. These trends conform to the findings of the EPV Index in Chapter 4.

Table B.4 summarises the various topics searched in Google and Yahoo![3] in different countries during 2004 and 2005, indicating the percentage of search queries from each category out of the total searches in a country.

The italicised numbers indicate a relatively high share of searches from a certain category. Hence, Table B.4 shows that searching for travel destinations (classified as recreation) is very popular in Denmark, Ireland and Australia. In Ireland, many users search also for business and computer-related information. In Canada as well as in Korea, most popular searches are for entertainment purposes (more than 60 per cent).

Table B.4 Percentage of searches by countries

	Arts	Sports	Games	Recreation	Society	Science	Shopping	News	Reference	Computers	Business
Australia	51.40	13.64	3.18	17.73	3.18	0.00	4.09	3.18	0.45	0.45	2.73
Brazil	46.90	6.86	1.71	3.43	31.43	0.00	1.71	4.57	2.86	0.00	0.00
Canada	61.60	4.74	2.11	11.58	5.79	0.00	3.16	5.79	0.00	0.53	4.74
China	54.80	8.89	2.96	0.74	11.11	0.00	0.74	4.44	8.89	0.00	0.00
Denmark	25.00	14.38	7.50	28.13	6.25	0.00	4.38	8.13	4.38	1.88	0.00
Finland	25.80	3.87	10.32	16.77	18.71	0.00	2.58	6.45	1.94	5.16	7.74
France	28.90	7.23	2.13	12.34	9.36	0.43	11.91	4.68	7.66	2.55	9.79
Germany	24.40	3.41	0.98	9.27	17.56	1.46	7.32	5.85	14.63	5.37	8.78
India	40.00	10.00	0.00	12.73	4.55	1.82	0.00	10.00	11.82	0.91	7.27
Ireland	28.20	2.35	4.71	23.53	0.00	0.00	5.88	5.88	5.88	9.41	10.59
Italy	30.00	21.36	2.73	16.82	10.91	1.82	1.36	10.45	2.27	0.91	0.91
Japan	42.30	3.64	2.73	3.64	9.09	0.00	2.27	16.82	12.27	3.18	4.09
Korea	64.10	6.90	3.45	2.07	5.52	0.00	0.69	10.34	2.07	0.00	2.76
Netherlands	45.90	26.36	2.73	5.45	8.64	0.00	5.45	3.64	0.91	0.45	0.45
New Zealand	38.00	9.00	2.00	14.00	11.00	0.00	8.00	10.00	3.00	2.00	3.00
Norway	43.10	15.38	9.23	10.00	3.08	0.77	0.77	12.31	1.54	1.54	0.00
Russia	18.00	7.33	0.67	15.33	20.00	0.67	11.33	4.00	3.33	6.00	8.00
Spain	22.70	19.09	4.55	15.00	8.18	0.91	5.91	9.09	4.09	0.91	9.09
Sweden	28.00	5.33	0.67	2.67	22.00	0.00	11.33	14.67	7.33	7.33	0.67
UK	44.60	9.14	5.14	12.00	6.86	0.57	5.14	5.71	6.29	1.71	1.71
USA	70.50	11.46	5.00	1.95	2.07	0.73	0.12	6.46	0.00	0.37	0.85

Similarly, in the USA findings indicate a higher share of entertainment-related searches (more than 70 per cent of the popular search queries). In China and India there are many search queries related to higher education and university examinations. These searches, which are classified as reference, are more frequent in China and India than in other countries. Finland and Norway indicate the highest share of games-related searches. In Finland there is also frequent search for chats and forums (classified as society). Both games and chats imply that the majority of searchers in these countries are relatively young. The other country with a relatively higher share of chat and forum-related searches is Sweden, which interestingly enough is a very close neighbour. Sweden also demonstrates a high share of news, shopping and computer-related searches. In France and Germany, again neighbours, searches are varied, and no category is exceptionally high at the national level. At the international level, however, queries about shopping, business and references are relatively frequent in both countries versus other countries. Many popular searches in the Netherlands, Italy and Spain are for sport-related information. In Brazil, which has the highest share of society-related queries, public administration appears among the top searches each month, entailing half of the society-related searches. In Japan there are frequent searches for references (mainly maps and translation tools) and news. Russia displays a high share of business, computer and shopping-related searches. Finally, in the UK there are no remarkable trends of information search.

This brief summary of search topics in different countries was obtained by calculating the percentage of popular search queries from each category in each country over 2004 and 2005. It can provide only a general notion of the different searches worldwide. The indices and statistical analyses in Chapter 4 were designed to address more comprehensively and accurately the search differences between countries and their possible implications for the digital divide.

Notes

1. As extracted from *http://www.clickz.com/showPage.html?page=151151* (accessed March 2007).
2. As the analysis of the different search queries is based on ratio scale (frequency of information uses) and both negative and positive correlations are expected to be found, a Pearson two-tailed correlation test was conducted. A Spearman correlation test yielded similar results.
3. Based on the information provided by Google Zeitgeist and Yahoo! Buzz.

Bibliography

ABC News (2007) 'Google Earth moves Chilean village to Argentina', 29 April, available at: *http://www.abc.net.au/news/stories/2007/04/29/1909200.htm* (accessed June 2008).

Adam, D. and Johnson, B. (2007) 'Google may use games to analyse net users', *The Guardian*, 12 May, available at: *http://technology.guardian.co.uk/news/story/0,,2078061,00.html* (accessed May 2007).

Adorno, T. W. (1991) *The Culture Industry: Selected Essays on Mass Culture*, London: Routledge.

Agarwal, A. (2008) 'Most popular Google subdomains', *Digital Inspiration*, 8 December, available at: *http://www.labnol.org/internet/popular-google-subdomains/5888* (accessed May 2009).

Ahituv, N. (2001) 'The Open Information Society', *Communications of the ACM* 44(6): 48–52.

Al Jazeera (2007) 'Thais to sue Google over king video', 9 May, available at: *http://english.aljazeera.net/NR/exeres/78C68794-FA87-4160-8316-692FEB50E054.htm* (accessed May 2007).

Aldenderfer, M. S. and Blashfield, R. K. (1984) *Cluster Analysis*, Beverly Hills, CA: Sage.

Alexa (2009) 'Site information for Yahoo!', available at: *http://www.alexa.com/siteinfo/yahoo.com* (accessed September 2009).

Anderson, B. (1983) *Imagined Communities*, London: Verso.

Anderson, C. (1977) *Statecraft: An Introduction to Political Choice and Judgment*, New York: John Wiley and Sons.

Anderson, C. (2006) *The Long Tail*, London: Random House Business.

Anderson, R. H., Bikson, T. K., Law, S. A. and Mitchell, B. M. (1995) *Universal Access to Email – Feasability and Societal Implications*, Santa Monica, CA: Rand.

Asadi, S. and Jamali, H. R. (2004) 'Shifts in search engine development: a review of past, present and future trends in research on search engines', *Webology* 1(2), available at: *http://www.webology.ir/2004/v1n2/a6.html* (accessed January 2007).

Astor, M. (2006) 'Google to shut down Orkut communities', *USA Today*, 24 May, available at: *http://www.usatoday.com/tech/news/2006-05-24-google-brazil_x.htm* (accessed October 200).

Auchard, E. (2007a) 'Google signs software deals in two African nations', *Reuters*, 19 March, available at: *http://www.reuters.com/article/technologyNews/idUSN1929294120070320* (accessed October 2009).

Auchard, E. (2007b) 'AFP, Google News settle lawsuit over Google News', *Reuters*, 7 April, available at: *http://www.reuters.com/article/ousiv/idUSN0728115420070407* (accessed June 2008).

Babe, R. E. (1995) *Communication and the Transformation of Economics*, Boulder, CO: Westview Press.

Bagdikian, B. (2004) *The New Media Monopoly*, Boston, MA: Beacon Press Books.

Bar-Ilan, J. (2004) 'The use of web search engines in information science research', in B. Cronin (ed.) *Annual Review of Information Science and Technology Vol. 33*, Medford, NY: Information Today, pp. 231–88.

Bar-Ilan, J. (2007) 'Google bombing from a time perspective', *Journal of Computer-Mediated Communication* 12(3), available at: *http://jcmc.indiana.edu/vol12/issue3/bar-ilan.html* (accessed November 2007).

Barabási, A. L. (2002) *Linked: The New Science of Networks*, Cambridge: Perseus.

Barbaro, M. and Zeller, T. (2006) 'A face is exposed for AOL searcher no. 4417749', *The New York Times*, 9 August, available at: *http://www.nytimes.com/2006/08/09/technology/09aol.html* (accessed June 2008).

Barlow, J. P. (1996) 'A declaration of the independence of cyberspace', available at: *http://www.eff.org/~barlow/Declaration-Final.html* (accessed November 2004).

Barnard, F. M. (2004) *Herder on Nationality, Humanity, and History*, Montreal, Quebec: McGill-Queen's Press.

Barnett, G. A. (2001) 'A longitudinal analysis of the international telecommunications network: 1978–1996', *American Behavioral Scientist* 44(10): 1638–55.

Barnett, G. A. and Kim, K. (1996) 'The determinants of international news flow: a network analysis', *Communication Research* 23(3): 323–52.

Barney, D. (2004) *The Network Society*, Cambridge: Polity Press.

Baron, N. S. (2008) *Always On: Language in an Online and Mobile World*, Oxford: Oxford University Press.

Barzilai-Nahon, K. (2006a) 'Gatekeepers, virtual communities and their gated: multidimensional tensions in cyberspace', *International Journal of Communications, Law and Policy* 11 (Autumn): 1–28.

Barzilai-Nahon, K. (2006b) 'Gaps and bits: conceptualizing measurements for digital divide/s', *The Information Society* 22(5): 269–78.

Battelle, J. (2003) 'An open source search engine', *Search Engine Watch*, 11 September, available at: *http://searchenginewatch.com/showPage.html?page=3071971* (accessed May 2007).

Battelle, J. (2005) *The Search: How Google and Its Rivals Rewrote the Rules of Business and Transformed Our Culture*, Boston, MA; London: Nicholas Brearley Publishing.

Bawden, D. (2001) 'Information and digital literacies: a review of concepts', *Journal of Documentation* 57(2): 218–59.

BBC News (2003) '"Miserable failure" links to Bush', 7 December, available at: *http://newsvote.bbc.co.uk/mpapps/pagetools/print/news.bbc.co.uk/1/hi/world/americas/3298443.stm* (accessed March 2006).

BBC News (2006a) 'Privacy fears hit Google Search', 10 February, available at: *http://newsvote.bbc.co.uk/mpapps/pagetools/print/news.bbc.co.uk/2/hi/technology/4700002.stm* (accessed March 2006).

BBC News (2006b) 'Hacker fears "UFO cover-up"', available at: *http://news.bbc.co.uk/2/hi/programmes/click_online/4977134.stm* (accessed June 2006).

BBC News (2006c) 'Google buys YouTube for $1.65bn', 10 October, available at: *http://news.bbc.co.uk/2/hi/business/6034577.stm* (accessed January 2007).

BBC News (2007a) 'How governments censor the web', 22 March, available at: *http://news.bbc.co.uk/2/hi/technology/6475911.stm* (accessed March 2007).

BBC News (2007b) 'Google ranked "worst" on privacy', 11 June, available at: *http://news.bbc.co.uk/1/hi/technology/6740075.stm* (accessed June 2008).

BBC News (2007c) 'Google Search challenge dismissed', 21 March, available at: *http://news.bbc.co.uk/1/hi/business/6474183.stm* (accessed March 2007).

BBC News (2009) 'All clear for Google Street View', 23 April, available at: *http://news.bbc.co.uk/2/hi/technology/8014178.stm* (accessed July 2009).

Beardsworth, A. (1980) 'Analyzing press content: some technical and methodological issues' in H. Christian (ed.) *Sociology of Journalism and the Press*, Keele: Keele University Press, pp. 371–95.

Bell, D. (2001) *An Introduction to Cybercultures*, London: Routledge.

Beniger, J. R. (1986) *The Control Revolution: Technological and Economic Origins of the Information Society*, Cambridge, MA: Harvard University Press.

Bennett, L. W. (1990) 'Toward a theory of press-state relations in the United States', *Journal of Communication* 40(2): 103–125.

Benton Foundation (1998) *Losing Ground Bit by Bit: Low-Income Communities in the Information Age*, Washington, DC: Benton Foundation and National Urban League.

Benton, M. and Frazier, P. (1976) 'The agenda setting function of the mass media at three levels of "information holding"', *Communication Research* 3: 261–74.

Bergman, M. K. (2001) 'The deep web: surfacing hidden value', *The Journal of Electronic Publishing* 7(1), available at: *http://www.press.umich.edu/jep/07-01/bergman.html* (accessed November 2005).

Berkman Center for Internet and Society (2002) 'Replacement of Google with alternative search systems in China: documentation and screen shots', available at: *http://cyber.law.harvard.edu/filtering/china/google-replacements/* (accessed October 2007).

Blakely, R. (2006) 'Google offers printable books online', *Times Online*, 30 August, available at: *http://business.timesonline.co.uk/article/0,,9075-2335189.html* (accessed June 2008).

Bohman, J. (2004) 'Expanding dialogue: The internet, the public sphere and prospects for transnational democracy', in N. Crossley, J. M. Roberts (eds) *After Habermas: New Perspectives on the Public Sphere*, Oxford: Blackwell, pp. 131–55.

Bonfadelli, H. (2002) 'The internet and knowledge gaps: a theoretical and empirical investigation', *European Journal of Communication* 17: 65–84.

Borgatti, S. P. (2002) *NetDraw: Graph Visualization Software*, Harvard, Cambridge, MA: Analytic Technologies.

Borgman, C. L. (2000) *From Gutenberg to the Global Information Infrastructure: Access to Information in the Networked World*, Cambridge, MA: MIT Press.

Borgmann, A. (1999) *Holding on to Reality: The Nature of Information at the Turn of the Millennium*, Chicago, IL: University of Chicago.

Bounds, A. (2007) 'Google searches for European lobbyists', *Financial Times*, 19 March, available at: *http://www.ft.com/cms/s/8134e52e-d655-11db-99b7-000b5df10621.html* (accessed March 2007).

Boyd, D. M. and Ellison, N. B. (2007) 'Social network sites: definition, history, and scholarship', *Journal of Computer-Mediated Communication* 13(1), available at: *http://jcmc.indiana.edu/vol13/issue1/boyd.ellison.html* (accessed May 2009).

Boyd-Barrett, O. and Tantanen, T. (eds) (1998) *The Globalization of News*, London: Sage.

Brannan, P. and Albright, D. (2006) 'ISIS imagery brief: new activities at the Esfahan and Natanz nuclear sites in Iran', *The Institute for Science and International Security*, 14 April, available at: *http://www.isis-online .org/publications/iran/newactivities.pdf* (accessed June 2008).

Broersma, M. (2001) 'AI gets down to business', *ZDNet*, 23 January, available at: *http://news.zdnet.co.uk/internet/0,1000000097,2083916,00 .htm* (accessed June 2008).

Bucy, E. P. (2000) 'Social access to the internet', *Press/Politics* 5: 50–61.

Butler, D. (2007) 'Google provides a view of Darfur tragedy', *San Francisco Chronicle*, 10 April, available at: *http://www.sfgate.com/cgi-bin/ article.cgi?f=/n/a/2007/04/10/national/w141547D31.DTL&type=poli tics* (accessed June 2008).

Callicott, B. and Vaughn, D. (2006) 'Google Scholar vs Library Scholar: testing the performance of Schoogle', *Internet Reference Services Quarterly* 10(3&4): 71–88.

Card, J. (2006) 'The geography of the Korean psyche', *Asia Times Online*, 6 June, available at: *http://www.atimes.com/atimes/Korea/ HF06Dg01.html* (accessed June 2006).

Cardon, D. and Granjon, F. (2005) 'Social networks and cultural practices: a case study of young avid screen users in France', *Social Networks* 27: 301–35.

Caves, R. (2000) *Creative Industries: Contracts between Art and Commerce*, Cambridge: Harvard University Press.

Castells, M. (1996) *The Rise of Network Society. The Information Age: Economy, Society and Culture Vol. 1*, Oxford: Basil Blackwell.

Castells, M. (1997) *The Power of Identity Vol. 2*, Oxford: Blackwell.

Castells, M. (2000) 'The global economy', in D. Held and A. McGrew (eds) *The Global Transformations Reader*, Cambridge: Polity Press and Blackwell Publishers, pp. 259–73.

Castells, M. (2004) 'Informationalism, networks, and the network society: a theoretical blueprinting', in M. Castells (ed.) *The Network Society: A Cross-Cultural Perspective*, Northampton, MA: Edward Elgar, pp. 3–48.

Chapman, M. (2006) 'Google News launches in Arabic', *Information World Review*, 19 June, available at: *http://www.iwr.co.uk/ information-world- review/news/2158533/google-news-launches-arabic* (accessed June 2006).

Chau, M., Fang, X. and Yang, C. C. (2007) 'Web searching in Chinese: a study of a search engine in Hong Kong', *Journal of the American Society for Information Science and Technology (JASIST)* 58(7): 1044–54.

Cho, J. and Roy, S. (2004) 'Impact of search engines on page popularity', paper presented at the 13th International Conference on the World Wide Web, 17–20 May, New York.

Chowdhury, S. (2007) 'Google to help Mumbai police track offenders', *The Indian Express*, 12 March, available at: *http://www.indianexpress .com/story/25427.html* (accessed June 2008).

Chrisafis, A. (2006) 'Chirac unveils his grand plan to restore French pride', *The Guardian*, 26 April, available at: *http://technology .guardian.co.uk/news/story/0,,1761482,00.html* (accessed January 2007).

Ciolek, T. M. (2003) 'The internet and its users: the physical dimensions of cyberpolitics in Eastern Asia', paper presented at From the Book to the Internet: Communications Technologies, Human Motions, and Cultural Formations in Eastern Asia, 16–18 October, University of Oregon, available at: *http://www.ciolek.com/PAPERS/oregon-2003- text.html* (accessed December 2005).

Claburn, T. (2006) 'Google Earth adds high-resolution images', *Information Week*, 19 June, available at: *http://www.informationweek .com/software/showArticle.jhtml?articleID=189500473* (accessed June 2006).

Cleaver, J. H. M. (1998) 'The Zapatista effect: the internet and the rise of an alternative political fabric (Mexican Zapatista National Liberation Army)', *Journal of International Affairs* 51(2): 621–22.

Clement, A. and Shade, L. R. (2000) 'The access rainbow: conceptualizing universal access to the information/communication infrastructure', in M. Gurstein (ed.) *Community Informatics: Enabling Communities with Information and Communications Technologies*, Hershey, PA: Idea Group Publishing, pp. 32–51.

Compaine, B. M. and Gomery, D. (eds) (2000) *Who Owns the Media? Concentration of Ownership in the Mass Communications Industry*, Mahwah, NJ: Erlbaum.

comScore (2009a) 'Google sites ranks as top internet property worldwide', 23 January, available at: *http://www.comscore.com/press/ release.asp?press=2698* (accessed March 2009).

comScore (2009b) 'comScore study highlights challenges and opportunities for Microsoft–Yahoo! Search partnership', 14 August, available at: *http://www.comscore.com/Press_Events/Press_Releases/ 2009/8/comScore_Study_Highlights_Challenges_and_Opportunities_ for_Microsoft-Yahoo!_Search_Partnership* (accessed September 2009).

comScore (2009c) 'YouTube surpasses 100 million US viewers for the first time', 20 March, available at: *http://www.comscore.com/Press_ Events/Press_Releases/2009/3/YouTube_Surpasses_100_Million_US_ Viewers* (accessed July 2009).

comScore (2009d) 'comScore releases June 2009 US search engine rankings', 16 July, available at: *http://www.comscore.com/Press_Events/*

Press_Releases/2009/7/comScore_Releases_June_2009_U.S._Search_ Engine_Rankings (accessed September 2009).

comScore (2009e) 'Global search market draws more than 100 billion searches per month', 31 August, available at: *http://www.comscore.com/ Press_Events/Press_Releases/2009/8/Global_Search_Market_Draws_ More_than_100_Billion_Searches_per_Month* (accessed September 2009).

Copping, J. (2005) 'Insurgents "using Google Earth"', *The Daily Telegraph*, 17 December, available at: *http://www.telegraph.co.uk/ news/main.jhtml?xml=/news/2005/12/18/ngoog18.xml&sSheet=/news/ 2005/12/18/ixhome.html* (accessed June 2008).

Cox, R. (1987) *Production Power and World Order: Social Forces in the Making of History*, New York: Columbia University Press.

Cronin, B. (2001) 'Hyperauthorship: a postmodern perversion or evidence of a structural shift in scholarly communication practices?', *Journal of the American Society for Information Science and Technology* 52(7): 558–69.

Cross, R., Borgatti, S. and Parker, A. (2002) 'Making invisible work visible: using social network analysis to support human networks', *California Management Review* 44(2): 25–46.

Crystal, D. (2003) *English as a Global Language* (2nd edn), Cambridge: Cambridge University Press.

Dahl, R. (1985) *A Preface to Economic Democracy*, Berkley, CA: University of California Press.

Danet, B. and Herring, S. C. (2007) *The Multilingual internet: Language, Culture, and Communication Online*, Oxford: Oxford University Press.

Darby, T. (2006) 'Nakba – the Palestinian catastrophe', *Google Earth Community*, available at: *http://bbs.keyhole.com/ubb/showflat.php/ Cat/0/Number/310630/an//page//vc/1* (accessed April 2008).

De Swaan, A. (1991) 'Notes on the emerging global language system: regional, national and supranatural', *Media, Culture and Society* 13(3): 309–24.

De Vries, L. (2006) 'Feds seek Google records in porn probe', *CBS News*, 19 January, available at: *http://www.cbsnews.com/stories/2006/01/19/ tech/main1221309.shtml* (accessed June 2008).

Deans, J. (2002) 'Chinese government backs down on Google', *The Guardian*, 13 September, available at: *http://www.guardian.co.uk/ internetnews/story/0,7369,791772,00.html* (accessed November 2005).

Dearing, J. W. and Rogers, E. M. (1996) *Communication Concepts 6: Agenda-Setting*, London: Sage.

Deshpande, R. (2007) 'Google Earth agrees to blur pix of key Indian sites', *The Economic Times*, 4 February, available at: *http://economictimes .indiatimes.com/articleshow/1559349.cms* (accessed June 2008).

DiMaggio, P. and Hargittai, E. (2002) 'From the digital divide to digital inequality', paper presented at The Annual Meeting of the American Sociological Association, 16–19 August, Chicago, IL.

DiMaggio, P., Hargittai, E., Neuman, W. R. and Robinson, J. P. (2001) 'Social implications of internet', *Annual Review of Sociology* 27: 307–36.

DiMaggio, P., Hargittai, E., Celeste, C. and Shafer, S. (2004) 'From unequal access to differentiated use: a literature review and agenda for research on digital inequality', in K. Neckerman (ed.) *Social Inequality*, New York: Russell Sage Foundation, pp. 355–400.

Dmoz (2005) 'Open Directory Project', available at: *http://dmoz.org/about.html* (accessed January 2005).

Dordoy, D. and Mellor, M. (2001) 'Grassroots environmental movements: mobilisation in an information age', in F. Webster (ed.) *Culture and Politics in the Information Age: A New Politics*, London: Routledge, pp. 167–82.

Downs, A. (1957) *An Economic Theory of Democracy*, New York: Harpers and Row.

Entman, R. (2004) *Projections of Power: Framing News, Public Opinion, and US Foreign Policy*, Chicago, IL: The University of Chicago Press.

Estadao (2007) 'Polícia Usa Google Earth Para Achar Criminoso no RS', 9 January, available at: *http://www.estadao.com.br/tecnologia/internet/noticias/2007/jan/09/70.htm* (accessed January 2007).

Evans, T. (ed.) (1998) *Human Rights Fifty Years on: A Reappraisal*, London: St. Martin's Press.

Fabrikant, G. Hansell, S. (2007) 'Viacom tells YouTube: hands off', *The New York Times*, 3 February, available at: *http://www.nytimes.com/2007/02/03/technology/03tube.html* (accessed October 2009).

Fallows, D. (2005) 'Search engine users: internet searchers are confident, satisfied and trusting – but they are also unaware and naïve', *Pew Research Center for the People and the Press*, 23 January, available at: *http://www.pewinternet.org/pdfs/PIP_Searchengine_users.pdf* (accessed September 2006).

Fallows, D. (2008) 'Almost half of all internet users now use search engines on a typical day', *Pew Research Center for the People and the Press*, 6 August, available at: *http://www.pewinternet.org/~media/Files/Reports/2008/PIP_Search_Aug08.pdf.pdf* (accessed April 2009).

Falun Dafa (2006) 'About Falun Dafa', available at: *http://www.falundafa.org/eng* (accessed June 2006).

Feldman, M. P. (2002) 'The internet revolution and the geography of innovation', *International Social Science Journal* 54: 47–56.

Fleischer, P. (2007) 'Privacy at Google', *http://www.google.com/events/ docs/policyblog_uk_privacy_booklet.pdf* (accessed April 2008).

Florida, R. (2002) *The Rise of the Creative Class*, New York: Basic Books.

Foster, R. J. (1991) 'Making national cultures in the global ecumene', *Annual Review of Anthropology* 20 (October): 235–260.

Fox, B. (2005) 'Google searches for quality not quantity', *New Scientist*, 30 April, p. 24, available at: *http://www.newscientist.com/article .ns?id=mg18624975.900* (accessed January 2007).

Franklin, B. (1994) *Packaging Politics: Political Communications in Britain's Media Democracy*, London: Edward Arnold.

Freedom House (2005) 'Freedom in the world country ratings', New York: Freedom House', available at: *http://www.freedomhouse.org/ratings/ index.htm* (accessed January 2006).

Gamble, A. (1990) 'Theories of British politics', *Political Studies* 38: 404–20.

Gandal, N. (2001) 'The dynamics of competition in the internet search engine market', *International Journal of Industrial Organization* 19: 1103–17.

Garnham, N. (2001) 'Information society theory as ideology: a critique', *Information, Communication and Society* 3(2): 139–52.

Gaunt, P. (1990) *Choosing the News: The Profit Factor in News Selection*, Westport, CT: Greenwood Press.

Geens, S. (2006) 'Bahrain bans Google Earth', *Ogle Earth*, 7 August, available at: *http://www.ogleearth.com/2006/08/bahrain_bans_go.html* (accessed April 2008).

Geens, S. (2007) 'Did Google censor Basra imagery?', *Ogle Earth*, 14 January, available at: *http://www.ogleearth.com/2007/01/did_google_ cens.html* (accessed January 2007).

Gerhart, S. (2004) 'Do web search engines suppress controversy?', *First Monday* 9(1), available at: *http://firstmonday.org/issues/issue9_1/ gerhart/index.html* (accessed February, 2007).

Ghanem, S. (1997) 'Filling in the tapestry: The second level of agenda setting', in M. McCombs, D. L. Shaw and D. Weaver (eds) *Communication and Democracy*, Mahwah, NJ: Erlbaum, pp. 3–14.

Gharbia, S. B. (2007) 'Morocco: stop internet censorship!', *Global Voices Advocacy*, available at: *http://advocacy.globalvoicesonline .org/2007/10/29/morocco-stop-internet-censorship* (accessed April 2008).

Gilpin, R. (1987) *The Political Economy of International Relations*, Princeton, NJ: Princeton University Press.

Ginsberg, J., Mohebbi, M. H., Patel, R. S., Brammer, L., Smolinski, M. S. and Brilliant, L. (2009) 'Detecting influenza epidemics using search engine query data', *Nature* 457: 1012–14.

Gluck, C. (2005) 'Taiwan protests over Google map', BBC News, 4 October, available at: *http://news.bbc.co.uk/go/pr/fr/-/2/hi/asia-pacific/4308678.stm* (accessed October 2005).

Golan, G. and Wanta, W. (2001) 'Second-level agenda setting in the New Hampshire primary: A comparison of coverage in three newspapers and public perceptions of candidates', *Journalism and Mass Communication Quarterly* 78: 247–59.

Google (2005) 'Google 2004 and 2005 Zeitgeist Archive', available at: *http://www.google.com/intl/en/press/zeitgeist/archive2004.html* (accessed March 2005).

Google (2006a) 'Statistical machine translation live', available at: *http://googleresearch.blogspot.com/2006/04/statistical-machine-translation-live.html* (accessed December 2007).

Google (2006b) 'Google Toolbar privacy notice', available at: *http://www.google.com/support/toolbar/?quick=privacy* (accessed June 2006).

Google (2006c) 'Gmail privacy policy', available at: *http://mail.google.com/mail/help/intl/en/privacy.html* (accessed June 2006).

Google (2006d) 'Happy birthday, Google Earth', available at: *http://googleblog.blogspot.com/2006/06/happy-birthday-google-earth.html* (accessed January 2008).

Google (2007a) 'Google history', available at: *http://www.google.com/corporate/history.html* (accessed March 2007).

Google (2007b) 'Corporate information: Google management', available at: *http://www.google.com/intl/en/corporate/execs.html* (accessed June 2008).

Google (2007c) 'Google Earth coverage', available at: *http://web.archive.org/web/20071215121224/http://earth.google.com/data.html* (accessed October 2009).

Google (2007d) 'Company overview', available at: *http://www.google.com/intl/en/corporate/index.html* (accessed March 2007).

Google (2008) 'Our search: Google technology', available at: *http://www.google.com/technology* (accessed June 2008).

Google (2009a) 'About Google Scholar', available at: *http://scholar.google.com/intl/en/scholar/about.html* (accessed May 2009).

Google (2009b) 'Google Maps – Sources of information', available at: *http://maps.google.com/support/bin/answer.py?hl=en&answer=7103* (accessed October 2009).

Google (2009c) 'Using GPS devices with Google Earth', available at: *http://earth.google.com/userguide/v4/ug_gps.html* (accessed July 2009).

Grabill, J. T. (2003) 'On divides and interfaces: access, class, and computers', *Computers and Composition* 20(4): 455–72.

Graham, S. (1998) 'The end of geography or the explosion of place? Conceptualizing space, place and information technology progress', *Human Geography* 22(2): 165–85.

Hafner, K. and Rai, S. (2005) 'Governments tremble at Google's bird's-eye view', *The New York Times*, 20 December, available at: *http://www.nytimes.com/2005/12/20/technology/20image.html?ex=1292734800&en=91529f7772801391&ei=5088* (accessed June 2008).

Hafner, K. and Ritchel, M. (2006) 'Google resists US subpoena of search data', *The New York Times*, 20 January, available at: *http://www.nytimes.com/2006/01/20/technology/20google.html* (accessed October 2009).

Haines, L. (2005a) 'Google Earth threatens democracy', *The Register*, 13 September, available at: *http://www.theregister.co.uk/2005/09/13/google_earth_threatens_democracy* (accessed June 2006).

Haines, L. (2005b) 'South Korea throws strop at Google Earth', *The Register*, 31 August, available at: *http://www.theregister.co.uk/2005/08/31/google_earth_korea* (accessed April 2008).

Harding, T. (2007a) 'Terrorists "use Google maps to hit UK troops"', *The Daily Telegraph*, 13 January, available at: *http://www.telegraph.co.uk/news/main.jhtml?xml=/news/2007/01/13/wgoogle13.xml* (accessed June 2008).

Harding, T. (2007b) 'Google blots out Iraq bases on internet', *Daily Telegraph*, 21 January, available at: *http://www.telegraph.co.uk/news/main.jhtml?xml=/news/2007/01/20/wgoogle20.xml* (accessed June 2008).

Hardt, M. and Negri, A. (2000) *Empire*, Cambridge, MA: Harvard University Press.

Hargittai, E. (2000) 'Open portals or closed gates? Channeling content on the world wide web', *Poetics* 27: 233–53.

Hargittai, E. (2002) 'Second-level digital divide: differences in people's online skills', *First Monday* 7(4), available at: *http://firstmonday.org/htbin/cgiwrap/bin/ojs/index.php/fm/article/view/942/864* (accessed October 2009).

Hargittai, E. (2003) 'The digital divide and what to do about it', in D. C. Jones (ed.) *New Economy Handbook*, San Diego, CA: Academic Press, pp. 822–41.

Harley, B. J. (1988) 'Secrecy and silences: the hidden agenda of state cartography in early modern Europe', *Imago Mundi* 40: 57–76.

Harrigan, K. R. (1985) 'An application of clustering for strategic group analysis', *Strategic Management Journal* 6: 55–73.

He, B., Patel, M., Zhang, Z. and Chang, K. C. (2007) 'Accessing the deep web: a survey', *Communications of the ACM* 50(5): 94–101.

Headrick, D. R. (1991) *The Invisible Weapon: Telecommunications and International Politics 1851–1945*, New York: Oxford University Press.

Held, D. and McGrew, A. (eds) (2002) *Governing Globalization: Power, Authority and Global Governance*, Cambridge: Polity Press.

Helft, M. (2007) 'Google zooms in too close for some', *The New York Times*, 1 June, available at: *http://www.nytimes.com/2007/06/01/technology/01private.html?_r=2&oref=slogin&oref=slogin* (accessed April 2008).

Helft, M. and Stelter, B. (2009) 'Google puts small ads on pages of news site', *The New York Times*, 26 February, available at: *http://www.nytimes.com/2009/02/27/technology/internet/27google.html* (accessed June 2009).

Herman, E. S. and Chomsky, N. (2002) *Manufacturing Consent: The Political Economy of the Mass Media*, New York: Pantheon Books.

Herman, E. S. and McChesney, R. (2000) 'The Global Media', in D. Held and A. McGrew (eds) *The Global Transformations Reader*, Cambridge: Polity Press and Blackwell Publishers, pp. 216–29.

Hess, C. and Ostrom, E. (2006) 'Introduction: an overview of the knowledge commons', in C. Hess and E. Ostrom (eds) *Understanding Knowledge as a Commons: From Theory to Practice*, Cambridge, MA: MIT Press, pp. 1–26.

Hill, K. A. and Hughes, J. E. (1998) *Cyber-politics: Citizen Activism in the Age of the Internet*, Lanham, MD: Rowman and Littlefield.

Hillis, S. (2007) 'Google combines search types', *Reuters*, 16 May, available at: *http://www.reuters.com/article/technologyNews/idUSN1625056220070516* (accessed May 2007).

Hills, J. (2002) *The Struggle for Control of Global Communication: The Formative Century*, Urbana, IL: University of Illinois Press.

Himanen, P. (2001) *The Hacker Ethic and the Spirit of the Information Age*, New York: Random House.

Himanen, P. (2004) 'Challenges of the global information society', a report for the Committee for the Future, the Parliament of Finland', available at: *http://www.eduskunta.fi/efakta/vk/tuv/challenges_of_the_globalinformationsociety.pdf* (accessed July 2006).

Hindman, M., Tsioutsiouliklis, K. and Johnson, J. (2003) 'Googlearchy: How a few heavily-linked sites dominate politics on the web', paper presented at the Annual Meeting of the Midwest Political Science Association, 3–6 April, Chicago, IL.

Hinman, L. M. (2005) 'Esse est indicato in Google: ethical and political issues in search engines', *International Review of Information Ethics* 3: 20–5.

Hinton, S. (1999) 'Portal sites: emerging structures for internet control', Research Report No. 6, La Trobe University Online Media Program, available at: *http://www.latrobe.edu.au/teloz/reports/hinton.pdf* (accessed December 2007).

Hirst, P. Q. and Thompson, G. F. (1999) *Globalization in Question: The International Economy and the Possibilities of Governance* (2nd edn), Cambridge: Polity Press.

Hoffman, D. L. and Novak, P. T. (1998) 'Bridging the racial divide on the internet', *Science* 280(5362): 390–1.

Hoffman, D. L. and Novak, P. T. (1999) 'Examining the relationship of race to internet access and usage over time', in B. M. Compaine (ed.) *The Digital Divide: Facing a Crisis or Creating a Myth?* Cambridge, MA: MIT Press, pp. 47–97.

Holtz-Bacha, C. and Norris, P. (2001) 'To entertain, inform and educate: still the role of public television in the 1990s?', *Political Communications* 18(2): 123–40.

Hopkins, H. (2007) 'Search engines larger than adult sites – stats from London internet peeps event', *Hitwise Intelligence*, 30 January, available at: *http://weblogs.hitwise.com/heather-hopkins/2007/01/ search_engines_larger_than_adu.html* (accessed March 2007).

Horrigan, J. B. (2006) 'Online news: For many home broadband users, the internet is a primary news source', available at: *http://www .pewinternet.org/pdfs/PIP_News.and.Broadband.pdf* (accessed March 2006).

Howard, P., Rainie, L. and Jones, S. (2001) 'Days and nights on the internet: the impact of a diffusing technology', *American Behavioral Scientist* 45(3): 383–404.

Hurlbert, W. (2004) 'Authority sites and necessary content', *SEO Chat, Free Developer Magazine*, 28 April, available at: *http://www.seochat.com/index .php?option=content&task=view&id=78* (accessed September 2004).

Ignatieff, M. (2003) *Empire Lite: Nation Building in Bosnia, Kosovo, Afghanistan*, London: Vintage.

Innis, H. A. (1951) *The Bias of Communication*, Toronto: University of Toronto Press.

Innis, H. A. (1972) *Empire and Communication*, Toronto: University of Toronto Press.

International Telecoms Union (ITU) (2006) 'Strategic plan for the union 2004–2007', available at: *http://www.itu.int/aboutitu/strategic_plans/ 04-07/index.html* (accessed August 2006).

Internet World Stats (2009) 'World internet users and population stats', available at: *http://www.internetworldstats.com/stats.htm* (accessed November 2009).

Introna, L. D. and Nissenbaum, H. (2000) 'Shaping the web: why the politics of search engines matters', *Information Society* 16(3): 169–86.

iProspect (2004) Search engine marketing firm iprospect survey confirms search engine loyalty exists', 14 April, available at: *http://www.iprospect.com/media/press2004_04_14.htm* (accessed September 2009).

IRIN (2006a) 'SOMALIA: Year in review 2005: Still waiting for change', available at: *http://www.irinnews.org/report.asp?ReportID=51137* (accessed May 2006).

IRIN (2006b) 'IRAQ-SYRIA: Expatriates begin voting', available at: *http://www.irinnews.org/report.asp?ReportID=50680* (accessed May 2006).

IRIN (2006c) 'UZBEKISTAN: Year in review 2005 – Growing isolation', available at: *http://www.irinnews.org/report.asp?ReportID=51078* (accessed May 2006).

IRIN (2006d) 'WEST AFRICA: China tours region to boost strategic ties', available at: *http://www.irinnews.org/report.asp?ReportID=51240* (accessed May 2006).

Izadi, F. and Saghaye-Biria, H. (2007) 'A discourse analysis of elite American newspaper editorials', *Journal of Communication Inquiry* 31(2): 140–65.

Jacso, P. (2005) 'As we may search – comparison of major features of the Web of Science, Scopus, and Google Scholar citation-based and citation-enhanced databases', *Current Science* 89(9): 1537–47.

Jacso, P. (2008) 'Google Scholar revisited', *Online Information Review* 32(1): 102–14.

Jamison, K. H. and Campbell, K. K. (1988) *The Interplay of Influence* (2nd edn), Belmont, CA: Wadsworth.

Janetzko, D. (2008) 'Objectivity, reliability, and validity of search engine count estimates', *International Journal of internet Science* 3(1): 7–33.

Jansen, B. J. and Spink, A. (2003) 'An analysis of web information seeking and use: documents retrieved versus documents viewed', paper presented at the 4th International Conference on Internet Computing, 23–26 June, Las Vegas, NV.

Jansen, B. J. and Spink, A. (2004) 'How are we searching the world wide web? A comparison of nine-search engine transaction logs', *Information Processing and Management* 42: 248–63.

Jansen, B. J., Spink, A. and Saracevic, T. (2000) 'Real life, real users and real needs: A study and analysis of users' queries on the web', *Information Processing and Management* 36(2): 207–27.

Johnson, B. (2006) 'Britain turns off – and logs on', *The Guardian*, 8 March, available at: *http://www.guardian.co.uk/technology/2006/mar/08/news.broadcasting* (accessed July 2007).

Johnson, S. C. (1967) 'Hierarchical clustering schemes', *Psychometrika* 38: 241–54.

Kalman, M. (2007) 'Israel's top secret sites on Google Earth', *San Francisco Chronicle*, 10 October, available at: *http://www.sfgate.com/cgi-bin/article .cgi?f=/c/a/2007/10/10/MNVASLM01.DTL* (accessed June 2008).

Kaplan, R. (1994) *Freedom Review*, New York: Freedom House.

Kavassalis, P., Lelis, P., Rafea, M. and Haridi, S. (2004) 'What makes a website popular?', *Communications of the ACM* 47(2): 50–5.

Kellerman, A. (2002) *The Internet on Earth: A Geography of Information*, London: Wiley.

Kennedy, P. (1989) *The Rise and Fall of the Great Powers: Economic Change and Military Conflict from 1500 to 2000*, New York: Vintage Books.

Kiousis, S. (2004) 'Explicating media salience: a factor analysis of *New York Times* issue coverage during the 2000 US presidential election', *Journal of Communication* 54(1): 71–87.

Knight, C. S. (2007) 'The top 100 alternative search engines', *Read/Write Web*, 29 January, available at: *http://www.readwriteweb.com/archives/top_ 100_alternative_search_engines.php* (accessed February 2007).

Knight, W. (2004) 'Google omits controversial news stories in China', *New Scientist*, 21 September, available at: *http://www.newscientist .com/article/dn6426-google-omits-controversial-news-stories-in-china.html* (accessed June 2008).

Kopytoff, V. (2007a) 'Google surpasses Microsoft as world's most-visited site', *San Francisco Chronicle*, 25 April, available at: *http://www .sfgate.com/cgi-bin/article.cgi?f=/c/a/2007/04/25/GOOGLE.TMP& type=business* (accessed June 2008).

Kopytoff, V. (2007b) 'Top secret, in plain view Google Earth may blur the image, but others don't', *San Francisco Chronicle*, 18 May, available at: *http://www.sfgate.com/cgi-bin/article.cgi?f=/c/a/2007/05/18/ GOOGLE.TMP&feed=rss.news* (accessed April 2008).

Kroes, R. (2003) 'The internet: an instrument of Americanization?' in U. Beck, N. Sznaider and R. Winter (eds) *Global America? The Cultural Consequences of Globalization*, Liverpool: Liverpool University Press, pp. 235–77.

La Monica, P. R. (2007) 'NBC, News Corp. team up against YouTube', *CNN*, 22 March, available at: *http://money.cnn.com/2007/03/22/ news/companies/nbc_newscorp/?postversion=2007032212* (accessed March 2006).

Laclau, E. (ed.) (1994) *The Making of Political Identities*, London: Verso.

Lance, G. N. and Williams, W. T. (1967) 'A general theory of classificatory sorting strategies', *Computer Journal* 9: 60–4.

Lash, S. (2002) *Critique of Information*, London: Sage.

Lawrence, S. and Giles, L. (1998) 'Searching the world wide web', *Science* 280(5360): 98–100.

Lawrence, S. and Giles, L. (1999) 'Accessibility of information on the web', *Nature* 400: 107–9, available at: *http://clgiles.ist.psu.edu/papers/Intelligence-2000-Nature-reprint.pdf* (accessed October 2007).

Lazarus, W. and Mora, F. (2000) *Online Content for Low-Income and Underserved Americans: The Digital Divide's New Frontier*, Santa Monica, CA: The Children's Partnership.

Lessig, L. (1999) *Code and Other Laws of Cyberspace*, New York: Basic.

Leung, K. C. (2007) 'Google Map in China', available at: *http://www.think different.to/googlemap/googlemapchina_c.pdf* (accessed April 2008).

Levy, S. (2005) 'Living by Google rules', *Newsweek* 145(15): 72–4.

Lewandowski, D. and Mayr, P. (2007) 'Exploring the academic invisible web', *Library Hi Tech* 24(4): 529–39.

Licoppe, C. and Smoreda, Z. (2005) 'Are social networks technologically embedded? How networks are changing today with changes in communication technology', *Social Networks* 27(4): 317–35.

Liedtke, M. (2007) 'Google tightens privacy measures', *USA Today*, 13 March, available at: *http://www.usatoday.com/tech/news/internet privacy/2007-03-14-google-privacy_N.htm* (accessed October 2009).

Litterick, D. (2005) 'Chirac backs Eurocentric search engine', *The Daily Telegraph*, 31 August, available at: *http://www.telegraph.co.uk/ money/main .jhtml?xml=/money/2005/08/31/cnsearch31.xml* (accessed June 2008).

Logan, R. K. (1986) *The Alphabet Effect*, New York: Morrow.

Lrae (2004) 'Do's and not do's', available at: *http://bbs.keyhole.com/ ubb/showthreaded.php/Cat/0/Number/16288/an/0/page/0#16288* (accessed April 2008).

Lundvall, B. A. and Johnson, B. (1994) 'The learning economy', *Journal of Industry Studies* 1: 23–42.

Lyman, P. and Varian, H. R. (2003) 'How much information?' available at: *http://www2.sims.berkeley.edu/research/projects/how-much-info-2003* (accessed June 2006).

Machlup, F. (1973) *The Production and Distribution of Knowledge in the United States*, Princeton, NJ: Princeton University Press.

Mackinnon, R. (2005) 'Yahoo! and Chinese censorship', *R Conversation*, 18 September, available at: *http://rconversation.blogs.com/rconversation/ 2005/09/yahoo_chinese_c.html* (accessed November 2005).

MacMillan, R. (2004) 'Google bets the house on banner ads', *The Washington Post*, 13 May, available at: *http://www.washingtonpost.com/ wp-dyn/articles/A23536-2004May13.html* (accessed June 2008).

Manheim, J. B. (1986) 'A model of agenda dynamics', in M. L. McLaughlin (ed.) *Communication Yearbook Vol. 10*, Newbury Park, CA: Sage, pp. 499–516.

Markoff, J. and Hansell, S. (2006) 'Hiding in plain sight, Google seeks more power', *The New York Times*, 14 June, available at: *http://www.nytimes.com/2006/06/14/technology/14search.html?ei=5090&en=d96a72b3c5f91c47&ex=1307937600* (accessed June 2008).

Mathaba (2006) 'Sudan blocks Google Arabic translation', 21 December, available at: *http://www.mathaba.net/news/?x=547588* (accessed January 2007).

Martinson, J. (2007) 'China censorship damaged us, Google founders admit', *The Guardian*, 27 January, available at: *http://business.guardian.co.uk/davos2007/story/0,,1999994,00.html* (accessed March 2007).

Mattelart, A. (1980) *Mass Media, Ideologies and the Revolutionary Movement*, Brighton: Harvester Press.

Mattelart, A. (2003) *The Information Society: An Introduction*, London: Sage Publications.

Mattelart, A. (2008) 'Communications/excommunications: an interview with Armand Mattelart by Costas M. Constantinou', *Review of International Studies* 34: 21–42.

Mattelart, A. and Mattelart, M. (1998) *Theories of Communication: A Short Introduction*, London: Sage.

May, C. (2002) *The Information Society: A Sceptical View*, Cambridge: Polity Press.

McCarthy, C. (2007) 'Microsoft acquires equity stake in Facebook, expands ad partnership', *CNET*, 24 October, available at: *http://news.cnet.com/8301-13577_3-9803872-36.html* (accessed May 2009).

McCullagh, D. (2002) 'Google excluding controversial sites', *CNET*, 23 October, available at: *http://news.com.com/2100-1023_3-963132.html* (accessed November 2004).

McGuire, P. and Granovetter, M. (1998) 'Business and bias in public policy formation: Civic Federation and the social construction of electric utility regulation', paper presented at the Annual Meeting of the American Sociological Association, 21–25 August, San Francisco, CA.

McLeary, P. (2006) 'International news, falling by the wayside', *CJR Daily*, 17 May, available at: *http://www.cjrdaily.org/behind_the_news/international_news_falling_by.php* (accessed December 2006).

McLuhan, M. (1962) *The Gutenberg Galaxy: The Making of Typographic Man*, Toronto: University of Toronto Press.

McLuhan, M. (1964) *Understanding Media: The Extensions of Man*, Cambridge, MA: MIT Press.

McMahon, P. (2002) *Global Control: Information, Technology and Globalization Since 1845*, Cheltenham: Edward Elgar.

McManus, J. (1993) *Market Driven Journalism: Let the Citizen Beware?*, Thousand Oaks, CA: Sage Publications.

McNair, B. (2005) 'The global public sphere: fourth estate or new world information disorder?', in M. J. Lacy and P. Wilkin (eds) *Global politics in the Information Age*, Manchester: Manchester University Press.

Millward Brown (2007) 'Google rises to the top of the BRandZ? ranking with a brand value of $66,434 million', 23 April, available at: *http://www .millwardbrown.com/Sites/Optimor/Content/News/OptimorPressReleases .aspx* (accessed April 2007).

Mosco, V. (1989) *The Pay-Per-View Society: Computers and Communication in the Information Age*, Norwood, NJ: Ablex Publishing.

Mosco, V. (1996) *The Political Economy of Communication: Rethinking and Renewal*, London: Sage.

Mosco, V. and Wasko, J. (eds) (1988) *The Political Economy of Communication*, London: Sage.

Mowshowitz, A. and Kawaguchi, A. (2002) 'Bias on the web', *Communications of the ACM* 45(9): 56–60.

Mumford, L. (1964) 'Authoritarian and democratic technics', *Technology and Culture* 5(1): 1–8.

Negroponte, N. (1995) *Being Digital*, New York: Knopf.

Nemeth, R. J. and Smith, D. A. (1985) 'International trade and world-system structure: A multiple network analysis', *Review* 8(4): 517–60.

Neuhaus, C., Neuhaus, E., Asher, A. and Wrede, C. (2006) 'The depth and breadth of Google Scholar: An empirical study', *Libraries and the Academy* 6(2): 127–41.

Ngugi, W. T. (1986) *Decolonizing the Mind: The Politics of Language in African Literature*, London: J. Currey; Portsmouth, NH: Heinemann.

Nguyen, D. T. and Alexander, J. (1996) 'The coming of cyberspacetime and the end of polity', in R. Shields (ed.) *Cultures of Internet: Virtual Spaces, Real Histories, Living Bodies*, London: Sage, pp. 99–124.

Nielsen/NetRatings (2009) 'Nielsen announces July US Search share rankings,' 12 August, available at: *http://en-us.nielsen.com/main/news/ news_releases/2009/august/Nielsen_Announces_July_U_S__Seach_ Rankings* (accessed September 2009).

Noman, H. and Zarwan, E. (2008) 'Internet filtering in the Middle East and North Africa', available at: *http://opennet.net/research/regions/mena* (accessed April 2008).

Nordenstreng, K. and Varis, T. (1974) 'Television traffic – a one way street?', *Reports and Papers no. 70*, Paris: UNESCO.

Norris, P. (2000) *A Virtuous Circle: Political Communications in Post-Industrial Societies*, New York: Cambridge University Press.

Norris, P. (2001) *Digital Divide: Civic Engagement, Information Poverty, and the internet Worldwide*, New York: Cambridge University Press.

North, A. (2007) 'Iraqis use internet to survive war', BBC News, 13 February, available at: *http://news.bbc.co.uk/1/hi/world/middle_east/6357129.stm* (accessed February 2007).

Nunberg, G. (2003) 'As Google goes, so goes the nation', *The New York Times*, 18 May, available at: *http://people.ischool.berkeley.edu/~nunberg/google.html* (accessed June 2008).

Nystedt, D. and McCarthy, K. (2006) 'Google launches censored Chinese search', *TechWorld*, 25 January, available at: *http://www.techworld.com/applications/news/index.cfm?NewsID=5233* (accessed June 2008).

O'Brien, K. J. (2006) 'Europeans weigh plan on Google challenge', *International Herald Tribute*, 18 January, available at: *http://www.iht.com/articles/2006/01/17/business/quaero.php* (accessed January 2007).

O'Brien, K. J. and Crampton, T. (2007) 'Germany quits search engine project', *International Herald Tribute*, 2 January, available at: *http://www.iht.com/articles/2007/01/02/business/search.php* (accessed January 2007).

Ofori-Attah, K. D. (2007) 'A brief review of United States' efforts in international education with respect to UNESCO', *Comparative and International Education Society Newsletter* No. 143, available at: *http://www.cies.ws/newsletter/jan%2007/Ofori-Attah.htm* (accessed February 2007).

O'Neill, E. T., Lavoie, B. F. and Bennett, R. (2003) 'Trends in the evolution of the public web: 1998–2002', *D-Lib Magazine* 9(4), available at: *http://www.dlib.org/dlib/april03/lavoie/04lavoie.html* (accessed July 2009).

OpenNet Initiative (2005) 'Internet filtering in China in 2004–2005: a country study, 14 April, available at: *http://www.opennetinitiative.net/studies/china* (accessed November 2005).

Osinga, D. (2004) 'The future of searching', available at: *http://douweosinga.com/blog/0403/2004Mar26_1* (accessed August 2006).

Pain, J. (2007) 'Dictatorships get to grip with Web 2.0', *CNET*, 2 February, available at: *http://news.com.com/Dictatorships+get+to+grip+with+Web+2.0/2010-1028_3-6155582.html* (accessed February 2007).

Palmer, M. (2005) 'Low-cost laptop aims to bridge digital divide', *Financial Times*, 16 November, available at: *http://www.ft.com/cms/s/2/af810ab0-56f0-11da-b98c-00000e25118c.html* (accessed January 2007).

Pan, B., Hembrooke, H., Joachims, T., Lorigo, L., Gay, G. and Granka, L. (2007) 'In Google we trust: users' decisions on rank, position and relevance', *Journal of Computer-Mediated Communication* 12(3), available at: *http://jcmc.indiana.edu/vol12/issue3/pan.html* (accessed May 2007).

Paolillo, J. C. (2007) 'How much multilingualism? Language diversity on the internet', in B. Danet and S. C. Herring, *The Multilingual Internet: Language, Culture, and Communication Online*, Oxford: Oxford University Press, pp. 408–30.

Pastore, M. (2000) 'Web pages by language', available at: *http://www.clickz.com/showPage.html?page=408521* (accessed November 2007).

People's Daily (1999) 'China bans Falun Gong', 22 July, available at: *http://english.people.com.cn/special/fagong/1999072200A101.html* (accessed June 2006).

People's Daily (2006) 'Thoroughly exposing Falun Gong', translated by Google Translate, available at: *http://translate.google.com/translate?sourceid=navclient-menuext&hl=en&u=http://www.people.com.cn/GB/shizheng/252/2139/index.html* (accessed June 2006).

Perraton, J., Goldblatt, D., Held, D. and McGrew, A. (1997) 'The globalization of economic activity', *New Political Economy* 2(2): 257–77.

Perri 6 (2002) 'Global digital communications and the prospects for transnational regulation', in D. Held and A. McGrew (eds) *Governing Globalization: Power, Authority and Global Governance*, Cambridge: Polity Press, pp. 145–70.

Pew Project for Excellence in Journalism (2009) 'The state of the news media: An annual report on American journalism', available at: *http://www.stateofthemedia.org/2009/narrative_online_audience.php?cat=2&media=5* (accessed June 2009).

Picard, R. G. (ed.) (2000) *Measuring Media Content, Quality and Diversity: Approaches and Issues in Content Research*, Turku: Turku School of Economics and Business Administration.

Pickles, J. (2004) *A History of Spaces*, London: Routledge.

Porter, C. (2003) 'US outlines priorities for World Summit on the Information Society', US Department of State, 3 December, available at: *http://usinfo.state.gov/xarchives/display.html?p=washfile-english&y=2003&m=December&x=20031203163730retropc0.0570032* (accessed June 2008).

PriceCollins (2006) 'Data problems: censorship', *Google Earth Community*, 27 February, available at: *http://bbs.keyhole.com/ubb/showthreaded.php/Cat/0/Number/330444/page/0/vc/1* (accessed April 2008).

Pritchard, D. (1986) 'Homicide and bargained justice: the agenda-setting effect of crime news on prosecutors', *The Public Opinion Quarterly* 50(2): 143–59.

Pu, H. T., Chuang, S. l. and Yang, C. (2001) 'Subject categorization of query terms for exploring web users' search interests', *Journal of the American Society for Information Science and Technology* 53(8): 617–30.

Punj, G. and Stewart, D. W. (1983) 'Cluster analysis in marketing research: review and suggestions for application', *Journal of Marketing Research* 20(2): 134–48.

Putnam, R. D. (2000) *Bowling Alone: The Collapse and Revival of American Community*, New York: Simon and Schuster.

Ramana, R. (2004) 'From IR to search and beyond', *ACM Queue* 2(3): 66–73, available at: *http://www.acmqueue.com/modules.php?name=Content&pa=showpage&pid=148* (accessed August 2006).

Renkema, J. (2004) *Introduction to Discourse Studies*, Amsterdam: Benjamins.

Resnik, D. (1998) 'Politics on the internet: the normalization of cyberspace', in T. W. Luke and C. Toulouse (eds) *The Politics of Cyberspace*, New York: Routledge, pp. 48–68.

Reuters (2007a) 'Google rivals urge antitrust scrutiny of deal', 16 April, available at: *http://uk.reuters.com/article/technologyNews/idUKN 1524189120070416* (accessed April 2007).

Reuters (2007b) 'Google focus now includes business software-CEO', 10 May, available at: *http://www.reuters.com/article/technology-media-telco-SP/idUSN1047876720070510* (accessed May 2007).

Rheingold, H. (1993) *The Virtual Community: Homesteading on the Electronic Frontier*, Reading, MA: Addison-Wesley.

Riley, D. (2007) 'Google News: the end of news indexing as we know it?', *TechCrunch*, 20 May, available at: *http://www.techcrunch.com/ 2007/05/20/google-news-the-end-of-news-indexing-as-we-know-it* (accessed April 2008).

Riley, T. B. (2001) *Electronic Governance and Electronic Democracy: Living and Working in the Connected World*, London: Commonwealth.

Riley, T. B. (2004) *E-Government, The Digital Divide and Information Sharing: Examining the Issues*, Ottawa, ON: Commonwealth Centre for E-Governance and Riley Information Services Inc.

Roberts, J. (2000) 'From know-how to show-how? Questioning the role of information and communication technologies in knowledge transfer', *Technology Analysis and Strategic Management* 12(4): 429–43.

Robertson, R. (1992) *Globalisation, Social Theory and Global Culture*, London: Sage.

Robinson, J. P., DiMaggio, P. and Hargittai, E. (2003) 'New social survey perspectives on the digital divide', *IT and Society* 1(5): 1–22.

Rodgers, Z. (2006) 'Google opens audio ads beta', *ClickZ News*, 8 December, available at: *http://clickz.com/showPage.html?page=3624149* (accessed February 2007).

Rogers, E. M. (2003) *Diffusion of Innovations*, New York: Free Press.

Rogers, R. (2004) *Information Politics on the Web*, Cambridge, MA: MIT Press.

Ronfeldt, D., Arquilla, J., Fuller, G. E. and Fuller, M. (1998) *The Zapatista Social Netwar in Mexico*, Santa Monica, CA: Rand.

Ross, N. and Wolfram, D. (2000) 'End user searching on the internet: an analysis of term pair topics submitted to the excite search engine', *Journal of the American Society for Information Science* 51(10): 949–58.

Saatchi & Saatchi (1986) *Annual Report Year Ending September 30*, London: Saatchi & Saatchi.

Samson, A. (1996) 'The crisis at the heart of our media', *British Journalism Review* 7(3): 42–51.

Schenk, D. (1997) *Data Smog: Surviving the Information Glut*, New York: Harper-Collins.

Scheufele, D. A. (2002) 'Being a citizen online: new opportunities and dead ends', *The Harvard International Journal of Press/Politics* 7(3): 55–75.

Schiller, H. I. (1992) *Mass Communications and American Empire* (2nd edn), Boulder, CO: Westview Press.

Schiller, H. I. (1996) *Information Inequality: The Deepening Social Crisis in America*, New York & London: Routledge.

Schmidt, R. (2006) 'Microsoft, AOL, Google asked by US to keep internet records', *Bloomberg*, 1 June, available at: *http://www.bloomberg.com/apps/news?pid=10000103&sid=af87XTpBzphA&refer=us* (accessed June 2006).

Sciadas, G. (ed.) (2003) 'Monitoring the digital divide … and beyond', *Technical Report, Orbicom*, Montreal: Orbicom International Secretariat, available at: *http://www.orbicom.uqam.ca/projects/ddi2002/2003_dd_pdf_en.pdf* (accessed December 2007).

SearchCIO (2006) 'Unique users', available at: *http://searchcio.techtarget.com/sDefinition/0,,sid19_gci912421,00.html* (accessed September 2006).

Search Engine Watch (2006) 'comScore Media Metrix search engine ratings', 21 August, available at: *http://searchenginewatch.com/2156431* (accessed September 2009).

Segev, E., Ahituv, N. and Barzilai-Nahon, K. (2007) 'Mapping diversities and tracing trends of cultural homogeneity/heterogeneity in cyberspace',

Journal of Computer-Mediated Communication 12(4), available at: *http://jcmc.indiana.edu/vol12/issue4/segev.html* (accessed July 2007).

Senellart, P. and Senellart, J. (2005) 'SYSTRAN Translation Stylesheets: Machine Translation driven by XSLT', paper presented at XML Conference & Exposition, 14–18 November, Atlanta, GA.

Shade, L. (2002) 'The digital divide: From definitional stances to policy initiatives', paper prepared for the Department of Canadian Heritage P3: Policy and Program Forum, Ottawa, available at: *http://www.fis.utoronto.ca/research/iprp/publications/shade_digitaldivide.pdf* (accessed January 2008).

Shankland, S. (2007) 'Google Earth shows Chinese nuclear sub', *CNET*, 5 July, available at: *http://news.cnet.com/8301-10784_3-9740023-7.html* (accessed October 2009).

Shankland, S. (2008) 'Google begins blurring faces in Street View', *CNET*, 13 May, available at: *http://news.cnet.com/8301-10784_3-9943140-7.html* (accessed July 2009).

Shapiro, C. and Varian, H. (1999) *Information Rules: A Strategic Guide to the Network Economy,* Boston, MA: Harvard Business School Press.

Sherman, C. (2004) 'Yahoo announces content acquisition program', *Search Engine Watch*, 2 March, available at: *http://searchenginewatch.com/searchday/article.php/3320071* (accessed June 2008).

Sherman, C. and Price, G. (2001) *The Invisible Web: Uncovering Information Sources Search Engines Can't See,* Medford, NJ: CyberAge Books.

Shillingsburg, P. L. (2006) *From Gutenberg to Google: Electronic Representations of Literary Texts,* Cambridge, New York: Cambridge University Press.

Shrader, K. (2007) 'Curbs on satellite photos may be needed', *San Francisco Chronicle*, 8 May, available at: *http://www.sfgate.com/cgi-bin/article.cgi?f=/n/a/2007/05/08/national/w140605D01.DTL&type=politics* (accessed April 2008).

Silverstein, C., Henzinger, M., Marais, H. and Moricz, M. (1999) 'Analysis of a very large web search engine query log', *ACM SIGIR Forum* 33(3): 6–12.

Simmons, C. (2007) 'The interconnected web: media consolidation, corporate ownership, and the world wide web', paper presented at the annual meeting of the Association for Education in Journalism and Mass Communication, 8 August, Washington, DC.

Skydsgaard, J. E. (1968) *Varro the Scholar: Studies in the First Book of Varro's De re rustica,* Copenhagen: Munksgaard.

Smith, A. M. (1994) *New Right Discourse on Race and Sexuality,* Cambridge: Cambridge University Press.

Snyder, D., Kick, E. (1979) 'Structural position in the world system and economic growth. 1955–70: A multiple network analysis of transnational interactions', *American Journal of Society* 84: 1096–126.

Spink, A., Jansen, B. J., Wolfram, D. and Saracevic, T. (2002a) 'From e-sex to e-commerce: web search changes', *IEEE Computer* 35(3): 107–11.

Spink, A., Ozmutlu, S., Ozmutlu, H. C. and Jansen, B. J. (2002b) 'US versus European web searching trends', *SIGIR Forum* 36(2): 32–8.

Star, S. L. and Ruhleder, K. (1996) 'Steps toward an ecology of infrastructure: design and access for large information spaces', *Information Systems Research* 7(1): 63–92.

Strover, S. (1999) *Rural Internet Connectivity*, Columbia, MO: Rural Policy Research Institute.

Sullivan, D. (2006) 'comScore Media Metrix search engine ratings', *Search Engine Watch*, 21 August, available at: *http://searchenginewatch.com/showPage.html?page=2156431* (accessed June 2008).

Sunstein, C. (2001) *Republic.com*, Princeton, NJ: Princeton University Press.

Sussman, L. R. (2000) 'Censor dot gov: The internet and press freedom 2000', New York: Freedom House, available at: *http://www.freedomhouse.org/pfs2000/sussman.html* (accessed May 2005).

Taylor, S. (2007) 'Google, Baidu race to set up online library in China', *Reuters*, 7 March, available at: *http://www.reuters.com/article/technology-media-telco-SP/idUSSHA36364720070308* (accessed March 2007).

Techtree (2006) *Kalam Concerned over Google Earth*, 19 October, available at: *http://www.techtree.com/techtree/jsp/article.jsp?article_id=68712&cat_id=582* (accessed June 2008).

Thompson, J. B. (1995) *The Media and Modernity*, Cambridge: Polity Press.

Thompson, J. B. (2000) 'The globalization of communication', in D. Held and A. McGrew (eds) *The Global Transformations Reader*, Cambridge: Polity Press and Blackwell Publishers, pp. 202–15.

Tianliang, Z. (2005) 'Google "kowtows" to the Chinese government', *The Epoch Times*, 8 February, available at: *http://english.epochtimes.com/news/5-2-8/26332.html* (accessed June 2008).

Torfing, J. (1991) 'A hegemony approach to capitalist regulation', in R. Bertramsenet, J. Thomsen and J. Torfing (eds) *State, Economy and Society*, London: Unwyn Hyman, pp. 35–93.

Tulving, E. (1983) *Elements of Episodic Memory*, Oxford: Clarendon Press.

Tumber, H. (2001) 'Democracy in the information age: the role of the fourth estate in cyberspace', in F. Webster (ed.) *Culture and Politics in the Information Age: A New Politics?*, London: Routledge, pp. 17–31.

Turow, J. (2005) 'Audience construction and culture production: marketing surveillance in the digital age', *Annals of the American Academy of Political and Social Science* 597: 103–21.

Ulken, E. (2005) 'Non-traditional sources cloud Google News results', *USC Annenberg Online Journalism Review*', available at: *http://www .ojr.org/ojr/stories/050519ulken/* (accessed February 2007).

Ullmann, L. and Gorokhovich, Y. (2006) 'Google Earth and some practical applications for the field of archaeology', *CSA Newsletter* 18(3), available at: *http://www.csanet.org/newsletter/winter06/nlw0604.html* (accessed June 2006).

UN News (2006) 'New list of "10 stories the world should hear more about" released at UN', 15 May, available at: *http://www.un.org/apps/ news/story.asp?NewsID=18486* (accessed December 2006).

Underwood, D. (1993) *When MBAs Rule the Newsroom*, New York: Columbia University Press.

UNESCO (2005a) *Towards Knowledge Societies*, Paris: United Nations Educational, Scientific and Cultural Organisation, available at: *http:// unesdoc .unesco.org/images/0014/001418/141843e.pdf* (accessed on March 2006).

UNESCO (2005b) 'Convention on the protection and promotion of the diversity of cultural expressions', available at: *http://portal.unesco.org/ culture/en/ev.php-URL_ID=11281&URL_DO=DO_TOPIC&URL_ SECTION=201.html* (accessed August 2006).

UNESCO (2006) 'In focus: measures and indicators', available at: *http:// portal.unesco.org/ci/en/ev.php-URL_ID=20973&URL_DO=DO_ TOPIC&URL_SECTION=201.html* (accessed July 2009).

United Cities and Local Governments (UCLG) (2006) 'Information society', available at: *http://www.cities-localgovernments.org/uclg/ index.asp?pag=template.asp&L=EN&ID=21* (accessed August 2006).

USA Today (2007) 'Google and cable firms warn of risks from web television', 7 February, available at: *http://www.usatoday.com/tech/ news/2007-02-07-google-web-tv_x.htm* (accessed June 2008).

Van Couvering, E. (2004) 'New media? The political economy of internet search engines', paper presented at the Annual Conference of the International Association of Media and Communications Researchers, 25–30 July, Porto Alegre.

Van der Pijl, K. (1984) *The Making of an Atlantic Ruling Class*, London: Verso.

Van Dijk, J. (2005) *The Network Society: Social Aspects of New Media* (2nd edn), London & Thousand Oaks, CA: Sage.

Van Eijk, N. (2004) 'Regulating old values in the digital age', paper presented at the Guaranteeing Media Freedom on the Internet OSCE- Conference, 27–28 August, Amsterdam, available at: *http://www.ivir .nl/publications/vaneijk/osce-27082004-nve1.pdf* (accessed December 2007).

Vanhanen, T. (1997) *Prospects of Democracy: A Study of 172 Countries*, New York: Routledge.

Vass, S. (2008) 'Google reaches deals with news websites', *Sunday Herald*, 10 April, available at: *http://www.sundayherald.com/business/businessnews/display.var.1411787.0.google_reach_deals_with_news_websites.php* (accessed April 2008).

Vaughan, L. and Thelwall, M. (2004) 'Search engine coverage bias: evidence and possible causes', *Information Processing and Management: an International Journal* 40(4): 693–707.

Virni, P. and Hardt M. (1996) *Radical Thoughts in Italy*, Minneapolis, MN: University of Minnesota Press.

Vise, D. A. and Malseed, M. (2005) *The Google Story*, New York: Bantam Dell.

W3Schools (2008) 'OS platform statistics', available at: *http://www.w3schools.com/browsers/browsers_os.asp* (accessed June 2008).

Walker, J. (2002) 'Links and power: the political economy of linking on the web', paper presented at the ACM Hypertext Conference, 11–15 June, Baltimore, MD.

Walker, L. (2006) 'Forgot what you searched for? Google didn't', *The Washington Post*, 21 January, p. D01, available at: *http://www.washingtonpost.com/wp-dyn/content/article/2006/01/20/AR2006012001799.html* (accessed June 2008).

Wallis, W. (2006) 'Google looks to expand in Middle East', *Financial Times*, 22 June, available at: *http://www.ft.com/cms/s/0d890250-0215-11db-a141-0000779e2340.html* (accessed June 2006).

Ward, J. H. (1963) 'Hierarchical grouping to optimize an objective function', *Journal of the American Statistical Association* 58(301): 236–44.

Warschauer, M. (2004) *Technology and Social Inclusion: Rethinking the Digital Divide*, Cambridge, MA: MIT Press.

Washington Times (2006) 'Commercial photos show Chinese nuke buildup', 16 February, available at: *http://www.washingtontimes.com/national/20060216-020211-7960r.htm* (accessed June 2008).

Wasserman, S. and Faust, K. (1994) *Social Network Analysis: Methods and Applications*, Cambridge: Cambridge University Press.

Waxman, J. (2000) 'The old 80/20 rule takes one on the jaw', *Internet Trend Report 1999, Review*, San Francisco, CA: Alexa Research. Cited in P. DiMaggio, E. Hargittai, W. R. Neuman and J. P. Robinson (2001) 'Social implications of internet', *Annual Review of Sociology* 27: 307–36.

Webber, S. (2000) 'Conceptions of information literacy: new perspectives and implications', *Journal of Information Science* 26(6): 381–397.

Weber, T. (2007) 'YouTubers to get ad money share', BBC News, 27 January, available at: *http://news.bbc.co.uk/2/hi/business/6305957.stm* (accessed January 2007).

Webster, J. G., and Lin, S. F. (2002) 'The internet audience: web use as mass behavior', *Journal of Broadcasting & Electronic Media* 46(1): 1–12.

Weinberg, T. (2007) 'Google Maps: invading your privacy? (Not anymore!)', *Seround Table*, 8 June, available at: *http://www.seroundtable.com/archives/013780.html* (accessed April 2008).

Wellisch, H. H. (1991) *Indexing from A to Z*, New York: The H. W. Wilson Company, available at: *http://www.asindexing.org/site/history.shtml* (accessed August 2006).

Wilkin, P. (2001) *The Political Economy of Global Communication: An Introduction*, London: Pluto Press.

Wilkin, P. and Beswick, D. (2005) 'The revolution will now be televised – strategies of communication and class conflict in Brazil', in M. J. Lacy and P. Wilkin (eds) *Global Politics in the Information Age*, Manchester: Manchester University Press, pp. 131–51.

Williams, J., Sligo, F. and Wallace, C. (2005) 'Free internet as an agent of community transformation', *The Journal of Community Informatics* 2(1), available at: *http://ci-journal.net/viewarticle.php?id=77&layout=html* (accessed August 2006).

Williams, W. (1985) 'Agenda setting research', in J. Fletcher and J. Dominick (eds) *Broadcast Research*, Boston, MA: Allyn and Bacon, pp. 189–201.

Wolfram, D., Spink, A., Jansen, B. J. and Saracevic, T. (2001) 'Vox populi: The public searching of the web', *Journal of the American Society for Information Science and Technology* 52(12): 1073–4.

Wolfstad (2006) 'Google Maps updated, and Dutch government buildings obscured', available at: *http://www.wolfstad.com/2006/04/google-maps-updated-and-dutch-government-buildings-obscured* (accessed June 2006).

Wray, R. (2007) 'NBC and News Corp unite to challenge YouTube', *The Guardian*, 23 March, available at: *http://technology.guardian.co.uk/news/story/0,,2041002,00.html* (accessed March 2007).

WSIS (2003) 'Declaration of principles, building the information society: a global challenge in the new millennium', World Summit on the Information Society, Document WSIS-03/GENEVA/DOC/4-E, available at: *http://www.itu.int/wsis/docs/geneva/official/dop.html* (accessed October 2007).

Wu, D. H. (2000) 'Systematic determinants of international news coverage', *Journal of Communication* 50(2): 113–30.

Yahoo! (2005) 'Buzz Index – Top Yahoo! Web Searches', available at: *http://buzz.yahoo.com* (accessed March 2005).

Yoon-Mi, K. (2007) 'KOREA: Google Earth criticized over geographical names', *Asia Media*, 15 August, available at: *http://www.asiamedia.ucla.edu/article.asp?parentid=75993* (accessed October 2007).

ZDNet (2006) 'Search engine loyalty: Google – 71%, Yahoo – 48.1%, MSN – 27.8%', 24 February, available at: *http://blogs.zdnet.com/ITFacts/?p=10262* (accessed September 2009).

Zeller, T. (2006) 'Republicans hit in "Google bombing"', *International Herald Tribune*, 26 October, available at: *http://www.iht.com/articles/2006/10/26/business/google.php* (accessed November 2006).

Zook, M. and Graham, M. (2007) 'The creative reconstruction of the internet: Google and the privatization of cyberspace and digiplace', *GeoForum* 38(6): 1322–43, available at: *http://dx.doi.org/10.1016/j.geoforum.2007.05.004* (accessed April 2008).

Index

Breinigsville, PA USA
14 February 2010
232430BV00003B/1/P